Who's Yer Daddy?

Terrace Books, a trade imprint of the University of Wisconsin Press, takes its name from the Memorial Union Terrace, located at the University of Wisconsin–Madison. Since its inception in 1907, the Wisconsin Union has provided a venue for students, faculty, staff, and alumni to debate art, music, politics, and the issues of the day. It is a place where theater, music, drama, literature, dance, outdoor activities, and major speakers are made available to the campus and the community. To learn more about the Union, visit www.union.wisc.edu.

Who's Yer Daddy?

Gay Writers Celebrate Their Mentors and Forerunners

Edited by

Jim Elledge

and

David Groff

Terrace Books

A trade imprint of the University of Wisconsin Press

Terrace Books
A trade imprint of the University of Wisconsin Press
1930 Monroe Street, 3rd Floor
Madison, Wisconsin 53711-2059
uwpress.wisc.edu

3 Henrietta Street
London WCE 8LU, England
eurospanbookstore.com

Printed in the United States of America

Library of Congress Cataloging-in-Publication Data

Who's yer daddy? : gay writers celebrate their mentors and forerunners / edited by Jim Elledge
and David Groff.
p.   cm.
Includes bibliographical references.
ISBN 978-0-299-28940-9 (cloth: alk. paper)
ISBN 978-0-299-28943-0 (e-book)
1. Gay authors—United States—Biography.
2. Gay men's writings, American.
I. Elledge, Jim, 1950–   II. Groff, David.   III. Title.
PS647.G39W48   2012
810.9′352664—dc23
2012015510

Permission has been granted to reprint the following essays that were previously published, some
in slightly different versions: Kenny Fries's "How I Learned to Drive: The Education of a Gay
Disabled Writer" from The Progressive; Aaron Hamburger's "The Mentor I Never Met: Janet
Frame" from Poets & Writers; Randall Mann's "Thom Gunn: A Memoir of Reading" from The
Kenyon Review Online; and Dale Peck's "My Mother's Grave Is Yellow" from Conjunctions.
A different version of Mark Doty's "Walt Whitman: Glow on the Extremest Verge" originally
appeared in Seneca Review. Also, "Buckley" by Paul Monette is reprinted from West of Yesterday, East
of Summer: New and Selected Poems (1973–1993) (St. Martin's). Copyright © 1994 by Paul Monette.
Reprinted by permission of David Groff and Wendy Weil for The Estate of Paul Monette.

For

David

&

For

Clay

Contents

Acknowledgments

The editors of this volume thank the editors of the journals listed on the copyright page for their permission to reprint essays that initially appeared in their pages.

At the University of Wisconsin Press, we thank our editor, Raphael Kadushin, for his early and enthusiastic support of this book. We are grateful to copyeditor Sue Breckenridge and appreciate the entire team at the press, including its director Sheila Leary, as well as Andrea Christofferson, Matthew Cosby, Carla Marolt, and Sheila McMahon, for their dedication, hard work, professionalism, and good humor.

Our thanks as well to our writers, who approached the question of literary influence with such imagination, insight, wit, and gravity.

Who's Yer Daddy?

Introduction

All Our Daddies — and Then Some

Jim Elledge and
David Groff

M ost books, even anthologies, grow out of an individual's private concerns or interests, loves or hates, typically from something that has "moved" the writer or editor into action. In that regard, this book is totally different.

Who's Yer Daddy? Gay Writers Celebrate Their Mentors and Fore-runners grew out of a panel Jim Elledge organized and moderated in Chicago during the 2009 annual conference of the Association of Writers and Writing Programs. The panel included poets Mark Bibbins, Peter Covino, David Groff, and Brian Teare, and it drew some eighty attendees, an S.R.O. crowd—atypical of audiences at most conferences. The response was so strong and the listeners so engaged that, during the Q&A that followed, many in the audience asked if copies of the essays would be available in a journal or as a book. At that moment, Elledge decided that he needed to expand the project, and he joined with David Groff to edit this collection of gay men remembering the literary fore-runners, real-life mentors, comrades, cultural and social icons, fictional characters, and even genuine biological progenitors who made them the writers they have become.

The *Who's Yer Daddy?* panel grew quickly from those four initial essays to a collection of thirty-nine pieces by a broad representation of today's gay writers—of all ages, races, levels of recognition, gender expression, class, and literary aesthetic. We directly solicited all of the work in this collection, and it includes only five essays that were previously published. The writers here include fiction writers, poets, and performance artists, and range from venerable figures in contemporary literature to those who have just begun blazing their own trails. The essayists exhibit diverse literary sensibilities, aesthetics, prose strategies, racial and ethnic heritages, geographies, and approaches to gay male sexuality. Their work is as true a depiction as possible of the variety of voices within the gay literary community. As with the four essays presented at AWP, the essays range from the humorous to the serious, and often combine the two. A few are scholarly, while others are more conversational and spontaneous in style; several of them play with the very form of the essay itself. All, broadly defined, are memoirs that are both personal (although never solipsistic) *and* aesthetic in aim.

Who are the daddies for these gay writers? Everybody in this collection had biological parents, of course, and those are typically, but not exclusively, heterosexual. But these writers also have a literary ancestry, one that is at least as important to their literary sensibilities as their biological ancestry, if not more. By "literary ancestry," we don't mean simply previous writers who were gay and who influenced our contributors, but all sorts of other individuals who had a hand in their development. Many but not most of those individuals are writers, gay and straight. Quite often, those who influenced our contributors were, as readers will expect, literary icons of the past: Whitman, say, or Gide.

But the question of literary progenitorship led these essayists to a startlingly wide roster of figures—including many who aren't in any way direct literary ancestors. (And many "daddies" are engendering figures who belong elsewhere on the family tree: some aunts, uncles, even siblings. Many daddies are mommies.) In these pages are not just the great Abrahams and Isaacs of queer literature. Certainly Whitman and Wilde and Melville, and such twentieth-century masters as Frank O'Hara and Edmund White, are all present here, but no colossus stands astride the collective literary consciousness of gay male writers today. Many of these essayists offer us literary guides and scouts whose creative territories are far less known to us. If the contributors to *Who's Yer Daddy?* explore their literary roots in the wellsprings of the canon, the anthology also showcases a number of generally unknown forerunners and influences—queer and non-queer—who are not mainstream figures and have, in fact, been ignored, even submerged, by the mainstream but who have nevertheless gained a tenuous and marginal visibility, at least among gay writers. In the process, the book's contributors draw attention to the work and importance of these "outsiders" as profound and surprising literary influences.

Some of the essayists in *Who's Yer Daddy* chronicle an entire tribal council, a lineage of exemplars whose lives and books inspire and sustain. Others offer a transformative encounter between one particular figure and the nascent writer—an encounter that might later move from the page to real life, when that young writer meets face to face the poet or novelist who so influenced him. Still others celebrate a particular fore-runner through a personal review-essay. And threaded through many of these essays is a direct or implied coming-out narrative, when a young man's connection to a work of art, a pop cultural icon or phenomenon, or a writer's personal story crystallizes his sexual identity and the creative sensibility that will arise from it.

Not every "daddy" in *Who's Yer Daddy* is a writer. The essayists here also explore other figures in their lives, or in the arts, as well as concepts, schools, and texts—gay and non-gay alike—that have been influential in their development. A number of them reach into pop culture to retrieve their "daddy" or sometimes "daddies." Gay male writers today feel entitled to commandeer creative energy not just from Andre Gide and James Merrill but also Bobbie Gentry and Bette Midler.

Certain essayists have found their literary inspiration in real people in their lives. Several writers honor the teachers who shepherded them to books, authors, and the very possibility that they themselves could write. They also speak of friends and comrades whose living example—often dramatic and sometimes problematic—cracked open their own creative selves. And perhaps most moving of all are those half-dozen writers who take literally the question "Who's Your Daddy?" and write vividly and intimately of their own fathers and other parental figures—and the challenging, often knotty literary inheritance they leave their progeny.

Who made us whoever it is we are? These questions of identity, lineage, and creative and psychic influence are essential not just to queer writers but to the readers of this anthology—the literate, engaged, and bothered men and women, queer and un-queer, seeking entertainment and insight from writers you already know and those you don't. You'll find in these pages writers familiar and new to you, and in their work—whether homage, exposé, literary exploration, journey, or meditation—you'll discover an issue that remains vital to every thoughtful person, whether a writer or reader, whether straight or queer: the question of identity.

Writing—all art, for that matter—should transcend, and does transcend, such limitations as sexual orientation and gender. Think, for example, of the influence of Walt Whitman, the great-great-great-granddad of all U.S. poets, whether queer or not, male as well as female. Or consider, more recently, the impact of Frank O'Hara, Allen Ginsberg, Anne Sexton, Sylvia Plath, and many, many others, across sexual lines. And yet at the same time, gay writers know, if no one else does, that sexual orientation is extraordinarily important to those for whom it is, for lack of a better word, an *issue*. Art is transcendent, of course, but at the same time, because it's created by a human being, a sexual animal, it's fueled by sexuality and, specifically, by sexual identity. One doesn't exist without the other.

The concept of identity, especially *gay* identify, is just as much a slippery slope as is that oft-used term "gay sensibility." And as we read these wonderful essays that probe into areas that have kept all gay writers that we've ever met pondering for hours and hours at some point in their lives, we become aware that we are reading not just the conclusions of each writer's explorations but, in many cases, only the middle of the process. Each day, we discover new daddies, some even younger than us, and so the process of identifying our heritage—and thus, identifying ourselves and our place in something far larger than any one of us—is a never-ending one. It's also rarely linear, although we often describe it that way. We also expect that if nothing else, all of the contributors would agree that, to misquote one of their compatriots of this volume: No, there is no such thing as gay identity, and yes, it is very important.

Jim Elledge and *David Groff*

Who we are and where we come from defines our similarity and constructs our relationship to the mainstream as well as our distinctiveness from it. Whether you are a writer or a reader, no matter your aesthetic or sexual orientation, from one generation to the next, the construction of identity remains a significant aesthetic, political, and cultural challenge. The community of queer writers and their readers serves not only as the site for expression of the gamut of genders, sexual orientations, and sexual manifestations, but at the same time, it is the arena where the wide range of races, ethnicities, ages, body types, heath statuses, economic levels, educational achievements, beliefs, and employment conditions exist side by side, contending for definition and attention.

—◦—

A word on the title. As we asked writers to contribute to this anthology, we found that most of them were delighted by the phrase *Who's Yer Daddy?* Some even laughed out loud when they first heard it. A few writers, however, pushed back, saying that the sexual insinuation of the title was inappropriate for a collection of literary personal essays, that it reinforced the stereotype that gay men write a literature that is reflexively sexualized and thus easily trivialized. Others thought the title was misleading, suggesting a collection of erotic daddy–son stories. As the editors of this anthology, we thought hard about those reactions. We concluded, however, that while we understand and respect the opinions of those who squirm at our title, we feel it captures the energy and spirit that we sought—and found—as we assembled the anthology's essays. We think it's fun. If there is one thing that gay men are good at, it is taking a received notion and queering it. We like the complexity and *frisson* of *Who's Yer Daddy?* and we hope that you do too. It you don't, just pretend that the anthology's subtitle is the title.

As its title implies, *Who's Yer Daddy?* is part tease, part confession, part acknowledgment; part testimonial, part birth certificate; part ode, part curse. We love our parents, literary and otherwise. We hate our parents. We owe them our very being. We owe them the briefest of footnotes in the most boring chapter of our autobiographies. Our relationship with our literary forebears is no less complicated, no less complex, and, for some of us, just as disturbing as the bond we have with our real parents. The only real difference is that our literary parents have never made us take castor oil. As participants and witnesses in the queer cultural scene, all of us have the chance to explore how our forerunners shape our own characters, awareness, and identities. The daddies of *Who's Yer Daddy?*—and our brothers who write about them—can lead the way for all of us.

Jim Elledge and *David Groff*

Culture Club in Space

An Anecdotal Poetics

Benjamin S. Grossberg

When I was twelve or thirteen or fourteen, I dressed up as Boy George for Halloween. It was 1983 or '84 or '85. "Karma Chameleon" was on the radio, and I was ready for drag. I had gathered pieces over a series of weeks, and my oldest brother's girlfriend, Fran, helped me assemble the costume in his bedroom. She and I sat on his bed, chatting as we worked. Together, we combed out a cheap black Halloween wig and then braided it with metallic ribbon. When Fran put the wig around my head—there was no top to it, just a rubber band that encircled my forehead—I jumped up and ran to the mirror, saying, "This makes the costume!" Then she brought over the hat, a plastic bowler I had found for a few dollars at CVS. I placed it on and said again: "This makes the costume!" Finally—Fran must have lowered it over my head—I was draped in a long blue-felt smock that reached to my knees, probably an old housedress. I jumped up and down, ricocheted around the room, saying it over and over: "This makes the costume! This makes the costume!"

And then my small band of heterosexual friends and I went trick-or-treating: me as Boy George, my Roman Catholic friend Arnaldo as a priest, my friend Ashish, a last-minute pirate, a curling mustache drawn on his brown skin. (God how the football team would have mocked us.)

When I remember that night, I see myself moving like a marionette—springing by the lift of a puppeteer's hand from house to house, taking each suburban lawn in one bounce, the sudden bright blue of my smock materializing from door to door.

The blue glowing like a transporter beam. Like the radar dish on the front of a starship. Like a starship on *Star Trek*.

When I was twelve or thirteen or fourteen, I dressed up as Captain Kirk for Halloween. It was 1983 or '84 or '85, and I regularly pushed my bedtime past eleven o'clock. That's when *Star Trek* came on, and I could watch it downstairs with my three older brothers. *Star Trek* was on at 11:00 and again at midnight. If I could stay awake and finesse my parents, I could watch both episodes.

I had gathered pieces for the costume over a series of weeks. The proper insignia—representing command—purchased from a convention. A plain Russell sweatshirt, command yellow, and gold braid to be sewn around each sleeve. Black cloth for my mother to stitch around the collar. And the crowning prop: a phaser—black plastic, solid, heavy, correctly sized for the fist. And when you pulled the trigger, it emitted a convincing whine—in waves like a police siren—and a beam of light shot from the front. The same group of friends, the same neighborhood. This time I was constantly stopping, dropping to one knee, aiming the phaser—thrusting the weapon with brow-knitted surety. I remember the weight of it in my hand. It must have been the two D batteries in the handle. The phaser felt real.

I don't know which of these Halloweens came first, or what my friends made of my transformations. Did they feel uncomfortable with a twirling Boy George, and subsequently reassured by the starship captain? Or was the order reversed, making them feel that I'd somehow backslid? In any case, they didn't let me know. And my family? Well, my mother sewed my Captain Kirk sweatshirt; my oldest brother and his girlfriend helped me become Boy George. The early 1980s—the Way Back Then of gay life—was undeniably more repressive, but if there was a sense of judgment or shame, it happily passed me by. I remember in these years the syndicated comic *For Better or For Worse* included a strip in which the son, Michael, also wanted to dress as Boy George for Halloween.[1] If my choice of Boy George was controversial, it clearly wasn't beyond the boundaries of what the Sunday *Asbury Park Press* deemed appropriate for its comics section.

My identification with Boy George was not my "gay self," my identification with Captain Kirk not my "straight self." The dichotomy is false on at least two fronts: gayness and straightness are not distinct sides or selves, and they do not directly correlate to behavior. And even if they were and if they did, Boy George and Captain Kirk would not make a neat fit. For a start, Boy George was a good three inches taller than Captain Kirk. Brawnier, too. But that said, these figures did speak to aspects of my personality that, back then, I could only express and explore separately.

Certainly some of my identification with Boy George must have related to an inchoate sense of myself as "other" in terms of sexual desire. Though I was not aware of myself as gay until I was eighteen, I must have had an inkling of difference even before then, at twelve or thirteen. But while Boy George was a model of nonnormative desire, he also had a personal style that wasn't so much feminine as unbounded by the rigidity of the masculine. He was gay, sure, but he was also saturated color, quips, flirtatiousness, and a freer expression of the body. When Culture Club won the 1983 Grammy for Best New Artist, Boy George (via satellite) addressed America on prime-time television. "Thanks America," he said. "You've got style, you've got taste, and you know a good drag queen when you see one." Perhaps the statement reveals a "gay sensibility." But even if it doesn't, this is a sensibility that samples widely—that enjoys a brashness and playfulness that were unsafe for boys in the early 1980s.

And Captain Kirk? Not my straight side, no. But a love of fantasy, adventure, exploration; the yearning for new worlds and those experiences that seem to broaden the possibilities of perception. In Richard Wilbur's poem "Mind," he compares thought to a bat flitting about in a cave, both free within and bound by the stone walls. The poem turns: "in the happiest intellection / A graceful error may correct the cave."[2] *Star Trek*—Captain Kirk—regularly corrected my cave.

So I suppose, like Whitman, I "contain[ed] multitudes"—or at least parts of myself that were difficult to reconcile. Whitman encounters the possibility that parts of himself won't fit with other parts simply by imagining (writing) a self large enough to contain them all: a mythic figure, "a kosmos." Despite his encouragement, I'm not sure that's a solution available to most of us.[3] But the challenge remains: how to come to terms with the multitudes of the self—how to understand that complexity and still feel whole, and build toward a single identity. And I suspect this task is especially difficult when the strands of ourselves find no models for integration, when we have to take up the task as if from scratch.

Perhaps it was as late as 1986 that I, in imitation of my older brother Joe, decided to make a movie. Joe is a special effects designer now; he's worked on a score of major Hollywood releases. Back then, he crafted a movie set in our basement to film an adaptation of the Ray Bradbury story "—And the Moon be Still as Bright." I served as his apprentice, learning craft, enjoying time with him. And after Joe's movie set was finished, I decided I would make my own movie, build my own set in an unused nook of our basement.

My film, never shot, was to be called *Culture Club in Space*. A couple of years afterward, Joe, unwilling to see the flattery in imitation, told me how much he hated my project, how offensive he found it. My plan was for a short film: three or four minutes. I wrote a script that combined a space battle with song clips that I and my fellow actors would lip sync. Between phaser shots and damage reports, we'd break into song. During pre-battle negotiations, a few bars of "Do You Really Want to Hurt Me?" A failed phaser attack and—you can picture this as captain-to-captain communication—the chorus of "Miss Me Blind." Then perhaps we'd narrowly avoid getting blown apart, and the crew would burst into "It's a Miracle." The set was standard going for a basement space ship. Tupperware containers spray-painted silver were affixed to desks. Cardboard panels painted yellow created futuristic wall texture. There was a captain's chair and a viewscreen with red, gold, and green panels above it.

Perhaps there are no random choices, and we are always, exhaustively, working at being ourselves. Unawares, I was pursuing a first attempt at synthesizing what everything in my life—like my brother Joe's sneering—told me should be kept distinct. A friend of mine, Cody, once told me he'd fantasized about sex with Mr. Spock. Another friend said of *Lost in Space* that he'd identified in equal parts with Dr.

Smith and the Robot. But nowhere in the world was there a model of integration—of how to make from what seemed like two roads, one road for one traveler. As a teenager, I wouldn't have said that I didn't feel whole. I wouldn't have described a schism within myself, said that I didn't understand how my different interests and concerns (my "multitudes") would ever unify to make a single man, but I look at my actions, and they suggest that, even back then, I was trying to find a wholeness.

For some of us, the work of our teenage years was not coming out to ourselves and not a struggle to repress or hide sexual orientation. (Though my friends and I certainly took our share of grief over being gay.) For some of us, the work of our teenage years was integration, synthesis, finding a way to be gay and to explore a fuller range of styles and behaviors that didn't crowd out or exclude everything else we were: that is, finding a way to be a whole self.

Twenty-five years later, integration is still the task I am about. Becoming a gay adult—becoming a gay poet—has meant seeking a whole self among those parts of me that society constructed as sharply distinct, to engage all of what compels, to bring all that I am to the page.

Imagine the episode. Spock raises an eyebrow, Kirk slowly lowers his phaser as the brightly painted Boy George steps out from behind one of the planet's dusty rock formations. It's a moment out of *The Wizard of Oz*; the black-and-white TV set suddenly flashes to color. This is Boy George of "The War Song": in a frilly black blouse, hair curled and red as a tulip. Of course Captain Kirk wouldn't understand cross-dressing. It was 1966: who had heard of such a thing? And of course there'd be lust: the tall, plumed, striding other; the soulful croon. Then some months later, egg tooth at the ready, I chew out of the calcium shell in a nest of straw: dreadlocked, humming, phaser on stun.

So what kind of poetry does that make for? Well, neither the likes of Captain Kirk nor Boy George find much place in the world of literature— that privileged but bound class to which poetry in our moment seems consigned. And when I first started writing, I didn't know how to reach outside the world of poetry for models. I therefore concentrated my search within canonical figures. As an undergraduate, I found one model in Christopher Marlowe, sixteenth-century playwright and poet—and sexual other, subversive, wit. The Boy George of the English

Renaissance. I wrote an undergraduate thesis on *Dr. Faustus* and *Edward II*, which allowed me to read gorgeous verse and learn about historical classifications of same-sex desire: what was excoriated, what celebrated. Behind my fascination was the figure of Marlowe, who reportedly said, "All they that love not tobacco and boys are fools."[4] Marlowe's zingers didn't always seem as good as Boy George's (I wasn't a smoker), but the iconoclastic heart was there—and the power of dramatic statement to usher in its own punctuating silence. From Boy George, from Marlowe, and later from Shakespeare and Whitman, I became a student of the stylishly telling phrase—and so began to work toward a poetry that was never very far from the dramatic. About half the poems in my first book, *Underwater Lengths in a Single Breath*, are dramatic monologues; all the poems in my third book will be. I saw how each quip, each clever line, was itself a kind of poem: with an image, a turn, a surrounding silence in which to resonate. In 1984 Boy George famously compared sex to "eating a bag of crisps." Therein was a lesson simile: about the leap between tenor and vehicle, about how simile is play, and about how that play can be complicated. After all, what's more boring and common than a bag of potato chips? And—as the advertising told us—what's more addictive?[5]

Finding a literary Kirk was harder. In his essay "On Science Fiction," Kurt Vonnegut wrote of his career, "I have been a sore-headed occupant of a file drawer labeled 'science fiction' . . . and I would like out, particularly since so many serious critics regularly mistake the drawer for a urinal."[6] Despite the high quality of contemporary practitioners like Margaret Atwood, "literary science fiction" remains an oxymoron. I think of Tolkien's transformative essay "*Beowulf*: The Monsters and the Critics," in which he argued that the criticism of his day minimized the fantasy elements of the epic, which, he insisted, are central to its meaning. It seems Tolkien was already fighting to make space for his own great work, *The Lord of the Rings*, still a decade away from composition. But like Vonnegut, Tolkien too ended up in that file drawer—lesser, somehow, than the literary. So I turned to Edith Hamilton and the world of classical mythology, to what Whitman called "those immensely overpaid accounts" of Greece and Rome.[7] I agree with Whitman's assessment, and I would avoid those stories now. But look for Captain Kirk in the world of literature, and you may come no closer than Odysseus. Also, the world of poetry has no shortage of precedents for the use of classical imagery (*overpaid* accounts), and the classical heritage has the added benefit of an already existing space for male–male desire.

My first book, then, was enabled and tamed by its models. Seeking to make a new thing through the work of integration, I wrote a book deeply indebted to old things: Renaissance literature, classical mythology. *Underwater Lengths in a Single Breath* clearly belongs in the realm of poetry. The book consists of dramatic monologues by classical figures, male–male desire draped in togas, and a few poems about Christopher Marlowe. I combined Boy George, Captain Kirk—and the *Norton Anthology of Poetry*. In the early 1990s, in a University of Houston workshop, a fellow student once broke class rules to address me directly as my poem was being discussed. She looked at me across the seminar table and asked, "Why don't you just say the word 'AIDS' in this poem?" I had no answer. Looking back, I think that I didn't know how to do that and still engage my imagination, or how to do that and still be writing poetry—or at least, what I thought of as poetry. *Underwater Lengths* offers one method of integration: one way I found wholeness as a gay writer, and I am proud of the book. But it is also the work of a young writer, as deeply immersed in his reading as in the world.

Over time, I have come to attempt the task of synthesis more directly, increasingly drawing on contemporary tropes and sensibilities. My current project is a book-length series of dramatic monologues from the perspective of a "space traveler" character—an alien who travels the galaxy observing phenomena that lead him to meditation on problems of the heart. He describes black holes and binary stars. He quips. He ruminates on frustrated desire. Interestingly, I find that to address my concerns in this more immediate manner triggers an anxiety—in myself, at least—that the project may not be "poetry." But perhaps this is the nature of letting popular culture directly influence your work: to explore a new mode in an art is to risk discontinuity, to risk that your work won't seem like art at all.[8] Being true to Boy George and Captain Kirk— and worrying less about the *Norton Anthology*—has led me to a poetry less recognizable as such. But that said, these poems also come closer to unifying my full self: and that means they contain strains of complication and tonal richness that I haven't been able to get on a page before. In other words, the poems feel more honest than my earlier work; they feel more true.

But this project, *Space Traveler*, is also just an interim solution. The task of synthesis continues. For my work as a poet, that means trying to find ways to bring progressively more of what I am to the page—new approaches that might manifest themselves as subsequent books. If Boy George were my shoulder angel and Captain Kirk my shoulder devil (or would that be reversed?), I'd like to imagine each whispering in an ear, but in unison, twin muses with increasingly harmonized voices—and harmonizing with other parts of myself, too. Eventually, this might lead me to the work that only I can do, the contribution that can be made only by this particular combination of characteristics in this particular moment. I think that's something we all hope for—to bring all of our richness, all of our resources to bear in any given situation, to give form to our full selves, before we pass on.

Notes

1. This strip appeared on October 17, 1984.

2. "Mind" was originally published in *Things of This World* (New York: Harcourt, Brace, 1956).

3. "Song of Myself" may be more inspiration than practical. The quoted language is from sections 51 and 24, respectively.

4. This line—along with a few dozen other fun heresies—was attributed to Marlowe by Richard Baines, government informer. There's a good deal of evidence to suggest Baines was lying.

5. Lays introduced its slogan "betcha can't eat just one" in 1963.

6. Vonnegut's "On Science Fiction" was published in the *New York Times*, September 5, 1965.

7. This phrase comes from "Song of the Exposition," first published in the 1872 edition of *Leaves of Grass*.

8. T. S. Eliot discusses the relationship between innovation and tradition in "Traditional and the Individual Talent," arguing that too great a conformity with the writing of the past disqualifies a work from being considered art, as art is by nature revolutionary.

Benjamin S. Grossberg

Walt Whitman

Glow on the Extremest Verge

Mark Doty

Sunday morning in Mendocino, the driving rain off the Pacific's been scouring the bluffs all night, cascading wildly over the band of moorland before the dreamy little town begins. We're in a coffee shop reading e-mail when a homeless man enters—or so I'd assume, anyway, a late middle-aged man, with a sun-tightened face, with backpacks and rolled and belted blanket, leading a slow-walking, serious black lab. He chooses a corner, kneels down, unhitches and unrolls the blanket, spreads it on the floor for her, talks softly to the dog, saying something like We'll get warm in here, we'll dry out in here. He gets her settled, then goes for a cup of coffee and comes back. He goes outside for a minute; she watches the door with a fixed gaze, eyes the color of wet bark unwavering, muzzle lifted. Suddenly I so do not want to be left; I have one companion whom I require; what if he doesn't come back this time? He's always come back though sometimes it's a long wait, and you can't ever be certain, and who besides me would take care of him if he didn't come back.

Then I shake my head and there's a beautiful nervous dog on the floor and I'm sitting on a stool in front of my laptop screen reading my mail.

—⌒—

"I know I am deathless," Walt Whitman writes, in his great signature poem, a claim he can make because he is already everywhere, pouring out of the limits of his singular body into the life of the whole. He is of a piece with all being. Each individual thing perishes; the whole continues. And so does the poem:

> I know this orbit of mine cannot be swept by a carpenter's compass,
> I know I shall not pass like a child's carlacue cut with a burnt stick at night.

When I was a kid I used to love the July evening pleasure of drawing in the air with "sparklers," those little fountains that hissed a continuous stream of sparks an inch or two from their tip till they burned down to a smoky, blackened stick. You could make a "carlacue" that would seem to linger in the air for seconds after the source of the light was gone. It's a stunning image for the fleeting nature of the self—just a little scribbling on the dark—and it's somehow enriched by the beauty of the paradox. If one stands at a little distance in time, the individual really *is* as fleeting as that track of light. But the life of the whole, the larger life that seems, impossibly, to speak to us from this strange poem, does not pass.

Or, you could say, the writing persists, at least for a while, though the hand that writes fades into darkness.

—⌒—

If you're already everything, already complete, then what need could there be to speak, to write a poem? But in truth Walt Whitman's great song of himself is suffused with longing, a fervor for the only thing that isn't me: you. It's you who must be won over, you the reader whom the writer and his book desire, you the lover whom the soul seeks. The book wishes to free you from the illusion that you're separate; it wants you to remember what you know, already, on some level: that you are me. Or, more precisely, we are it.

From the position of heightened, benevolent distance at which the singer of "Song of Myself" stands, there's no real difference between us, and yet he understands that it's human not to be in that state, so the poem's central gesture is one of reaching to us—the poet's arm around our shoulder, the poet's hand in ours, the poet's lips whispering in our ear. (*I was chilled with the cold type and cylinder and wet paper between us*, he writes, wanting not the awkward intermediary of the printed page but the warm congress of voice with ear, skin with skin.)

What is this level of distance? Surely it's the friendliest incarnation of the voice of the absolute ever; compare it to the voice out of the whirlwind in Job and you hear immediately the difference between the sublime indifference of the universe and an avatar of human warmth. Whitman's a man with a whirlwind within him, not a disembodied spirit, so his poem is both human and somehow above the human at once. "Song of Myself" is poised at a level where individuality is an entertaining spectacle—it is the source of the marvelous variety of the world the poem sets out to enumerate in Whitman's famous catalogues. But since the self speaking is the great multifarious life of the whole, the loss of any individual doesn't really matter: *there is really no death, / And if ever there was it led forward life* . . .

A friendly incarnation. There's a central figure in the Buddhist pantheon, a character so beloved you can find his or her name in a dozen forms, since Avalokitesvara or Chenresig or Quan Yin seems to cross lines of culture and language and gender effortlessly. We know that Whitman read Vedanta, and was aware of the new influx of translated religious texts from Asia in the spiritual and cultural hotbed of new ideas that was the East Coast of the United States in 1850, but who knows what he knew of Buddhism? To my mind what matters is imaginative sympathy, and Whitman would have seen in Avalokitesvara a kindred inclination. The historical figure transfigured into countless images and a godly stature was a monk who, on the edge of complete enlightenment, vowed not to enter into that state until all sentient beings had gone before him. Therefore, he became a figure of limitless compassion, the infinitely loving one who looks down from his position of understanding to the struggles of all creatures who have not yet realized their identity with an enormous heart, with a great outpouring of kindness. The speaker in "Song of Myself" is a kind of homespun American Avalokitesvara; he recognizes with enormous joy his own realization of unity, and that vision leads to a tenderness toward all things:

Swiftly arose and spread around me the peace and joy and
    knowledge that pass all the art and argument of the earth;
And I know that the hand of God is the elderhand of my own,
And I know that the spirit of God is the eldest brother of my own,
And that all the men ever born are also my brothers . . . . and the
    women my sisters and lovers,
And that a kelson of the creation is love;
And limitless are leaves stiff or drooping in the fields,
And brown ants in the little wells beneath them,
And mossy scabs of the wormfence, and heaped stones, and elder
    and mullen and pokeweed.

Surely Avalokitesvara is the "elderhand" of Walt Whitman; these lines overflow with a kind of unlimited, expansive tenderness. A "kelson" is the long, central beam of a wooden ship, the central structural element that holds a vessel together, and thus the great warmth of this passage extended from men and women, from the breadth of creation down to the tiniest things. It's a mark of Whitman's genius that he doesn't allow this passage to remain purely rhetorical. Suppose he'd stopped after "a kelson of the creation is love"? What convinces us that this is true is the way that love goes pouring out to the tiniest, least significant things in the world. Whatever a "wormfence" is, it must be something tiny indeed, not even easy to see, much less the "mossy scabs" upon it, but they are as beloved here as everything else, caught up in the expansive character of the ecstatic, which links everything, as Elizabeth Bishop put it, "by *and* and *and*." The material world of the poem is entirely lit up with this sense of splendor, of the radiant worth of each element of the world:

I believe a leaf of grass is no less than the journeywork of the stars,
And the pismire is equally perfect, and a grain of sand, and the egg
    of the wren,
And the tree-toad is a chef-d'œuvre for the highest,
And the running blackberry would adorn the parlors of heaven,
And the narrowest hinge in my hand puts to scorn all machinery . . .

Radiant, and endless: I am all and all never ceases.

Mark Doty

But this awareness does not erase the other self, the more limited consciousness; no one, save perhaps Avalokitesvara, who's become a god, after all, lives at that height. Walt Whitman could experience what passes *all the art and argument of the earth* and then return from that *extremest verge* to his mother's crowded house in Brooklyn, to his need to pay the bills. The gift of an encompassing vision so radical as to crack the foundations of the self does not change, at least not entirely, the life of the man that goes on after the veil's been parted. The self that slipped out of the limits of individuality, time, and place dwelled beside that self still bound by limit, the Whitman who loved his poor, mentally disabled brother, who struggled with attachment and desire, whose heart and health were broken by the endless suffering of the wounded soldiers in the temporary hospitals of D.C., become what Emily Dickinson called, horrifyingly, *a pile of moan*. The god in him saw everything as *flashing sparks from the wheel*, but the man himself was haunted, understanding that the particular is always perishing, and therefore all the more to be cherished.

If I can stand somewhere near the level of "Song of Myself," I understand that my dog's a glorious incarnation of the world, one of the endless flashing bright points of the universe unfolding itself. The abiding being that is the world takes pleasure in the disguise of matter, in the long adventure of incarnation, disappearing and then rediscovering (him)self again.

If I look at the same creature from my more familiar, limited vantage point, he's purely himself, a set of endearing gestures and characteristics that will never come again, and thus his disappearance is tragic—in the way that all the world is, all its parts forever going away. How, without the limits of perceived separateness, without the poignant agency of time, how could the adventure of living have poignancy, how could individuality really matter? (As if to illustrate my text, just now as I write, out the window a bit of shining green seems to break itself off the flowering vine that covers the fence and hurry away—hummingbird!)

Thus the poet feels a certain doubleness. He knows the vision of the higher self to be real, but he can't feel it all the time. He writes, in the preface to his first edition, that the poet "glows a moment on the extremest verge." And years later he would say to his friend John Burroughs that his early poems were written in a kind of trance, to which he could not will himself to return. So a discrepancy between selves haunts a number of poems:

> Trippers and askers surround me,
> People I meet . . . . . the effect upon me of my early life . . . . of the
>   ward and city I live in . . . . of the nation,
> The latest news . . . . discoveries, inventions, societies . . . .
>   authors old and new,
> My dinner, dress, associates, looks, business, compliments, dues,
> The real or fancied indifference of some man or woman I love,
> The sickness of one of my folks [. . .] or depressions or exaltations,
> They come to me days and nights and go from me again,
> But they are not the Me myself.
>
> Apart from the pulling and hauling stands what I am . . .

—❦—

I'm not sure when I first read Whitman—high school, I think, and in truth I didn't get it, though there were lines I understood to be remarkable, as when the poet looks at grass and says, "And now it seems to me the beautiful uncut hair of graves." That was unmistakably poetry, the deep bracing thing itself, but it took many years for me to really enter into Whitman's astonishing, cumbersome, magnificent project. It took me years to recognize his courage, to take in the fact that he'd written remarkable affirmations of the flesh and of sexuality and even of same-sex love, and published them in 1855 and in 1860. Where did such nerve come from? And though he'd dutifully try to write poems praising heterosexual congress, and rather carefully cover his tracks in his conversation and his correspondence—well, the astonishing frankness, the bravely visionary claim of the unity of body and soul, they take my breath away.

Over the years I read them again and again, especially the great ones, which are practically all written by 1860: the dazzling trumpet call of floor of the Soundview housing projects where I lived, with its cool blue walls, beige government-issued tiles, my twin-sized captain's bed and the reading lamp that I rescued when my friend Tony was about to toss it. And the bookshelf, quickly filling up with books, rested on top of my dresser where my daddies could watch over me as I slept. They opened me up to gay worlds I had never imagined. And like all good daddies should, they showed this young Puerto Rican man from the Bronx possibilities in life and love.

Given that my encounters with these daddies began in 1985 before there was an Internet, I am amazed now that I hooked up with them at all. I was a good student and a reader since as far back as I can recall, but how did I come across them? Desktop computers existed, but they weren't on the tops of many desks. There was no Google back then and certainly no GayDaddy.com. But like most cruising spots, one learns where to go and with patience and desire discovers what one seeks. These writers lived on the shelves and many of them weren't hidden. They were mixed in the fiction section and I would comb the shelves looking for homoerotic covers, especially the Plume Book/New American Library covers with their soft faded images, pastel colors, and men looking coy or distracted off to the side, to pick up daddy after daddy.

Whether it was solving mysteries in California, partying it up on Fire Island, pining for passion in the East Village, falling in and out of love in Boston, having sex in bathhouses, discovering that one's father is gay also, witnessing gay men dying of AIDS, convalescing in a family's Cape May beach house, navigating the pre–World War I gay subculture in Britain, being the lover of Alexander the Great, strolling the pre-dawn streets of the Manhattan, following a shallow Speedo-clad clan sailing and sexing it up on an elaborate yacht, or experiencing coming-out story after coming-out story set in the '50s, '60s, '70s and '80s and in the South, the East Coast, the West Coast, or on construction sites, in schools again and again, my daddies shared their lives, stories, and experiences, and like a good son, I lapped it all up with relish. Staying up late, missing train stops, and taking long bathroom breaks to take in more and more of them. It was the height of AIDS when there were still many questions about the virus, so although I had begun to ease my way into the club scene at the time, going to Better Days, the Paradise Garage, the Pyramid

"Song of Myself," the great long view of our places in time in "Crossing Brooklyn Ferry," the magnificent evocation of the origin of song in grief in "Out of the Cradle Endlessly Rocking," and then the plainspoken, achingly direct love poems of the Calamus sequence. In truth, as I get older, there are no American poems that seem to matter to me more; no one else broke such ground, delved so deeply, risked so completely. Everything I would wish to be is there on the page, in Walt Whitman. And so, I will admit, is much I wouldn't want to emulate: the long-windedness, the kneejerk patriotism, the tiresome sentimentality of the later poems. He becomes a public poet, and his desire to be seen as a sage is entirely at odds with his radicalism. But after all, the man ruined his health, in the nightmare hospitals of the Civil War, and suffered an awful stroke, and understood himself as a sexual radical in an age when homosexuality as we understand it was just being defined, medicalized, and proscribed. As is sometimes the case with artists, he made his great work in a kind of visionary exaltation, a sort of trance—you can see it in his face, in the ethereal daguerreotype portrait of him taken in Brooklyn in the 1850s; he looks as if every defense he might have had has been dissolved, and his eyes shine with a radiant compassion. He could no more will himself to return to this state than he could decide to be thirty-five again.

—❦—

The child writes with a burnt stick on the night. Whitman writes in pencil and in ink, in his small green notebooks. Then he begins, at a printing office in Manhattan, to set them in type, arranging the stanzas and the lineation himself, choosing where to wrap the words so that a long line moves continuously on the page, arranging the white space between stanzas so as to reflect the motion of thought. He will not pass like the child's illuminated scrawl because he has made his poem solid; he has, as Frank Bidart puts it, "fastened" his voice to the page.

—❦—

What emerges from his body—and, we might say, from the bodies of his lovers and cameradoes, his streetcar conductors and stagecoach drivers and hearty boys—is language. The emanation of all that skin is language; out of our collective physical being comes a voice, and the genius of Whitman's poem is to incarnate that voice. That is why every line of the poem can be read as spoken by that which is all of us, the collective, pervasive presence that is speech, that is language experiencing us. Maybe we are simply vehicles, and language itself is the living thing.

Source

Whitman, Walt. *Walt Whitman: Selected Poems, 1855–1892.* Edited by Gary Schmidgall. New York: St. Martin's, 1999.

Latin Moon Daddy

Charles Rice-González

I've had many daddies. I used to pick them up at the Barnes & Noble on Eighteenth Street and Fifth Avenue on my lunch break from my first job after I'd graduated from college. I'd give them ten to fifteen minutes before deciding whether I'd take them home. I always did. I was easy.

Edmund White, Andrew Holleran, David Leavitt, Robert Ferro, Felice Picano, Alan Hollinghurst, John Reid (Andrew Tobias), Rita Mae Brown, Christopher Bram, Ethan Mordden, Gary Indiana, Stephen McCauley, Mary Renault, Gordon Merrick, Joseph Hanson, even Anne Rice with her sexy vampires, accompanied me on the number six train during my morning and evening commutes. Often, I'd get undressed and curl up in bed with them. Snuggling under the warmth of blankets, tangling my legs up in sheets as my eyes took in all the words on those smooth white pages. Although I read wherever I could—waiting in line at the bank, walking down the street from the subway, on a bench in Washington Square Park—I liked being in bed best of all lying on my back holding my daddy up in the air or resting on my side with my hand pressing down on the book keeping my daddy in place. It was way better than standing around the musty rows of books at Barnes & Noble. My room was my world, they were on my turf, up on the fif

Club, and the Tunnel, it was safer to go to bed with Ethan Mordden's *Buddies* than to go home with a real one. There were many images that were imprinted in my mind, but there are two that are the strongest. One is from Andrew Holleran's *Dancer from the Dance*, where that character Malone is gazing at a young beautiful Puerto Rican man sitting in a bathtub surrounded by candles and reading a book. Even though the character was not a major one and there was a sense of objectification, he was there. The other image comes from Douglas Sadownick's *Sacred Lips of the Bronx*, where the main character, Michael, a young Jewish man, is about to run off with his Puerto Rican boyfriend. They race up the steps to the number four train. The young Puerto Rican man gets on the train, but Michael doesn't. The doors close and the elevated train leaves the station. Michael watches it until it is a dot in the distance, then disappears, and the Puerto Rican character does too.

But it wasn't until I read Jaime Manrique's *Latin Moon in Manhattan* that I connected to the experience, the language, the culture of the characters Manrique portrayed. I wasn't standing in my world and looking into another. And although he was writing about a Colombian enclave in Jackson Heights, Queens, New York, and I lived in a Puerto Rican and black neighborhood in the Bronx, I got it. I reflected the rhythms and the cultural references. The experiences he described of living in the world of our families and the worlds of the big city was visceral, sensual.

From the moment the book opened with the number seven train leaving Manhattan to begin its crawl to Queens, this daddy had me, because each day, after I left my job in the promotions department of Human Sciences Press on Thirteenth Street and later at Universal Pictures on Fifty-Seventh Street, I rode the number six train home to the Bronx. The shaking and rumbling train vanished as I slipped deeper into his text. He compared Manhattan to Oz and described the reflections of the setting sun on the Twin Towers as "gold leaf entrances to huge hives bursting with honey." I shuddered upon reading that. His words and descriptions were like tender strokes sparking electricity over my skin. This daddy's hug felt warm and familiar. There were no explanations needed. Nos entendimos, we understood one another. I had to imagine what a bathhouse was like or what it would be like to be blond, beautiful, and desired by every man sailing on the yacht. But I knew what it was like to sit in a living room of older Latina women gossiping in Spanish. I knew the feeling of embracing a world greater than the one at home and yet keeping home close to the heart. When Manrique described how his cousins back in Colombia made fun of how clumsy he was at all the country activities for boys, I recalled trips to Puerto Rico where cousins or their friends laughed when I darted in terror from a giant iguana or couldn't handle a machete to slice open a coconut. My cultural connection to this daddy was comforting and thrilling.

I looked for more of his work and read *Colombian Gold* and his poetry books, although I was not necessarily *into* poetry. A version of his collection *Tarzan, My Body, Christopher Columbus* has a picture of Manrique, shirtless, on the cover. He holds up both arms, flexes his biceps, holds his head cocked to the right and has a mock macho snarl on his face. Wow! A beefcake shot of my daddy. The collection itself was not like reading *Latin Moon*, because I like to take my time with the foreplay fiction affords, whereas poetry tends to go right to the sex. But it was still very satisfying to take in all the words because they resonated with my queer, Latino sensibilities, and after all, they were his words.

By the mid-'90s I had many more daddies, including Federico García Lorca, Manuel Puig, and Reinaldo Arenas, all subjects of the essays in Manrique's *Eminent Maricones: Arenas, Lorca, Puig, and Me.* Now, I loved them, too, but they wrote mainly about experiences in Latin America or the Caribbean (except for Arenas's memoir *Before Night Falls*, which includes his coming to New York City). James Baldwin was another daddy I discovered through his big queer novel *Giovanni's Room*, but it was about a white American expatriate in Paris (and I didn't read *Another Country* until my MFA program in 2006). So, Baldwin with his emphasis on race became a hero more in terms of civil rights than gay rights.

Another major daddy was Abraham Rodriguez Jr., author of *Spidertown, Boy without a Flag, Buddha Book*, and *South by South Bronx*. He came the closest to Manrique in the hierarchy of daddies. Rodriguez's novels and stories all take place in the Bronx, and they pulse with the sounds, smells, and sights of the borough. I've walked the streets he writes about, and I related to his young, hopeful, mischievous, and street savvy characters. They were my friends, cousins, neighbors, and classmates. Rodriguez was also Puerto Rican, so culturally there was a

Charles Rice-González

natural fit, but his characters or stories weren't gay. Rodriguez was one of my straight daddies. Later in the '90s Junot Díaz came on the scene with *Drown*. I became a groupie, following him around to reading after reading at KGB and in bookstores, including Seri Colon's Agüeybana in the Lower East Side. I savored his words and the experiences of his characters in the Dominican Republic and in the United States, but missed a strong, central, queer positive storyline.

Since first reading Manrique, I've read other queer Latino works including Rigoberto González's *Butterfly Boy: Memories of a Chicano Mariposa*, Erasmo Guerra's *Between Dances*, Emanuel Xavier's *Christ Like*, and the queer Latino anthologies that came out in 1999, Manrique's *Bésame Mucho* and Jaime Cortez's *Virgins, Guerillas and Locas*. Still, Jaime Manrique remains my main daddy despite the fact that his latest book, *Our Lives Are the Rivers*, did not have a gay theme, and his next book, which I will read, will be about the iconic Spanish writer Miguel de Cervantes.

Manrique is the bridge. He is queer, Latino, and New York City. He was the first writer who brought all those elements together for me. And even though his writing was literary and at times poetic it was also straightforward and cinematic. Scenes from his books play like clips from a movie in my memory. I can see the old, grungy Times Square in *Latin Moon in Manhattan* and the sassy midget prostitute Hot Sauce working the streets. Manrique was the ultimate daddy, inspiring me to write my story and from my perspective.

I had to wait nearly five years after *Latin Moon in Manhattan* before my daddy's next love letter, *Twilight at the Equator*, which had a profound effect on me. With this book, Manrique continued to write from a queer, Colombian perspective. He allowed that perspective to color his experiences without necessarily writing about them as issues.

Santiago, the main character, often found himself straddling his Latino and gay worlds and finding places where they intersected. One way it shined brightly was when exploring the culture clashes between living in New York City and living in Barranquilla or Bogotá, Colombia. Both were large metropolitan cities, but in New York he found more acceptance for himself as a gay man and more obstacles as a Latino, whereas in Colombia being Latino was not an issue, but he could be killed for being a homosexual. His characters existed in our worlds, and the duality or multiplicity of who they are was just an element that propelled action, shaped character, and offered me a connection.

That is demonstrated in a sense of nostalgia that the main character has for his homeland of Colombia while he is living in New York City, where he'd been living for most of his adult life, yet there is this pull to go back home. He doesn't quite understand the pull, because he clearly knows that he left fearing being killed for being gay, nor did he want the other alternative, which was to live in Colombia hiding his homosexuality. Yet memories of old towns and friends called to him. That was true for me, too. Even though I've never lived in Puerto Rico, that pull to go "home" is a very common feeling for many immigrants and for their children who've never lived in the native lands of their parents, but have lived there through hearing countless stories.

Midway through the book, the main character does go home, after his sister has died tragically in New York. At first, he slips into the nostalgia of moonlight on water, tropical breezes, and memories of old loves. But the sepia-toned experiences erupt into full color when an uncle he remembers as a prominent businessman turns out to be a ruthless drug dealer. The action between the two characters escalates, and the uncle's homophobia drives him over an emotional edge to where he is prepared to kill Santiago. Santiago escapes, and is reminded that there were solid, concrete reasons he left his country, and that it should remain as part of his past. As a Latino man, he embraces his freedom to pursue his writing and to live in New York City as a gay man.

With this book, my daddy had won my eternal devotion. Even though it was one-sided, all the drama and excitement of our relationship was full on.

In 2005, I attended my first Publishing Triangle Awards ceremony and noticed Manrique seated in the audience. It was the first time I had seen him in person. My heart thumped throughout the whole presentation, and I kept stealing glances at him. The room was pretty full and there was speech after speech, and award after award. At the end of the ceremony, I saw him making his way through the auditorium. *My daddy is tall and burly.* I recalled the beefcake cover of the *Tarzan, My Body, Christopher Columbus* collection. He wore an elegant jacket with a silk scarf draped around his neck. I kept thinking, "Holy shit, that's Jaime Manrique. Holy shit, that's Jaime Manrique." I didn't know anybody else in the hall, but the one person I recognized was my daddy! I took a deep breath, intercepted him, and introduced myself. I didn't tell him how much he influenced and inspired me, I just rambled on about an artist friend we both knew and about a book I was writing. He politely nodded and listened. Then he spoke. *My daddy has a deep baritone voice that echoes in his broad chest.* He offered to read my novel when I was done with it. Then he politely excused himself and offered his hand for me to shake. *My daddy has large hands that could completely cup my entire bald head.*

I've met my daddy many times since. Once at a party for *Ties That Bind: Familial Homophobia and Its Consequences* by Sarah Schulman, one of my latest daddies. And I've gone to hear him read around the city. We've exchanged e-mails and telephone conversations, and once he even invited me as his date to a PEN American event.

I did finish that novel that I rambled on about the first time we met. And, as he offered then, he looked it over and gave me a quote.

Now loving Manrique doesn't mean that I don't love White, Holleran, Bram, Brown, Schulman, and all my other daddies. I suppose in this realm it's natural for me to be polyamorous. They all offer something to me in my development as a writer.

I can't recall if I have ever truly expressed to Jaime Manrique how important he was to me, as he was to many queer Latino readers. So in a way, this essay is my appreciative love note to my main daddy.

Making a Man
Out of Me

Richard Blanco

I'm six or seven years old, riding back home with my grandfather and my Cuban grandmother from my *tía* Onelia's house. Her son Juan Alberto is effeminate, "*un afeminado*," my grandmother says with disgust. "*¿Por qué?* He's so handsome. Where did she go wrong with dat *niño?*" she continues, and then turns to me in the back seat: "Better to having a granddaughter who's a whore than a grandson who is *un pato* faggot like you. Understand?" she says with scorn in her voice. I nod my head *yes*, but I don't understand: I don't know what a faggot means, really; don't even know about sex yet. All I know is she's talking about *me, me*; and whatever I am, is bad, very bad. Twenty-something years later, I sit in my therapist's office, telling him that same story. With his guidance through the months that follow, I discover the extent of my grandmother's verbal and psychological abuse, which I had swept under my subconscious rug. Through the years and to this day I continue unraveling how that abuse affected my personality, my relationships, and my writing. I write, not in the light of Oscar Wilde, Walt Whitman, or Elizabeth Bishop, but in the shadow of my grandmother—a homophobic woman with only a sixth-grade education—who has exerted (and still exerts) the most influence on my development as a writer.

I am seven, I think. My grandmother tells me I eat wrong: "Don't use a straw, ever. *Los Hombres* don't drink soda with a straw. Now throw dat away and sit up." I look wrong: "*Dios mío*, you nosin but bones. Dat's why the boys at school push you around. Even a girl could beat you up. Now finish your steak, or else." My friends are all wrong: "I no taking you to dat Enrique's house neber again. He's a Mamacita's boy. I don't want you playing with him. I don't care what you say, those GI Joes he has are dolls. Do you want to play with dolls; is dat what you want *señorita?*" I play wrong: "I told your mother not to get you those crayons for Christmas. You should be playing outside like *un hombre*, not coloring in your girly books like dat *maricón* Juan Alberto." I speak wrong: "*Hay Santo*, you sound like *una niña* on the phone. When is your voice going to change?" And I walk wrong too: "Stop clacking your sandals and jiggling like a sissy. Straighten up *por Dios*—we're in public." I am wrong ("I'll make a man out of you yet . . ."), afraid to do or say anything (". . . you'll see . . ."), scared to want or ask anything (". . . even if it kills me . . ."), ashamed to be alive.

At thirty-one, I sit at a candlelit table across from the man who will be my husband. I tell him about my grandmother and the coping mechanisms I developed; how they naturally led me to writing; mechanisms that became part of my very creative process. Becoming withdrawn and introverted, I grew to become an observer of the world, instead of a participant. In order to survive emotionally I learned to read my environment very carefully and then craft *appropriate* responses that would (hopefully) prevent abuse and ridicule from my grandmother. I explain to my husband-to-be that I am still that quiet, repressed boy whenever I am in a room full of people, trying to be as invisible as possible, but taking in every detail, sensory as well as emotional, that will eventually surface in a poem. My work is often described as vivid and lush; relatives often marvel at my recollection in my poems of family events and details. Qualities I attribute directly to the skills spawned from my coping with my abuse. But beyond that, I've come to understand why writing and me became such a great fit. It allowed me to participate in the world, to feel alive, while remaining an invulnerable observer, safe in my room, at my desk, in my imagination where no one, especially my grandmother, could hurt me.

I'm eight, definitely. I remember because my grandmother is horrified that I'm already *eight* and haven't learned to ride a bike yet. "*Qué barbaridad*, no wonder . . . ," she tells me, leaving me to fill in the blanks with her words: No wonder: I'm a sissy, effeminate, a weakling. I'm used to her words for me. "I'll teach you," she barks, "Put your sneakers on." We walk my bike to the empty parking lot at St. Jude's Church where I pedal and fall; pedal and fall; pedal and finally glide in perfect balance, leaving her behind clapping and cheering me on: "*¡Andale! Finally! ¡Andale!*" On the way back home, I ride my bike beside her as she praises me, "*Qué bien.* You did great! *¡Qué macho!*" and kisses my forehead. That night she makes chicken *fricasé*—my favorite—with extra drumsticks and olives just for me. For a moment I can almost believe she loves me, that she'll never call me a faggot again, that she'll let me play with my *sissy* Legos and watercolors. But that very night she shoos my cat Ferby off my lap: "Stop dat. You looking like *una niña* sitting there petting dat thing. Why don't you like dogs?" Apparently, I have the wrong pet, too.

Twenty-eight years later, I get a cat at the suggestion of another therapist, who says it would be good for me; I should indulge myself. I name him Buddha—a leopard-spotted stray who follows me everywhere around the house. He kneads my arms and stomach; he licks my eyebrows. Though he's an animal, his "love" feels unconditional, unlike my grandmother, who only loved me if I didn't strike out at little league games; if I didn't swing my arms as I walked; if I sat still and behaved like the straight little boy she wanted to turn me into. At an early age I came to believe that all love was conditional like my grandmother's. Consequently, I shut down my emotional communication with others, because in my mind no one could be trusted. I became afraid to love, because no one could truly love a faggot like me: not my father or mother, not my brother—or my lovers. But writing allowed me to connect emotionally with others, albeit as a substitute for the real thing. In a poem I could love from a safe distance, love virtually; *say* what I couldn't ordinarily say, make myself vulnerable.

I'm nine, maybe ten, sitting on the family room sofa, sneaking a look through the Sears catalog, again: pages and pages of men without shirts, men in tight briefs, men in boots. Wanting to touch them, I run my fingers across their smooth chests, their hairy chests, their arms, their crotches, pretending. It feels good. It feels terrible. I want to touch myself, but I can't because that's what my grandmother means by faggot, I know that by then. She knows I know and that I'm up to no good when she bursts into the room. Before I can stuff the catalog back into the magazine rack, she tears it from my hand, tosses it across the room, and yells: "Stop being such a *mariconcito*. You wanting me to put you in ballet classes? Is dat what you want? What's wrong with you? Go playing outside like a normal boy." Instead I dash to my bedroom. In tears I tear out a page from my composition book and write: *I, Ricardo De Jesus Blanco, swear to never do what I did today, ever, ever again, or else. As God as my witness.* I sign and date it; seal it in an envelope and place it under my mattress.

Thirty-two, maybe thirty-three years later, I'm remembering I couldn't even bring myself to write down exactly what it was I *did* on that day, afraid my grandmother might read it and find me out; that I would out myself through what I wrote. A fear I carried well into my thirties, through my first and second books of poetry, never daring to come out on the page. Those love poems I *did* dare to write, I wrote in second person, a gender-neutral "you"; and used only initials in my dedications: for M.K., for C.A.B., for C.S.B. All my beloved and almost beloved—Michael, Carlos, Craig—reduced to anonymous letters, acronyms for my sexuality that my grandmother would (hopefully) never figure out. I remained safely locked inside the literary closet. Though lately I've come to think it was a cultural closet I was hiding in. Since I couldn't even begin to entertain writing about my sexual identity, I focused my work on issues of cultural identity and negotiation as Cuban American instead. Not that these weren't important and honest concerns of mine (and continue to be); but in part it was my living in the shadow of my grandmother's abuse that kept me from investigating and identifying with gay writers, much less writing about my sexuality or my grandmother's abuse. I simply was not *one of them*, in my mind, but I was of course.

I'm twenty-six visiting Cuba for the first time. We are having lunch at *tía* Mima's house when I learn that her son Gilberto set himself on fire at eight years old, and died. I feel an instant kinship with this child, this boy I never met. In a flash, I remember what I meant/felt when I wrote *or else*: that desperate feeling of wanting to end my life, too; that deep, entrenched sadness that was my childhood. A sadness I have carried since then, according to yet another therapist who diagnosed me with dysthymia—a low-grade but persistent mild depression. At forty-one I realize I've been sad all my life and have always written from that psychological point of view. I am inspired by the melancholy I see mirrored in others, in the world, and the ways we survive it. I strive to capture sadness and transform it through language into something meaningful, beautiful. Although throughout most of my writing career I had never consciously written for or about the gay community, thematically I feel I've unconsciously been a very gay writer all along in this sense: trying to make lemonade out of lemons, castles out of mud, beauty out of pain.

Would I have become a poet regardless of my grandmother's abuse? Probably, but not the same kind of poet, nor would I have produced the same kind of work, I think. Nevertheless, in the end her ultimate legacy was to unintentionally instill in me an understanding of the complexities of human behavior and emotions. I could have easily concluded that my grandmother was a mean, evil bitch and left it at that. But through her I instead realized there are few absolutes when it comes to human relationships. People, myself included, are not always *good* or always *bad*. They can't always say what they mean; and don't always mean what they say. My grandmother loved me as best she could, the way she herself was loved, perhaps. Her trying to *make me a man* was an odd, crude expression of that love, but it inadvertently made me the writer I am today. And for that I feel oddly thankful, I realized fourteen years ago: I'm standing alone at her bedside at Coral Gables Hospital: She's drugged up. The tubes down her throat don't let her speak; she can't say terrible things to me anymore. Watching her, I flash back through all the sound bites of her verbal abuse, and start scribbling down a few lines for a poem I tentatively title "Her Voices." The first poem I will ever write for her, about her, and my sexuality. My first *out* poem. I'm twelve, I'm thirty-eight, I'm seventeen, I'm thirty-one, I am a man when she wakes up, opens her eyes wide for a moment, looks at me and squeezes my hand, then slips away, quietly, silently, without a word—and I let her go.

Under the Influence

Chip Livingston

I've come to consider myself a fifth-generation off-shoot of the New York School poets, and I count a couple of gay writers from earlier generations of that "school" among my primary influences and encouragers. It's impossible to even broach the subject without beginning with Kenward Elmslie, since he was my introduction to Poetry with a capital letter, and he was my introduction to becoming a New Yorker.

I moved to New York City in early 2003 to work as Kenward's personal assistant. Prior to meeting him, there were very few poets of the New York School that I was even aware of (John Ashbery, certainly; and the names Frank O'Hara and James Schuyler, but not their work). To be fair to myself, I didn't even consider myself a poet yet, but I knew taking the job with Kenward was to be part of my education.

I'd been a fiction writer up to that point, but I dabbled in and published some narrative poetry. One of my fiction professors, Lucia Berlin, was Kenward's good friend, and she had given me two of his books during my master's program at the University of Colorado. Lucia had said then that my writing, much of it focused on the recent loss of my boyfriend to AIDS, reminded her of Kenward's on losing his partner Joe, and she loaned me his book, *Bare Bones*, a remembrance of his life with the artist and writer Joe Brainard. The subject of Kenward's book and the way he expressed his grief resonated with me. So when I returned to Colorado after three years of teaching in the Virgin Islands, and Lucia called me to ask what was I doing for work—and would I consider moving to Manhattan to work as Kenward's assistant?—I jumped on this chance to experience a different world of art and poetry.

I tried to read Kenward's "new and selected" poems in *Routine Disruptions* before flying to New York for my live interview with him in late 2002. The language in his verse seemed so "out there" from my perspective, dislocated from any kind of narrative, almost as inaccessible for me as Ashbery's had proven to be (although I found Kenward's quicker, wittier, and not nearly so dense), and I worried that my failure to carry "poetry talk" with the seventy-four-year-old writer would blow the opportunity for me. I tried reading his book again on the plane.

As playful and irreverent as the poetry was, it also seemed somehow highbrow. I didn't think I'd be smart enough to be his assistant. I didn't think I was worldly enough. Or I thought that his privilege and Harvard education might have made Kenward arrogant and he would look down on me; maybe he'd think I had no place in his world, no place in poetry.

Within fifteen minutes of arriving at his West Village townhouse, I was completely at ease. There were no expectations that I was a fan—he seemed genuinely delighted that I'd even read any of his books. He'd greeted me at the door in a polo shirt, gray sweatpants, and white leather tennis shoes. He was a big man, soft-spoken but clear, and his home had a quiet feeling, lived-in, not pretentious although definitely grand. He sat across from me at the mahogany dining table, and he spoke to me as an equal. He was interested in my teaching at the University of the Virgin Islands, my giving up the sand and sun.

Kenward considered me a writer; and he had thoughtful questions about my work. I learned that Lucia had been mailing him copies of my published poems and stories. He complimented some by specific enough details that showed me he'd read them well and also that his memory for written lines was incredibly sharp. He asked about my influences.

Eight years ago when Kenward first asked me, I said I hadn't read enough poetry to be able to articulate that yet, but in fiction, I had my favorites. I said one of my earliest models had been the short stories of Brad Gooch. Kenward smiled. "Brad was my first assistant," he said.

"He worked upstairs for me and Joe." A sign, I thought. This was definitely where I was supposed to be.

My first night on the job was in January 2003. Kenward gave me four new poems that he'd written over Christmas week. He asked me if I'd look them over and see if anything was sticking out. Though I was flattered that he asked, it felt like an examination. Despite being exhausted from flying back and forth across the country, lugging my baggage from the airport and up the stairs to my room at Kenward's, I stayed up late struggling to parse out a meaning in the poems, a narrative from the opaque wordplay. I got online and Googled again his bio and Wikipedia'ed him trying to root the old man's material in some kind of experiential notion.

His thirty-year love affair with Joe Brainard had provided the grounding for *Bare Bones*, but his style of verse—at least in these four new samples—was experimental at best, L-A-N-G-U-A-G-E at worst, and in a vein I was afraid I couldn't cotton to. But I made a few notes, not suggestions but questions, relating to the content.

Kenward was sweet in his response, surprised at my invention of narratives to go with his abstractions. He complimented the flavors and presentation of my mushroom omelet, but assured me there was no storyline to follow in his poems, that they were just words he liked placed together, and that the pieces were for the ear, but he was interested in where I had taken them and said he thought he'd revisit them at the computer with my stories in mind.

The poems weren't altered to incorporate my ideas. I saw this when I took them to the mailbox. That three of the poems were immediately picked up for publication by *New American Writing*, one, "Agenda Melt," even going on to reappear in *Best American Poetry 2004*, just proved what I suspected. I wouldn't know real art or poetry if it was put under my nose.

My resolution for the new year had been to read at least twenty-six books of poems, A to Z alphabetically through a list of selected authors. I had been encouraged to browse and borrow from Kenward's library, and the letter "A" had been designated as Ashbery. Kenward and I talked of my difficulty with the work. Kenward instructed me to follow the sentence in John's poetry, that "J.A." wrote in grammatical sentence structure, and if I followed the lines in search of the architecture of the sentence, I'd be able to follow the meaning of the poem. Sometimes this works for me. I'd get more practice with Ashbery and O'Hara and Schuyler in my graduate program, which I entered that fall. Although I'd completed an MA in fiction writing at Colorado, I wanted both the terminal degree and the structured education that an MFA in poetry would comprise. Kenward's old friend in New York, Ron Padgett, who had taught at Brooklyn College, helped guide my coursework once I'd been admitted.

I am a dedicated student, and I applied myself heartily to my studies, determined to find "my line"—the way department head Lou Asekoff and I defined the difference between my prose and verse. And while my narrative poems continued to be published, I started experimenting with space, allowing a white pause to take the place of punctuation, and upon Kenward's suggestions to incorporate repetition of words for emphasis, for sound and rhythm. I started hearing a kind of lyric voice in my head, and it felt natural so I followed it.

My second semester at Brooklyn College, I took an independent study with Lisa Jarnot, who asked me if I was familiar with Tim Dlugos's work. She saw something in my poems that was "reminiscent of Dlugos's line," she said. Mentioning someone's "line" made me pay attention. I told her I hadn't heard of Tim and that I'd just been playing with space as punctuation. At our next weekly meeting she loaned me her copy of *Powerless*. I devoured it.

I felt a compulsive pull to every bit of this work. It felt like I had finally found "my poet," someone who made me laugh and cry, who wrote about being gay and about TV sitcom plots and about AIDS with both mundane humor and eloquent soliloquy. His poems had the easy affection of Joe Brainard's collages. They were instantly likeable. And while I was making a concentrated effort to read widely and really understand the different mechanics of language in all types of writing, I had never before connected with someone's poetry the way I did with Tim Dlugos and *Powerless*. I was desperate to know more about him. I wanted to read everything Tim had ever written. I searched the Internet for biography material. I ordered a copy of *Strong Place*.

I learned he'd grown up in Boston and had lived in New York and Washington, D.C.; that he'd died of AIDS complications in 1990; and that he'd entered Yale School of Divinity, late in his life, to study

Episcopalian religious doctrine. And I saw something in his poems, in the rhythm and spacing of his lines and in the subject matter—gay men's lives, gossiping about our friends, talking about our politics and movie stars—that was similar enough to my recent poems to warrant Jarnot's mention, and I'm eternally grateful that she did. Though I suspect I'd have discovered Tim one way or another. It was one of my greatest compliments to have even been mentioned in the same sentence as Tim, this "new" poet I thought was beyond fantastic. And I found his photographs handsome. He was someone I wish I'd had a chance to know.

I learned Tim had worked at the Poetry Project at St. Mark's Church, where I had taken a workshop and where I read poetry at Kenward's seventy-fifth birthday party. Tim had edited *The Poetry Project Newsletter*, which I subscribed to. It was a wonder I'd never heard of this third-generation New York School poet before Lisa mentioned him.

He became a quick obsession, as I traced every lead I could find online. My next day off, I went to Poets House and found some of Tim's chapbooks. Walking down Eighth Avenue, I recited some of his lines that had stayed with me—"I have not read anything by Proust, Dostoyevsky, Rimbaud, or Frank O'Hara." This was from "Day for Paul." I heard new lines in my head.

I got a chill up my spine. It felt like the words I'd "made up" had been whispered in my ear. I intentionally thought: *If that's your ghost, Tim, and you want to write a poem through me, like some sort of automatic writing, be my guest. I am totally okay with it.* And though my hair was standing up on my skin, it felt sensible that a ghost was beside me, and natural to suggest he might influence me. I got out my Post-it notes and wrote down what I heard: "Crawfish's idea digging the mud up." It didn't sound like Tim's work, but it didn't exactly sound like mine either.

That night, I tried to relax and open my mind to any kind of word rhythm or list sequence that might come through. I scribbled down a few ideas, new lines, almost a complete poem or two, chasing every word that appeared in my head, the words that I thought could possibly be Tim's.

The next morning, I realized I'd been a fool so far for not mentioning him to Kenward. I had the common sense to bring up his name at breakfast. "Kenward, I've become obsessed with this poet, and I want to know everything I can about him. I feel like his ghost is following me around town, even in this house. His name was Tim Dlugos."

Kenward howled. A good indication I would like his answer. He threw his head back and laughed. Then he straightened his face thoughtfully and said, "That makes sense. Tim used to live in your room."

I almost spit out my coffee. I knew I hadn't made it up. I'd spoken to a ghost.

Throughout breakfast and after, as I kept filling up our coffee cups, I listened as Kenward told me about Tim, how they'd met at a party, how he and Tim had become friends, and how Tim had come to stay at Kenward's house, the same one I lived in, from 1976 until sometime in '78, when Tim moved to Brooklyn, and one rowdy NEA weekend when Kenward visited him in D.C.

I've had the privilege to hear and read more stories about Tim since then. Ron Padgett gave me a copy of the spring 2000 issue of the *James White Review* that posthumously paid tribute to Tim. Through poet Aaron Smith, I met David Trinidad, who was a close friend of Tim's and who has tirelessly worked to keep Tim's poems in print. And though Tim died in December 1990, his previously unpublished poems still regularly appear in national journals and anthologies twenty years later—including *POETRY 2009*, *The American Poetry Review 2010*, and *Best American Poetry 2010*. His work keeps surfacing, and each "new" poem moves me, makes me want to get out a piece of paper and start a poem. As Kenward puts it, Tim's poems "still hold up."

May 2011 saw the debut of *A Fast Life: The Collected Poems of Tim Dlugos*, in which David Trinidad's efforts reward us with over six hundred pages of Tim's work, much of it never before published. I feel like I've been waiting for this collection since I first heard of Tim. And while I had no idea of its inception, it seems like I caught an early wave in a resurrection of Tim's poetry that's proving his literary importance. I can certainly trace his importance on my own poetry.

Not only are his late poems among the most artful and lyrical sources documenting AIDS in the 1980s, his New York School list poems illustrate with comedic poignancy our daily druthers—"The Young Poet," "Turning," and "On This Train Are People Who Resemble"—and to me cry out for updated imitations. I learn New York gay history from Tim, and I learn New York poetry.

Chip Livingston

The same continues with Kenward. The more I learn about the worlds he lived and lives in, and the more experience I have with his poetry, I've come to an understanding of how to read him, and how to enjoy his work. And while I no longer have the urgency of Tim's whisper in my ear, I do feel his presence and his influence around the house. Tim's work has become a continual source of inspiration, and from the shelf above my writing desk his collections and chapbooks are facing me, looking over me as I write, and sometimes I look up and ask him if I'm doing okay.

Usually, I imagine him shrugging, saying something like, "Eh? Who's to judge?" But in truth I know that is a mannerism of Kenward's, and I don't have a physical experience to animate Tim. But I'm told there are videos archived at the Poetry Project. The Tim Dlugos papers are housed in the Fales Collection nearby at an NYU library. I'm glad I have his personality and carriage yet to discover. I've also got his collected poems on order, and the rest of my life to study and keep learning from him.

My Mother's Grave
Is Yellow

Dale Peck

I first discovered Shirley Jackson's *We Have Always Lived in the Castle* in my high school library. "Discovered" seems a grand word for the experience: the library in Buhler High School was hardly a place where one "discovered" anything. It was a single, brightly lit, drop-ceilinged room lined with walnut-stained particle-board shelves scaled down to the size of pre–growth spurt freshman arms. Devoid of mystery or charm or whatever it is that people who work with children like to call "wonder," the BHS library was little more than a room with books in it, in stark opposition to the grand libraries that haunted the books on its shelves, the dark dusty magical rooms found in the novels of C. S. Lewis or J. R. R. Tolkien (or, often, Shirley Jackson), but it was, nonetheless, what I had to work with, and I like to imagine I ferreted out what few secrets it actually possessed. I looked for books the way my stepmother shopped for vegetables: by picking them up one at a time and checking them for desirability. I went wall by wall, shelf by shelf, book by book, my search conducted under the watchful eyes of the high school librarian, a tall thin young woman whose name I can't quite remember— Sybil? Sybert? Seibert?—who could see virtually every book from her post at the check-out counter. The books were, of course, indexed by the Dewey Decimal System, but, in a gesture that both acknowledged and reinforced the mundanity of my school's low standards, handwritten translations had been added to the labels, viz., *900–999: reference*.

Buhler High School was itself a simplification of a more complex code: Buhler, Kansas, was a tiny town of conservative Mennonites— 888 as of the 1980 census and shrinking all the time—located a dozen or so miles northeast of the small city of Hutchinson, where most of its students actually lived. The only reason a high school had been built in Buhler at all was so that Hutch's more affluent residents, who lived on the northern and eastern sides of town, could bus their sons and daughters to a school free of the poorer—read: nonwhite—element that made up a large part of Hutch High. Only two black students actually enrolled during my time there, although there was a brief appearance by a Chilean exchange student who, after three or four solitary weeks, disappeared from our hallways. I remember being aware of this gerrymandering even then. I suppose I was so conscious of it because I had moved to Kansas from Long Island when I was seven; most of my peers regarded our school's virtual whiteness as a naturally occurring circumstance but to me it always seemed odd, especially given the number of blacks and Latinos that were visible just ten miles to the south. Not surprisingly, the school board that produced such a segregated institution was solidly religious and conservative, and, also not surprisingly, this school board banned books as a matter of course. I don't remember being able to find *The Color Purple* when the movie came out, nor was *The Catcher in the Rye* available in our library; every year, I remember, the protests of that year's rebellious student (I was 1988's) led to a short-lived debate on whether the novels of Kurt Vonnegut were appropriate reading material for teenagers, and every year the conclusion was that some of them were and some of there were not, but just to be on the safe side all of them were banned.

I doubt that Shirley Jackson was ever the subject of such debate simply because, by 1981, when I entered high school, she had been almost completely forgotten. Jackson published her first novel, *The Road through the Well*, and her most successful short story, "The Lottery," in 1948, and she remained a well-known, well-read writer until her death in 1965, at the age of forty-six. During her brief professional life she produced dozens of short stories, six novels, and two works of nonfiction—sly satires on family life that must have gone right over the heads of the

Leave It to Beaver crowd—but since her death her reputation had steadily declined. That decline continues: a recent collection of short stories was received respectfully but without enthusiasm; her novels are either out of print or languish in the young adult sections of public libraries— which is why I was able to find one. I stumbled across the single copy of *We Have Always Lived in the Castle* our library possessed in, as they say, my tender, formative years. I'm now convinced the experience scarred me for life.

—

Of course, there was "The Lottery." Everyone in America reads "The Lottery"; everyone, I should say, *must* read "The Lottery," just as everyone must read *To Kill a Mockingbird* and *Huckleberry Finn* and at least an abridged version of Anne Frank's *Diary of a Young Girl*, and as a result the story inhabits the invisible realm of over-scrutinized objects, shoelaces and toothbrushes and librarians, objects whose enormous effect on our lives is never quite acknowledged; I first read the story in eighth grade, and of that original reading I only remember gleefully noting that the surname of the woman who wins the lottery was Hutchinson.

Briefly, for those who somehow escaped the story, "The Lottery" is a sketch of an unnamed "village" whose citizens say "Dellacroy" rather than "Delacroix," "m'dishes" instead of "my dishes." The villagers are simple folk who grow crops and clean house and, each June 27, hold a lottery whose winner is stoned to death. This lottery is performed with a kind of mesmeric simplicity by rural stereotypes who, at story's end, kill their friend with the same automatic gestures with which they might till a field or cook a meal. On the one hand, their mindlessness is what makes the story so horrifying, but it's also, I think, what renders "The Lottery" nothing *more* than a horror story: characters identifiable only as types are dismissible for the same reason. Though the story might, on first read, be shocking, it's not haunting—or, at any rate, it didn't haunt me. I was a native New Yorker living among the stereotypes Jackson was describing. Kansans said "pop," "scoot," "put it up" where I was inclined to say "soda," "move," "put it away," but that didn't mean I ducked every time someone picked up a rock. Violence is relatively rare in the Midwest, although when it does come it's explosive. I remember

Dale Peck

a fellow third-grader having his leg broken when he was thrown across a table during the course of a classroom argument; the boy who sat catty-corner from me in ecology my junior year used a shotgun to blow the heads off his girlfriend and the twins she was baby-sitting because he thought she was cheating on him; the only reason the lynch mob didn't get the black date of a classmate during our five-year high school reunion was that its members were too drunk to find her hotel. Shirley Jackson was perceptive enough to realize that the balding farmer of Grant Wood's *American Gothic* might very well stab his daughter with the pitchfork he held, and it was this possibility that she explored and expanded upon in "The Lottery"; but even in eighth grade I recognized the more mundane truth, which is that Wood's farmer would probably go out to the barn and bale hay like he was supposed to, and maybe—*maybe*—sneak a nip from a flask hidden in the hay loft.

We Have Always Lived in the Castle is, in one sense, another version of "The Lottery"—in, say, the same sense that a *mousse au chocolat* is another version of Jell-O chocolate pudding. It tells the story of an eighteen-year-old orphan, Mary Katherine Blackwood, who lives with her older sister Constance and invalid uncle Julian in their family's ancestral home. The novel, like "The Lottery," is set in a rural backwoods; a contemporary setting is signaled by the presence of automobiles and telephones, but Jackson is deliberately vague in her descriptions of these and other modern machines, and as a result the novel could take place any time after 1925 or '30. This temporal reticence is crucial to the story's theme: despite the fact that the novel is set in contemporary America, the characters behave as though they live in the middle of the last century, much like the characters of "The Lottery." But where the story's setting is essentially its subject, in the novel the setting is merely the ominous backdrop for a turgid family drama, which is why the novel succeeds where the story falters—and also, I think, why it was so particularly powerful to me. My father had moved us to Kansas because his third marriage in as many years had ended, and if the bleak landscape and odd customs of my new home filled me with confusion and not a little fear, it was nothing compared to the strangeness of what went on in my house.

The Blackwoods are not proletarians like the cast of "The Lottery," but wealthy landowners living just outside their own unnamed "village," whose poorer residents, Mary Katherine declares in the opening pages of the novel, "have always hated us." Why that is so is never made clear; the assumption, of course, is that the typical antipathy between the rich and poor is at play here, but gradually it emerges that the situation is more complex. The Blackwoods are, well, weird; not just Mary Katherine's parents, but also her brother and Uncle Julian's wife are dead, all killed by arsenic put into the sugar bowl one evening at dinner. Constance, the family cook, was acquitted of the murders, but the villagers are convinced of her guilt; in fact, Mary Katherine was the culprit. Twelve years old at the time, she had been sent to bed without supper. In retaliation, she put the poison in the sugar bowl, knowing that her beloved sister Constance never touched sweet things (Uncle Julian's survival was nothing more than dumb luck: he didn't eat enough poison to die, merely to destroy his gastrointestinal tract and, as well, to upset a brain that seems already to have been addled). But the novel is hardly a mystery: Mary Katherine's emotions and observations are so peculiar that it's hard *not* to suspect her of something. On her twice-weekly walk through the village for household supplies, she is lost in a reverie of "catching scarlet fish in the rivers on the moon"—remember, this is an eighteen-year-old—when she

> saw that the Harris boys were in their front yard, clamoring and quarrelling with half a dozen other boys. I had not been able to see them until I came past the corner by the town hall, and I could still have turned back and gone the other way, up the main highway to the creek, and then across the creek and home along the other half of the path to our house, but it was late, and I had the groceries and the creek was nasty to wade in our mother's brown shoes, and I thought, I am living on the moon, and I walked quickly. They saw me at once, and I thought of them rotting away and curling in pain and crying out loud; I wanted them doubled up and crying in front of me.

Note the detail with which the alternate path is described: Mary Katherine knows each step she will take long before she takes it. The magic of passages like this is that even as Mary Katherine—Merricat, as Constance calls her—fantasizes about the violent, painful deaths of nearly everyone she comes into contact with, she also communicates an awestruck, childlike view of the world, so that when her guilt is finally revealed it still comes as a shock—not the shock of the unexpected, but the shock of recognition, of a long-denied truth. The moral triumph of the novel is that, by the time Merricat mentions her crime aloud, we have already justified it in our minds; she never needs to, and, indeed, if she did, she would be much less likely to win our sympathy.

All of this is, as it were, merely compelling back story, developed in tandem with the main narrative. As the novel opens, the murders are six years in the past, and Mary Katherine and Constance and Uncle Julian have settled into their Never-Never Land existence, with tomboy Mary Katherine cast in the role of Peter Pan, fair-haired Constance as Wendy, and wheelchair-bound, rambling Uncle Julian as a kind of grotesque Lost Boy. Into this perfect world, of course, comes Captain Hook: cousin Charles, an apparition so horrible that Merricat "could not see him clearly, perhaps because he was a ghost, perhaps because he was so very big." Merricat stresses Charles's resemblance to her dead father, and, in her eyes, he is more than the "intruder" she calls him: he is an unknown element in a world so fetishistically ordered that the simple patterns of housekeeping, bathing, and eating are imbued with magical force. Charles is an adult come to drag her from her childhood paradise, and Merricat deals with him accordingly.

> Eliminating Charles from everything he had touched was almost impossible, but it seemed to me that if I altered our father's room, and perhaps later the kitchen and the drawing room and the study, and even finally the garden, Charles would be lost, shut off from what he recognized, and would have to concede that this was not the house he had come to visit and so would go away.

"Altering" in this case means destroying; Merricat first does simple things like smash his watch and foul his bedding, but when that doesn't work she resorts to drastic measures: she sweeps his smoldering pipe into an open wastebasket full of paper (although Freudian interpretations are often overused, I think they're appropriate here). In Merricat's mind the room Charles inhabits—her dead father's room—is distinct from the house she lives in, but, of course, the whole building catches fire. Charles goes for help—the Blackwoods have no phone—and returns with the villagers. Some of them work to put out the fire but most watch the house burn; for his part, Charles tries to steal the safe, which contains whatever's left of the Blackwood fortune, but it's too heavy to move.

But the drama isn't quenched when the fire's extinguished. Like vampires, the villagers are empowered by their official invitation into the Blackwood home and, like vampires, put their power to ill use: what the fire hasn't destroyed the villagers do, in an orgy of Dionysian passion, and while they work adults and children both chant a local nursery rhyme:

> Merricat, said Constance, would you like a cup of tea?
> Oh, no, said Merricat, you'll poison me.
> Merricat, said Constance, would you like to go to sleep?
> Down in the boneyard ten feet deep.

I made up my own nursery rhyme when I was a child, when I was five or six, much younger than I was when I first read Jackson's novel. The "rhyme" was only one line long—"My Mother's Grave Is Yellow"—and I recited it sometimes in bed, more often when I crawled beneath the coffee table in our living room. The table's wooden underside had been branded with the letters MMGIY, and for a few years, for the two or three years after my mother's death and before I was too big to fit under the table, I cast about for the hidden message in those initials, finally alighting on that one line: "My Mother's Grave Is Yellow." In fact I didn't know what color my mother's grave was. I'd never been allowed to see it, just as I'd never been allowed to see my mother when she was dying in the hospital, just as I'd never been allowed to see my father's mother because they didn't speak, or see my mother's mother because she didn't want to have anything to do with her children or their lives, or see dozens of my other relatives because they were dead or missing or simply too far away. There were more secrets in my family than revelations, but what was hidden was nevertheless known. The hatred or violence or simple fear that produced and informed my family's silences could be felt if not named, and if it took me years to recognize this force as the operating principal of *We Have Always Lived in the Castle*, I nevertheless sensed it: the novel spooked me so badly that I returned it to the library and resolved to never read it, or Shirley Jackson, again; with the exception of the inescapable "Lottery," which I must have encountered at least a half dozen times in subsequent years, I kept that promise for fifteen years.

Jackson structures her novel so that its climax comes just after Merricat confesses her role in her family's death. The juxtaposition of the two events is what drives home the novel's true point: that the difference between ruler and ruled is one of means, not temperament (my father terrorized me because he was bigger than me, but if I'd been bigger than him . . . !). In one sense, "The Lottery" can be dismissed as a sophisticate's paranoia about the proletariat—Jackson and her husband, the critic Stanley Edgar Hyman, were both intellectuals based in rural North Bennington, Vermont, where Hyman taught at the college—but *We Have Always Lived in the Castle* presents a world view that is both more personal and more complex than that of "The Lottery." Just as the villagers' poverty is the justification, conscious or unconscious, for their ignorance, Merricat's hoarded wealth allows her to build her own shell of ritualized unknowing. Not surprisingly, after the villagers have trashed the Blackwood house, life resumes its former pattern. Charles, stymied, leaves; the villagers, spent, abandon all overt contact with the Blackwoods, but each night a basket of food is deposited on their porch in atonement; Mary Katherine, clothed in an old tablecloth and drinking from the last unbroken cup, speaks the novel's final words without a trace of irony: "'Oh, Constance,' I said, 'we are so happy.'"

The link between this book and another subversive fairy tale, Orwell's *Animal Farm*, might not be apparent, but in fact Orwell's is simply a politicized treatment of the theme Jackson confronts on a social level: ignorance is bliss. But it's rarely accidental. In an ironic gesture of fate that I'm sure she would appreciate if not exactly welcome, Jackson's relegation to high schools and rural libraries has left the intellectual audience she wrote for ignorant of her words, whereas the rural clod hoppers she wrote about have access to her books but pass by them unknowingly. Only their children read them, and, I imagine, learn from Merricat's example: if the life you see is ugly shut your eyes, and dream of a better one. My mother's grave is yellow, would you like a cup of tea? The poison in Jackson's cup is the dark side of the imagination, the unconscious, but it's also the bitter antidote to a more quotidian but no less certain death, of conservatism, or provinciality, or just plain old-fashioned boredom.

Some Notes, Thoughts, Recollections, Revisions, and Corrections Regarding Becoming, Being, and Remaining a Gay Writer

Justin Chin

I. How to Be a Gay Writer

1. Be Gay.
2. Write like a motherfucker.

II. How to Be a Writer Who "Just Happens" to Be Gay, Just Happens as if One Accidentally Stepped into a Pile of Gay, as if a Lark Pooped Gay on One's Head

1. Be Gay.
2. Write like a motherfucker.
3. Explain to all and sundry until their ears bleed how you're gay but not really gay but gay. Or adamantly refuse to.

III. To Read

These days, it's difficult to imagine a time before the Internet and its easy anytime access to porn. But for me as a wee pup, growing up in a seemingly sterile place like Singapore in the early '80s, where even

Cosmo was banned, finding a *Playboy* or *Playgirl* was nearly impossible. No, what pubescent boys—gay or not—had to settle for were "dirty" novels. Harold Robbins and Sidney Sheldon were kings at that time, Tom Sharpe to a lesser degree. What you'd do was go to a bookstore, find said author's book on the shelf, and let it fall open to the places where the spine was already cracked, and voila! the dirty bits.

This was, of course, before the game-changing advent of the International Male Undergear catalog.

What was the first gay book that I read? I do remember reading Oscar Wilde's fairy tales in high school, and I loved how gorgeous and poignant and tragic and heartbreaking and swoony they were. There weren't actually any Acts of Gay in those stories, so it's more of a flaming book than a gay one, really.

There is another book though, that I found it in the school library. But for the life of me, I cannot remember what it was, even as I've tried through the years to figure it out. All I remember is this: The two male characters marinate in a haze of ennui, there is an orgy of sorts, someone sticks a bottle up his ass, the bottle breaks and the character dies, and everyone swans about being super maudlin. It might have been Cocteau (though I can't seem to place it) or some other French writer, or possibly German, definitely European. I do recall how the whole thing felt so illicit: reading it late at night so no one would walk in on me, feeling that I needed to finish it and return it before . . . I don't know before what. As if being found in possession of that book would telegraph to the world what a big fat homo I was. And I was.

IV. It Begins

I would not be the writer that I am today if not for the poet Faye Kicknosway. That is the simple plain truth.

As a freshman at the University of Hawai'i at Manoa, I signed up for Intro to Creative Writing, picking the class section that suited my schedule best. And in one of those serendipitous strokes of life, I ended up in Kicknosway's class.

She was tough—boy, was she ever. I was fighting back tears after our first conference, when she redlined and pointed out all the flaws in the poem I submitted. But she was also encouraging, and if you did good work, she let you know. Midsemester, she invited me to sit in on her upper-division class. There're some people you should meet, she said, and she introduced me to two students in that class: R. Zamora Linmark and Lisa Asagi, who till this day remain my strongest supporters and I theirs, and who are gifted writers in their own right.

In class, Kicknosway made us write persona poems and sestinas. She stressed the importance of listening to the voice of the poem, and editing with the ear. At the time, I didn't quite know it, but looking back, her pedagogical strategy was quite brilliant.

Sestinas taught us the importance of choosing the right words, the best words. Too show-offy or too easy and the poem would run out of steam and sputter out. Sestinas also required a kind of discipline and commitment.

Writing in personas, in some other person's voice or thoughts, she effectively pushed us away from the I-Me-My Ego, My Angst, My Deep Feelings, My Hidden Meanings that so often oversaturates beginning writers, but she also knew no matter what persona, there was always going to be some sliver of us still in there.

I wrote poems in the voices of Billie Holliday, Josephine Baker, Marilyn Monroe, assorted tricks and barflys, a Road Runner cartoon-watching serial killer, a Midwestern Walmart cashier, a closeted bride-groom in China, Jeff Stryker, Mary Jo Kopechne, a slowly unraveling liquor store clerk, a voodoo shaman, ex-boyfriends and boyfriends that never were, and, eventually, myself.

She aimed me toward reading Ai, Ntozake Shange, Jessica Hagedorn's early performance work, Rothenberg, Victor Hernández Cruz, Waldman, Corso, Jackson Mac Low, Robert Peters, an assortment of European Dadaist and Surrealist writers, Latin American magical realists, and a lot of '70s and '80s performance poetry.

I know it's a futile exercise, but I do sometimes wonder what my writing life would be like now if I had ended up in any of the other eight sections offered up of that Intro class.

V. To Read Too

I figured out pretty early on that reading was a major part of being a writer. And since I was not an English lit major, I wasn't forced to read all those great canonical books that I probably wouldn't read on my own unless required to. Left to my own devices, I tried to read as wide a range as I possibly could. But what strikes me now about those early fledgling years is *how* I read, as much as what and how much I read.

There was such a sense of discovery and of newness to it all. It was such a distinct pleasure and joy discovering writers that were new to me even if they had been working or dead for decades.

The staggering wonderment of the first time I stumbled onto Calvino, or Genet. The eye-opening amazement when I first read Jeanette Winterson, Jane Bowles, Rikki Ducornet, Rushdie, Rebecca Brown, Adam Mars-Jones, and so many others.

Yes, I was like a virgin, touched for the very first time.

I rather do miss that spirited sense of constant discovery, though it does still flare up from time to time these days.

VI. Influent

As writers, we are often asked about our influences, and truth be told, it's everything we take in, really. All the books we read and reread, all the films and TV shows and assorted narratives we experience, all the art and theater and performance and music we engage with, it all feeds into us in some way, it's all stored somewhere inside us waiting to pull together, even the stuff we despise and think is unbearably lame.

There is the stuff that inspires us, the stuff that teaches and instructs us, shows us how to, and there's the stuff that cautions and reminds us how not to, and how never to.

VII. First

These days, there is enough queer Asian American writing to slap together academic and literary conferences. In those heady days of the early '90s, not so.

Was there an unspoken competition, a race to see who would be the first rose in the garden? Probably. Though the race was over before it even began. Dwight Okita, Tim Liu, Chay Yew, and Norman Wong got there around the same time, but even before that, Russell Leong (Wallace Lin) and Lonny Kaneko had already been there. And the women had been there way before the guys: there was Willyce Kim, Barbara Noda, Kitty Tsui, and Merle Woo. And I'm sure there must have been more even before all these, queer Asian writers whose work have been lost to time and history.

VIII. Gay Writer

Know that you'd be called that for all the years of your writing career. Like *Fucking Faggot* or *Filthy Slut* or *Performance Poet*, it is rarely said neutrally.

What it means to say is: This writer is limited, what he has to say can't be of any consequence to the larger society or world; be open-minded and read him if you want, it might prove amusing, entertaining even, but if you want something serious, something of import, maybe not.

What it means to say is: This writer is going to write about gay sex in explicit and offensive and possibly gross detail. Be warned.

Whether you let all that define you or stymie you is entirely your bag. Know that some readers and editors will dismiss you outright, without a second thought. Assumptions, prejudice, and preconceptions dig hard grooves.

But of course, it's kind of hard to argue with the label, since all its component parts are essentially true. Gay? Yep. Writer? Uh-huh. So protesting or objecting just seems a tad persnickety.

Perhaps what it means to say is: This is a writer, and this writer is gay.

Or is this another one of those cases where the parts don't add up to the whole? When it comes to people, in all their dizzying flaws and glory, when do the parts ever add up to the whole?

IX. Gathering

Perhaps he had seen me reading and rereading the page in *Outwrite Magazine* announcing the first Outwrite Conference. The faculty advisor to the university's gay and lesbian group offered, out of his own pocket, to pay for me to go to the conference in San Francisco. That, of course, set off the gossips. He said it was "an investment in the future for the cause."

I couldn't have known it quite so clearly then, but on some deeper internal level, being at that conference did light some spark in me. Not only had I never been among so many queer folk, but these were also writers, aspiring and accomplished and legendary.

I was in constant awe. Allen Ginsberg, Sarah Schulman, and Judy Grahn were keynote speakers. I remember seeing Robert Giard taking photographs of a flexing and posing John Rechy in the hotel corridor. I remember putting faces to the names of poets I had read in *Poets for Life*. I remember seeing Richard Labonte, who would years later become a dear friend, and thinking that he looked like a fat Walt Whitman. This was the conference were Edward Albee infamously and scandalously declared that being male, he was a minority in the world, and being gay, also a minority, and being white Anglo-Saxon Protestant, yet again a minority, and that all his minority statuses had not prevented him from attaining his successes. It was in the breakout caucus session where I first learned the words *issue* and *process*.

Being at that conference showed me what was possible, that I could find myself in a continuum, a lineage that was grand and literary, that needed no elucidation or defense, no vindication or apologia.

And so, it was, and I am.

My Three Dads

Charles Jensen

> Everything is in the poems.
>
> Frank O'Hara

> All my movies are difficult to classify because they are very eclectic in mixing genres.
>
> Pedro Almodóvar

I took writing workshops in college, although I decided early on I would not major in English. In one of those early workshops, my teacher brought in Frank O'Hara's poem "The Day Lady Died" as a means of getting us to write out of the everyday, the mundane, but to focus on meaningful details.

The poem grabbed me by the collar.

It wasn't the content of the poem itself, I think now, that spoke to me. Before I even knew O'Hara was gay, I knew that he was gay. I knew it in the approach to subject, in the monumental impact of this loss described in the poem, the inextricability of the camp with the sincere.

I *understood* the poem.

I *understood* why it was written.

It resonated in me the way other poems we read in that class did not. Some forms of language to me felt closed. The poems were wall-like structures I could neither see through nor over. Or they were boring—no investment in any kind of urgency. I struggled to contend with them. Most of them I rejected. But the O'Hara piece—that was a poem for me.

A few weeks later, combing through a local used bookstore for poetry books to read and having absolutely no idea what to look for, I found a new-looking copy of Frank O'Hara's collected poems. I took it home, dove in, and began a long investigation into the poet whose voice would continue to speak to me long after I'd exhausted available material to read.

_____

I believe we should all perceive our work as a series of manifestoes.

_____

I enrolled at the same high school my older brothers had attended years before, sat in the same classrooms they sat in, took instruction from many of the same teachers. My English teacher that first year was Ms. Oliver, who was known by her favorite students simply as Oliver. She opted to put a special focus on creative writing in our class; we were required to respond to writing prompts in neat little journals she handed out, and we all had to do a research report on a poet while also writing our own poems.

My poems that year were tragic.

Both in the sense that they were awful, and in the sense that it was very clear to Oliver that I was beginning to struggle with my sexual orientation. And that I was losing.

_____

The poems seem to tumble out of him.

_____

It was also in that small rural high school that I first encountered the films of Pedro Almodóvar. One year, my Spanish teacher thought it would be a good pedagogical decision to show *Women on the Verge of a Nervous Breakdown* to a group of students from farming and/or fundamentally religious families. While the decision may seem questionable in retrospect, at the time I was absorbed.

I was already a "movie" person, my walls decorated with neatly framed movie posters. I worked for a time at the local video store. I rented constantly, widely, as variously as I could from the store's tiny library and, when I outgrew it, began driving to the nearest Blockbuster twenty minutes away.

Like O'Hara, Almodóvar has never been afraid to rifle through culture's trash can to see what he can find in there. Like O'Hara, he's unafraid to place society's rejects alongside society's treasures, as he does in *All About My Mother*, where a staging of *A Streetcar Named Desire* might star a chain-smoking lesbian and her heroin-addicted lover, or where a male-to-female transsexual truck driver might impregnate a nun.

And yet, the result of these juxtapositions, to me, is not trash, but treasure.

―೦

I didn't like being outside of classrooms. Inside of them, I was generally safe.

It was in the hallways, between classes, or in the cafeteria, during lunch, that I was vulnerable. Oliver wasn't the only person to see something in me that year; apparently virtually the entire school had come to the conclusion that I was inevitably gay.

Taunts of "faggot" followed me in those halls.

Books dropped out of my hands, papers pooling across the floor like milk.

Sudden shifts of gravity threw my body against lockers. I frequently tripped.

I found a place very deep in my consciousness where I nested—the rest of the world saw my shell and not much else. It was my shell they taunted. I was somewhere else.

I remember Oliver asked me to stay after class during that first year. This was in the fall. The morning light was hot and orange through the window, despite the closed blinds. Her classroom, with its thickly painted cinderblock walls and tile floor, was always cold.

She pushed a copy of my handwritten poem across the desk. Each letter of the alphabet, in sequence, strung along the top to help me generate rhyming words. My cross-outs and scribbled out changes-of-mind.

"This is really good work," she told me. "You need to keep writing." Oliver had dark eyes, almost like the full-black of a dog's eye, which made her seem both exceptionally wise and inscrutable. It was hard to determine what was behind those eyes, an expression I would come to learn and engage myself over time.

O'Hara's poems for me almost always open up a dialogue between writer and reader, whether or not they are addressed to a person, or to a "you," or even to himself. They have the immediacy of stream of consciousness with the articulation of long-held theories and observations. This tension is something I was drawn to. Likewise, he makes room for both high and low culture, where mention of *Funny Face* precedes a mention of Breughel and is followed almost immediately by Richard Burton and de Kooning.

O'Hara never underestimated the scope of his page, using it to make sweeping, epic statements like in "Ave Maria" ("Mothers of America / let your kids go to the movies!") or his manifesto, "Personism." His audacity in these moments sets him apart from the more staid of his contemporaries and precursors, but his embrace of all levels of culture with equal measure makes him less earnest than other audacious poets who shunned the mundane.

For four years, I wrote my own "I do this, I do that" poems, mimicking O'Hara's immediacy and cultural irrelevance. He gave me license to write about my life as I lived it—honestly, tragically, with elation, with confusion—but fully myself.

I love work that has awareness of genre, those familiar conventions that serve as scaffolding to stories. Or perhaps the conventions of genre are like a dress form onto which we stitch our carefully manufactured garments. In any case, both O'Hara and Almodóvar have a playful relationship with genre and its expectations. For O'Hara, it's appropriating the diary, the daybook, the manifesto, the missive. For Almodóvar, it's braiding together film noir, soap opera, sex farce. In my own work, I don't want to cross these borders; I want to unify them. I want to connect public speech and private confession, blur distinctions between science fiction and historical fiction, to speak as both myself and as someone I've never met.

—⌒—

I continued writing in high school, and furiously. I wrote reams and reams of ridiculous teenage poetry, rife with its pressures of symbolism, reluctance to make meaning, and its focus on pattern. Each poem I wrote I took to Ms. Oliver. She dutifully read each one and gave me exactly the degree of criticism I could handle at that point, which ranged from blind praise early on to thoughtful prodding and outright editing when I was nearer graduation.

The University of Wisconsin–Whitewater held an annual statewide writing festival for high school students. Each year, Oliver gathered up her ducks, her misfit students, and took them. Each festival ended with an award ceremony, where students were recognized with first-, second-, and third-place awards for their poems, as well as honorable mentions. By the second year of attending, we knew which workshop leaders had the award-winning writers. By the third and fourth year, I was earning third place.

—⌒—

La Agrado takes the stage one night in *All About My Mother*, attempting to cover for one of the lead actress's devastating heroin overdoses. Rather than have the audience go home, she muses aloud that she'd like to tell them the story of her life. "I am very authentic," she tells them as she enumerates the surgical procedures she's undergone and their associated costs, from breast implants to eyebrow lifts and chin filing.

Our instinct is to judge these modifications as entirely *inauthentic*—she has, in essence, revised her body to suit her own self-perception. She has built an outside that reflects her inside.

The suggestion, of course, is that our inner beings are authentic. The implication is that the world, then, is full of people who lack the bravery and audacity to be fully, wholly themselves—to show this face to the world. To not apologize for it.

To name ourselves.

Agrado = pleasant, agreeable.

⸺☙

Oliver, I came to confirm later, was a secret rural lesbian. Let me rephrase: it was not secret. In fact, it was widely assumed. It was whispered constantly behind her back. It took the form of lewd jokes in the unstable voices of adolescent boys echoing against the cinderblock walls of the boys' locker room.

But it was never discussed. Not by her, not with her.

Oliver lived in a simple farmhouse outside of town with another teacher, her partner, my elementary school gym teacher. They had a cat named Loki.

That was the extent of what I learned about her life outside school. And most of that I learned after she died suddenly two years after I graduated.

⸺☙

"One of [Personism's] minimal aspects is to address itself to one person (other than the poet himself)."

⸺☙

I continued to write in college, where I came out almost immediately and began living as openly as my confidence and distance from home would allow. This was shortly after e-mail became commonplace for university students. In rural Wisconsin, it was still something of a novelty; dial-up access numbers still carried long-distance charges. Oliver, a bit of a geek, was an early adopter. Our e-mail accounts allowed us to stay in touch and for me to continue sharing my work with her.

It was through poetry, then, that I recorded, examined, and openly expressed my sexuality. "These are different," she wrote to me after getting the first batch of work. "I can definitely sense a maturing in both your style and your subject." One of those poems went on to appear in the student-run literary magazine for undergraduates the following year, after Oliver died. It was my first publication.

"I have something I need to tell you," she wrote later that fall. She went on to explain that doctors had identified some cancerous growth and that she'd be undergoing treatment. She assured me everyone expected her to be fine.

—⚬

In the years that followed my introductions to O'Hara and Almodóvar, I did what I always do with the things that obsess me: I collected.

I gathered books—the uncollected poems, a book of essays about Almodóvar's body of work.

I bought and devoured the Joe LeSeur biography in poems, *Digressions on Some Poems by Frank O'Hara*. It was this last one that brought me fully into his world, seeing him the way I would have seen him—from the sidelines. In the LeSeur book, O'Hara is like a burst of fireworks—flashy, beautiful, brash.

Or like a spotlight: when his attention was on you, it enveloped you. When it turned away, you were left cold.

—⚬

Since it was a small town and everyone knew everyone's business, everyone knew where Oliver lived.

Oddly, this did not do anything to confirm or squelch the rumors about her co-occupancy with the gym teacher. As it was, some people believed they were hot-and-heavy lesbian lovers while others seemed to accept, however blindly, they were roommates.

After graduation, two friends and I dropped in to see her unexpectedly, sacrificing a night that would have otherwise been spent lurking at the mall forty-five minutes away or toilet papering a former classmate's house.

We were, the three of us, favorite students; students with older siblings Oliver had also known and taught; students who were, for one reason or another, walking on the thin margin of outcastness so many of our classmates sought to avoid.

Oliver seemed both genuinely happy we stopped in and also a bit beside herself as these two discrete worlds of hers—the work world and the personal world—however blended they may have been in her mind, had infrequently occupied the same physical space.

For our end, we felt giddy with our transgression, unable to reconcile that a teacher could actually exist outside the walls of the school without seeming overly teacher-y. Despite her reluctance, Oliver, I think, felt for a moment like herself—like a person, not an occupation.

_cs_

Operatic highs and lows: the sudden death of a chanteuse has the emotional resonance of a deeply personal loss. A nurse's tender admiration for a comatose ballerina twists, carefully, delicately, into a horrifying obsession.

_cs_

O'Hara and Almodóvar share the sense that the world, when viewed through a queer lens, is in fact rarely about our intimate relationships and more about our relationship to the world at large.

And yet, while sexual encounters themselves are rarely included by these artists, O'Hara, for example, has a number of poems to Vincent that are loving, gentle, intimate. And Almodóvar is full of complicated relationships of all stripes, whether gay, straight, or other. Almodóvar is the real world on amphetamines and Technicolor—everything is blown up to ridiculous proportions. Simple break-ups become monumental civil wars. An artistic respect becomes obsession becomes transgression.

Almodóvar's world is our world stripped of its external logical rationality. It operates on an intuition, the sense of order that exists deep within us.

—◌—

The first year I won at the UW writing festival, Oliver took me to Walmart immediately after the festival to buy a frame for the parchment certificate I received as an award. I was also eager to spend my $10 award on a new album, something on tape. The following day at school, she placed a notice in the morning announcements about my award.

I still have those certificates, still in those frames.

—◌—

I don't think there's even anything significantly "gay" about the content of O'Hara's work. He rarely writes of his relationships in the *Collected Poems*, or, at least, not with direct treatment. It seemed from his work, as I worked through that long volume, that the only thing he loved more than art was living around art and artists. He nears what many would call a "gay sensibility," but what I would prefer to discuss simply as his sensibility.

He pulled me in with his confidential address, naming his friends casually as though I'd know them by first name, as in "The Day Lady Died," or name-dropping others so I'd understand the importance of what he was telling me ("Why I Am Not a Painter," for example).

He knew the artifice of the thing was as essential as the thing itself, that both had merit—that ultimately, we are all art and artifice.

—◌—

The last time I saw Oliver, it was winter break and I was home, putting body heat back into my high school job at the local Walmart. She and her partner came through a checkout line I was working, buying their dog food and their cat food and other little household necessities.

I felt oddly quiet, embarrassed. As if I were being seen for the first time. I was no longer experiencing the world from the dark end of a long hallway, as I had all those years of high school. I was standing in the doorway now, being seen. When she looked at me, I knew she was seeing me, all of me.

She wasn't visibly weak, but she was somehow *suppressed*. I don't know how to describe it more clearly than that. She looked at me. "You've grown up a lot in a short amount of time," she said. Her eyes, dark little coals, were smiling.

—⌒◦

How they are opposed: for O'Hara, authenticity lives and breathes in the lived moment, in the actual. He writes, "I can't think of more than one poem at a time, so I would end up with a 'poetics' based on one of my poems which any other poem of mine would completely contradict except for certain affections or habits of speech they might include." O'Hara does not speak for posterity; he speaks for *now*, this moment, this particular *suddenly* or this brief meditation that just struck. To me, this feels especially queer—the culture we've built for ourselves, the culture I was steeped in as I was coming out and reading O'Hara and watching Almodóvar—that is the culture of the now. What's fresh? What's the new black? Who is the current *America's Next Top Model* and when can we toss her over for something newer? What is next?

Too, we have been a culture of loss, but O'Hara couldn't have known this. He didn't live to see AIDS decimate our numbers. The best fight against oblivion? Capturing the now. Living in the now. Remembering these myriad moments, all of them a jumble of those operatic highs and lows—our urgency to live fully while we can—our demand to assert our authenticity.

Almodóvar, conversely, begins in the hyperbole and there finds our authentic truths. Pepa, in *Women on the Verge*, makes a career (with her errant lover) of dubbing dialogue for foreign films, romances. Their "conversation" is falsified, a performance—and even their in-person *authentic* conversations carry the tinge of soap opera in them. It isn't until Pepa snaps, sets fire to the apartment, stalks her lover, spikes the gazpacho, and generally creates mayhem that she discovers her authentic self, her authentic feeling: relief. She has voluntarily moved from the inauthentic world of feminine performance to the world of authentic selfhood.

My years of faulty performing heterosexuality were like this—in many ways, fooling no one but myself, a kind of drag where the seams all showed and the lighting was truly awful. But I took off that costume, changed into my real clothes, my real look, my real self. Poetry was and is always part of that. It is through poetry I document my lived (or imagined) experience. I am in search of the authentic: the authentic me, the authentic art.

Orpheus in Texas

Saeed Jones

Perhaps I am being presumptuous when I assume that every gay man has a complicated relationship with the idea of fatherhood. The word makes me look over my shoulder, expecting my father to be there, arms crossed and waiting for a good answer. He's probably smiling, knowing exactly how much it irritates me: that inappropriately bright grin. To bring poetry and the notion of influence into the room sets a spark in me.

While I write here, in this burning room, I want to tell you about my father, the way his absence has fathered my poems and why I think Orpheus might be to blame.

The first song Orpheus taught me was about regret. I cannot remember the last time I saw my father, only that—in the months before his disappearance—I took to telling anyone who would listen that he was no longer my father. He had disappointed me too many times in my fourteen years alive, I'd say. (Hours spent by the living room window, my eyes rising to meet every passing car that was not his. His gift for walking into the room immediately after the recital's conclusion, the school play's last line. *I'm sorry I'm late. How were you?*) And anyway, he had remarried and started a new family. I would tell people that the decision was mine: I didn't want him to be my father anymore.

I cannot remember how people responded to such a statement. How foolish I must have looked in front of them: a petulant teenager angry his father was not meeting his expectations. That was the nature of my conversations with and about him in the weeks before he went on a business trip and did not return.

Only in mythology does there seem to exist such a perfect equilibrium between an ill-conceived action and appropriate consequence. Arachne, far too proud of her work at the loom, is turned into a spider. Acteon, the unfortunate hunter who happens upon Artemis bathing in a grotto, is turned into a deer and attacked by his own hounds. A boy tells everyone he knows that he does not want a father anymore and his father disappears.

Here is what I do remember: Late night, a phone call from my grandmother, the receiver sticky in my sweaty palm, remembering—even then—that he always had sweaty palms, and listening but not understanding the words leaving my grandmother's fraught mouth. I did not know he had gone on a business trip just before Thanksgiving. All I knew was that he had not bothered to call me for my fifteenth birthday. "He didn't come back, Saeed. We've called all the hospitals and filed a report."

Guilt sharpens the senses, crystallizes every fragment of the moment: the soles of my feet sinking into carpet while I try to focus on each word, my mother watching me (and not understanding yet) from the other side of the room, the way the phone finally slips from my sweat-slick hand, the fact that it is not raining outside but should have been. I cried like a boy who knew exactly what he was being punished for.

In retrospect, it feels a bit too clever to say I started writing poems around this time. And though I am suspicious of the idea that a writer's life can be explained by one incident, that phone call and the weeks that became years of absence have left a residue on every poem I have written since then. Whenever I doubt the relationship between my poetry and my father's absence, I read one of my poems out loud to myself and can taste what has been lost.

The second song was about desire. What initially pulled me into the myth of Orpheus and Eurydice was the image of nature literally being moved by his song: rocks crawling along dirt roads to follow him, flowers craning their necks toward notes mistaken for sunlight, a river cutting through a field to be closer to his music.

Every living thing desired what he could do. I wanted to write poems that could be desired—not just wanted, but craved. More so than from watching people, reading this part of the myth taught me that desire could be translated into influence. His songs acted upon nature; his songs *were* actions.

Should we ask for a raise of hands: Who here, among the poets, started writing because of such a desire? Who wanted poems that would turn heads, or perhaps charm inked words into phone numbers and invitations?

I was a teenage boy after all. And if ever there is a time when one's body seems to be at the full mercy of nature, it is the years of acne, growing pains, new pubic and armpit hair, and awkward desire. I wanted control—over my body, over the boys who were already starting to walk into my erect dreams, and more importantly—over the sadness that seemed to be the underworld of all of my emotions.

I could not bring my father back or even get a clear explanation of what had happened, but I could at least try to write poems that were at the full mercy of my intentions. I felt in control when I was writing; each poem was an attempt to stave off helplessness. Whether, in the end, the poem "obeyed" those intentions was not the point exactly. Rather, it was during the act of writing itself that a calm settled over me. Even when a poem was difficult or words were uncooperative, the frustration seemed pleasant, a joust with a stubborn old friend.

At the time, though, I was not fully cognizant of what poetry meant to me. But the fact is that all of my poems were in the voices of figures from mythos. I wrote "Orpheus in Texas" and saw him wandering through a field of bluebonnets. I wrote poems in the voices of Medea and Penelope, giving them a chance to see their spouses for who they really were: men made of absence. In the same way that I felt more comfortable writing about desire for the male form in the voice of a female character, it was safer to write about their grief than my own. I did not know that "persona" was the name for what I was writing. Nor did I know that each poem was a mask I was wearing to act upon my life.

The third song was about heat. If you walk far enough into the tunnels of the dead, the earthen walls become hot to the touch, hotter than a heart full of blood. Perhaps that is why we have always confused that place with hell.

The image of Orpheus singing for Hades and Persephone in exchange for Eurydice's return is a metaphor for the use of poetry to bargain with loss itself. (The myth seems more interested in the narrative of loss than death; death is just one way to lose someone, but there are other ways.) His art has shifted from an act of desire to desperate persuasion.

Did he sweat while he was singing? And if sweat dripped down the sides of his face while he performed, was it because of the oppressive heat, his nerves, or the sheer intensity of his want?

When I say that my father's absence has "fathered" my poems, I do not mean that every time I sit down to write I am explicitly trying to write a poem that will bring him back. Rather, his absence has become a presence, a heat I feel when I am writing. Or perhaps, later in the process (months after I have walked away from the poem), I return to reread or revise and see my father staring back at me. Often I think a poem is about a particular idea—say a drowning victim, or kudzu—and later, I see him in the poem or the poem trying to become a conversation with him. The conversation is not always the same; it may be an argument, a plea, a reassurance, or maybe even just a shared moment of eye contact between me and the space (in the poem) where he should be standing.

Even in the poems that on the surface are about male desire and the body in ecstasy, there remains a vein of his blood. All of my desires seem to get mixed up, and before long he's everywhere but where he's supposed to be. I've become skeptical of my own desire, you see. (Are my poems about lust for the body, as in the male form, or is the body itself a ghost, an ersatz salvation?) In my poems, desire (and the almost existential hunger it implies) is all-consuming and transformative. Desire, like loss, ravages. Whatever is left after the fire is the poem.

I know the song Orpheus was singing just before he turned around. Loss is not unique; loss is not just mine. Being a young queer poet surrounded by myriad word-fathers and word-mothers, I've seen how writers can come together to fill in one another's blanks, to negate loss as destructive and revise it into a catalyst for art.

An entire generation of queer writers can tell you what it is to write and love your way through a plague, and then keep writing and loving after so much has been lost. And my word-brothers and word-sisters who have been turned away from homes they knew, they too are making poems out of loss; making loss into something worthwhile and breathable. Or at least trying.

And it is the attempt that keeps me here. As much as the myth is about loss, it is a story about an attempt. He *almost* brought her back. The sunlight was already beginning to warm the shadows they were walking through. He could smell the grass and wondered if she could smell it too.

And he had to ask.

His desire to recover what had been lost overcame the rules of his bargain.

Did she turn upon her heels right then and willingly walk back into the dark, or did hands grab hold of her? And what is the meaning of losing Eurydice a second time? Perhaps there are limits to poems after all. Perhaps the best I can do is use my poems to walk a short while with loss, but not bring it home.

(Could I bear to spend an hour with my father only to see him walk away again? What then? What poem would I make of myself then?) I do not know. And I do not think I want to know.

Here is where I stop reading the myth as instruction. Orpheus loses Eurydice and forsakes his art because there is no use for his song if it will not bring her back. And it won't bring her back. He will end as a gruesome head floating on a lyre down a river. And I am being perfectly honest when I say that I reject that ending. Well aware that this rejection may be my equivalent of looking over my shoulder and trying to ask loss one more question, all I know is that here at my desk this early April morning, with birds owning the dark hour before dawn and a candle lit, the fact is that I do not have any photographs of my father; his face is made of line breaks and slant rhymes and metaphors forever reaching.

"It does not
have to be yours"

Mark Bibbins

When I first heard from Jim Elledge what this project was to be called, I thought, well, Gertrude Stein of course. Mine is Stein. The Invert(ed) Past. Mount Fattie is my daddy. Easy. She's a battering ram made of truffles; she's an iron feather duster; or, as Lynn Emanuel put it, "a huge typewriter in a dress." Her three-year-old nephew, after meeting her and Alice B. Toklas, explained that he liked the man, but wondered why the lady had a mustache. And someone else's Papa, unflattered by her portrayal of him (and others) in *The Autobiography of Alice B. Toklas*, sent Stein a copy of *Death in the Afternoon* with an inscription: "A Bitch Is A Bitch Is A Bitch Is A Bitch. From her pal Ernest Hemingway." But I confess I tend to like bitches, in a flame/moth way, although it's not enough simply to be bitchy. Or a simple bitch, at least not for long. Or a month. Or a moth.

Wayne Koestenbaum writes, "Reading Gertrude Stein takes enormous patience. The skeptical reader might wonder: what if Stein is not worth this level of attentiveness? What if her writing doesn't reward close scrutiny? Ask of your own life the same hard question: what if you stare fervently into your own mind and discover nothing there?" Indeed. Reading Stein gives the illusion, if you let it, of perfect freedom—free from, free to. Or maybe the work *is* the illusion: nothing given or given away, though from it we are allowed to take and take away. What was family to her—until she crossed him off, she was closest to her brother Leo and then she wasn't and never again—but Alice and always. And a lot of soldiers and painters passing through, too. We make our own families, at times because we have to, at others because we want to. What can a marriage be? What does your daddy do? Perhaps you will have two.

And Cummings, too: how queer, in the old sense, but also how new. Let's make all of an outside better than the inherited in, a wilder place to play. As he must have been for many others, Cummings was my first poetic love—I was twelve? thirteen?—right around when I understood that I was fundamentally, maybe dangerously different (even if the danger was only to myself). And yes, he's unfashionable and uneven and occasionally infuriating, but I love him anyway for his work's oddity and camp and romance and satire. For the wild permission he gives, for forever altering the way I experience words.

Fast-forward twenty or so years to 1994, the Squaw Valley writers' conference in the mountains of northern California. I was still an under-grad (long story) majoring in sociology, planning to work in HIV education and counseling, ready to pursue a master's in social work. But after taking a few workshops, poetry, as it does, got in the way, as it will. Or perhaps *cleared* the way is a more apt thing to say.

At the time I knew approximately nothing about poems or the people who make their lives through making them, but I was most excited at the prospect of working at the conference with Galway Kinnell; I hoped he would become my Poetry Daddy. I was also somewhat terrified to learn of another poet who was teaching there that year, someone of whom I had not previously heard: Richard Howard—poet, translator, Pulitzer winner, *Paris Review* poetry editor (a line from his "Recipe for an Ocean" is the title of this essay). Very grand, thoroughly imposing, even on paper (though to what extent, I could have had no idea). My friends and I went to the library and checked out some of Richard's books of poems, which only increased my sense of dread. He was going to find me insufferable, flick me away: supernova to my moth. Once I was up in the Sierras, feeling lightheaded, I sat down at a picnic table for my meeting with Galway, who looked at a few of my poems and suggested, not unkindly—though at the time I felt a little crushed and a lot dismissed—that perhaps I should show them to Richard Howard. He didn't say "instead," but I got the message. (Mark Doty writes in *My Alexandria*: "Even the emblems of our own embarrassment / become acceptable to us, after a while, / evidence of someone we'd once have wished to erase.") It all turned out better than expected, and Richard the Incomparable has been a treasured friend ever since—no offense to Galway, who was right, after all—which taught me a lesson about expectations that I still haven't fully absorbed.

John Ashbery showed me, among innumerable other things, that "Certainly whatever funny happens to you / Is OK." I should of course note that O'Hara and Schuyler give me the same green light every time I read them. Richard once told John, after a Q&A with some students: "They wanted the key to your poetry, but you presented them with a new set of locks." I guess I've always seen John's books as houses with all the doors and windows flung open, even though that's an insufficient metaphor—a house can't contain poetry like John's, and neither can metaphor. As with Stein, the work itself shows you best how to read it; John's poems can function as telegrams handed to you in a dream, origami airplanes flown by handsome pilots over the Riviera, or a luxurious afternoon nap. We chase the pronouns around and it's, as they say, like herding cats. The pronouns were never really a source of confusion (let alone vexation) for me, but then I'd love to work as a cat herder. My cats are my family because I say so, though I am not their daddy. We get to make our own, per Stein, "because my little dog knows me," and thus we participate in the wild collaborations that become ourselves.

Finally a few queerish books I love (not daddies, but cousins, maybe): Anne Carson's *Autobiography of Red*, Carl Phillips's *Cortège*, Brenda Shaughnessy's *Interior with Sudden Joy*, Aaron Shurin's *Involuntary Lyrics*. Completely by accident, I typed those alphabetically by author; as an extra accident, they arrive in order by title too. You say there are no accidents; I say there is no completely. And then I run away.

A Hidden Life
(On Joy Williams)

Paul Lisicky

1. There was no shattering realization, no originating moment in which I knew her work would change my life. I'm sure the first story I read of hers didn't look that much different from the others in the anthology. I'm sure it was an anthology. I didn't yet have the eyes to see how her work was different from the stories it sat between, stories by Ann Beattie, Padgett Powell, Mary Robison, Raymond Carver, all the hot bright lights of the 1980s. When I asked a teacher of mine what she thought of Joy Williams's work, she said, Another minimalist, and shrugged, not resentful, but not with the respect she deserved either—I already knew that then. I'd learn that she was much much more than minimalist. Her work would give me the chart to see that, though it would take some time.

2. No one else wrote descriptions like Joy Williams did—that must have registered with me early on. The descriptions were funny, absurd, and beautiful, painterly, or like something from a film, a good film. They came back to me, in front of the piano, or walking down the beach at night, as if I'd dreamt them rather than read them. They moved with an inner music, dark, cold, clear. They seemed closer to my inner life than anything else I'd read, though I don't want to minimize the distance between my mind and the mind that made those stories. That mind

was learned, exquisite, rebellious, whereas I was just fumbling, trying to write at least one story that was more than a scattering, a spray of flung drops on the page. In truth, I cared less about the traditional elements of story in those years than I did about description and atmosphere. I was a poet, but I needed more room than a line or a stanza. If I could write something on the way to a Joy Williams description, maybe that would be enough. Maybe that might point me to where I needed to go.

3. List:

> —*Outside the sun was descendant and pressed fiercely against the window glass.*
> —*Under everything that summer . . . under the heat and the fitful breezes, the slide of leaves against one another and the soft, whipping sound the water made as it was flung in an arc from the sprinkler . . .*
> —*He made the sound of parachutes snapping thickly open.*
> —*They were the same bright colors as the fish in the aquarium— vermillion and green and blue. The pelvis was a chalky, scaly white.*
> —*In the moonstruck yard, the banyan directed a new pink-nosed root around its humped and twisted elders into a slender, mold-filled crack.*

4. Her use of place got under my skin. I'd always been interested in Florida; I'd always been stirred by wrecked beauty, pleasure on the skids, even though I knew it supposed to be beneath me to turn an eye toward such a coarse locale. When I first picked up her work, particularly *Breaking and Entering*, her third novel, I could tell she loved Florida too. Her Florida wasn't the Florida of the Walt Disney Corporation, or Daytona Spring Break, or Jimmy Buffet, or even Carl Hiaasen, but an absurd, untamable Florida where the wild collides with the manmade. As Elizabeth Bishop said, "the poorest postcard of itself." Her work made it clear that the culturally approved take on any place is just bullshit. Her work demonstrated that any landscape was ripe for the writer's imagination, especially those maligned, diminished, ignored places.

5. Her love of water, animals, trees—especially outlandish trees— roused my attention. Her novels and stories leveled the hierarchy

between humans and other living presences, though they went about that sneakily, not with anything you'd call an agenda. The work was suspicious of agenda, of anything that told the reader how to think. Agenda is not the work of fiction—I'm sure she'd say something like that. Mystery, incomprehensibility: now that's the muck into which fiction drives its pilings.

6. Everything had a felt life. Everything a pulse—leaves, snakes, cardinals, sand, palms—though the work didn't do that with Mary Oliver's reverence or Virginia Woolf's transcendence. The world was way past that. Too much had already gone down—greed, indifference, environmental poisoning—and we couldn't talk about our predicament without laughter, dark laughter, or else our time here would be too damn futile.

7. At the same time, laughter is never a safety net. Her work believes in tragedy, and it is never cool about lives harmed, though some might mistake her work for cool.

8. Most contemporary American fiction thinks it *knows*. The assumption: you see what I see—and that might explain why the word "believable" is bandied about so freely. "I don't *believe* this," says many a student in workshop. Say it, and you're a judge, a king: you're wearing a robe or a crown you've never put on before. But what fiction can stand up to such a claim? These stories shake their heads at judges and kings. They know the world is stranger than we pretend it is. They believe we don't know the half of it. They believe that a hidden life is panting behind every surface, every shut door, and our task is to acknowledge that.

9. The stories acknowledge that hidden life with—what other word can I say but grace? The sentences are never too worked. They're never ostentatious. They don't want to look like they're needy, or trying, even as they're impeccably crafted, all the breaths and pauses coming just when the mind needs to close down for an instant before opening up again. They're in sync with the aperture of thinking and perception. Read her work aloud and your tongue won't trip. Miraculously, the

sentences are okay with the construction of your palate, your breathing patterns. But they don't entirely disappear either, in the manner of Chekhov or any other writer who wants to stand out of the way. Her sentences are never beige, never understated for the sake of understatement. They're not afraid of leaving an impression in you. Good taste? If they have to burn a hole in your mouth, then so be it.

10.

Little Dot did not hold onto the fifty-dollar bill. She gave it to Rosie, who donated it to a large charitable organization. The large charitable organization funneled it into a drug rehabilitation clinic. It was taken from the clinic's account to purchase a toaster oven for the office staff. The owner of the appliance store where the toaster oven was purchased blew it at the track one muggy matinee on a dog named Bat Mister. The bill then commenced a round of payment for lingerie, biopsy results and brake linings. It suffered a life that the most lurid of imaginations could not conjure. It penetrated deep into the repulsive nature of banality. It traveled and was suckered more than once. It knew bright lights and dark pockets. It knew admissions to pornographic films. It brought ten pairs of Mexican bowling shoes, a cheap cashmere sweater and a down payment for a trip never realized. It went off like an orphan, wailing. The flashy coincidences it disclosed were made routine by repetition. It never looked life straight in the eye. Not once. And it never returned. (from Breaking and Entering, *1988)*

11. Strange things happen in the work: a dog drowns; a bitter wife rants from an afterlife; a dick gets blown off through the agency of Emily Bliss Pickless, visionary, precocious eight-year-old, but there's always a purpose behind strange things. Guilt and redemption animate the world, and the only story is how we stagger back and forth between those countries.

12. I will never have her rigor, spiritual or artistic. I will never have her fearlessness, her audacity, her willingness to keep looking into the cup of night. She is not afraid of holding it in her hands. And she'd never put down that cup simply for the sake of charming the reader, leaving

Paul Lisicky

him with a smile, a hint of hope. She's not beholden to you, Reader, and until you experience that on the page, you realize how rare that is.

13. Her darkness is never false darkness.

14. As she says in an interview: "Literature should alarm and elate. Cherish anything that wakes you up, if even for an instant."

15. Her heroes: William Gaddis, W. G. Sebald, Jane Bowles, Paul Bowles, J. M. Coetzee, Don DeLillo. Especially Don DeLillo.

16. Fourteen years ago I'm at a party in Key West. It's a crowded party in a tent. I'm hot, nervous, overstimulated, unable to process all the people walking by, talking people, gesturing, martinis in hand. I want to leave, though I don't know how to go about that. I'm about to take the first steps toward that when I notice Joy Williams—yes, that's her face, just like the author photos—walk into the far side of the room. I literally tremble and turn away at the sight of her. My partner, who doesn't yet know Joy Williams's work, gets a kick out of my trembling. He's never seen me like this, not before Louise Glück, not before Jorie Graham. He says, Do you want me to introduce you? I almost cry, *no*, for surely I'll be inadequate. I'll have nothing of value to say to her, I know it. She'll think I'm an idiot. At the same time it would be wrong not to tell her how much her work has meant to me. Does any writer get to hear that enough? The temperature inside the tent has reached intolerable levels. Soon enough, I am grabbing Joy's hand. I am looking into her face, her kind, effervescent smile, trying to say something of meaning amid the booming voices around us. I am sweating through the back of my shirt. I won't yet know that she and I will get lost on a walk through a dark Key West neighborhood a dozen years later. I won't yet know that she'll become a friend of mine, someone I'll see a few times a year, or that I'll sit down and write an essay about her, and in order to write this essay I'll have to separate the Joy I know from Joy Williams the Writer. Would I want her to read this? I don't think the cup would ever be full enough.

Positively Not

A Talk about Poetries and Traditions

Brian Teare

i. Reject

I'd like to offer you a question: is there a difference between hegemony and poetic tradition?

Suppose by *hegemony* we mean the dominance of one social group over another, dominance maintained by "a ruling class . . . [that creates] cultural and political consensus through unions, political parties, schools, media, the church, and other voluntary associations" (Gramsci, as quoted by Hainsworth, "Gramsci's Hegemony Theory"). And suppose by *poetic tradition* we mean both how "poetic history . . . is held to be indistinguishable from poetic influence since strong poets make history" *and* how the "relations between poets [are] . . . akin to what Freud called the family romance" (Bloom, *The Anxiety of Influence*, 5, 8).

It follows from these words of Antonio Gramsci and Harold Bloom that poetic tradition could be defined as one form of hegemony whose major controlling metaphor is that of the heterosexual family. Behind this metaphor is a structure that fuses nation, race, sex, gender, and sexuality into one ruling class whose lineage is a formula for dominance we learn by going to school, by browsing the shelves of our libraries and bookstores, by reading anthologies, and, potentially, essays such as this one. We learn, literally, to *reproduce* the heterosexist metaphor, the very one that underwrites the potential erasure of gay poetries.

Which behavior begs another question: just how voluntary *are* our associations? Perhaps hegemony is both more subtle and easier to achieve than we think; perhaps in choosing essays to read we might more be vigilant and self-critical! Perhaps we should keep in mind what feminist poet and critic Susan Howe writes in her introduction to *The Europe of Trusts*:

> Malice dominates the history of Power and Progress. History is the record of winners. Documents were written by the Masters. . . . This is my historical consciousness. (11, 13)

In this light, I'd like to offer a related, though perhaps more provocative question: what's the difference between hegemony and "gay poetic tradition"? What if, by borrowing the same familial metaphor and psychoanalytic vocabulary on which Harold Bloom relies, gay poetic tradition ends up being a document written by the Masters, a document in which only Power and Progress and Privilege write books that get in the hands of readers?

And further: what's to be gained by better defining our individual writings in relationship to *any* hegemony, especially a sexual, familial one, if, as Judith Butler writes in *The Psychic Life of Power*, the result will be that "whatever you say will be read back as an overt or subtle manifestation of your essential homosexuality"; what's the use if "the one who in defiant 'outness' declares his/her homosexuality only to receive the response, 'Ah yes, so you are that, and only that'" (93)?

In other words: who benefits most from a definition and practice of "gay poetic tradition"? Gay poets who, in mimicking the hegemonic structure of a heterosexist literary tradition, create community, history, and self-acceptance? Or the straight mind, who sees such a tradition as both separate and inferior, and with such a tradition delineated can thus better police the boundaries of their own?

Perhaps the problem is that "tradition" *needs* subordinates in order to remain dominant. Which is why, even within gay poetry, we've replicated the concept of a central lineage—Whitman, Crane, Ginsberg, etc.—while relegating others to the margins of illegitimacy. In *No Future: Queer Theory and the Death Drive*, Lee Edelman beautifully captures the catch-22 of queer hegemony when he writes that "those of us inhabiting the place of the queer may be able to cast off that queerness and enter the properly political sphere, but only by shifting the figural burden of queerness to someone else" (27). It's the first catch in making a bargain with hegemony.

The second catch? Meanwhile, outside of the well-policed boundaries of "gay poetic tradition," our community, history, and self-acceptance remain entirely contingent on those in power over "tradition," which is always already heterosexual and which retains the exclusive right to reproduce both itself and its metaphors of lineage and of illegitimacy, of Otherness. As Monique Wittig warns us in her essay "The Straight Mind": "Everybody tries to show the Other as different. But not everybody succeeds in doing so. One has to be socially dominant to succeed" (*The Straight Mind and Other Essays*, 29).

ii. Rejoice

What follows are brief quotations from five poets; when taken together, their words create a poetics of dissent that negates the hegemonic tendencies of "poetic tradition" and its Laws. Instead of reinforcing Freudian and heterosexist tropes of family, lineage, and reproduction, they offer alternative metaphors for thinking *through* and *with* poetry's histories:

Robert Duncan: "The first person plural—the 'we,' 'our,' 'us'—is a communal consciousness in which the 'I' has entered into the company of imagined like minds, a dramatic voice in which the readers and [the writer] are gathered into one composition . . . closer to our inner insistence than the thought and feeling of parents or neighbors. . . . Not only the boundaries of states or civilizations but also the boundaries of historical periods are inadequate to define the vital figure in which we are involved" ("Rites of Participation," in *A Selected Prose*, 99, 98).

Nathaniel Mackey: "Creative kinship and the lines of affinity it effects are much more complex, jagged, and indissociable than the totalizing pretensions of canon formation tend to acknowledge. My recourse to a figurative rubric admits that in our taxonomic practices, as Foucault has pointed out via Borges, we stand on poetic—that is, made-up—ground" (*Discrepant Engagement*, 3–4).

Brenda Hillman: "Though rejoicing in community, we speak to the agonizing questions as individual artists: how it is possible for language to represent and not to represent, to be the deepest solitude and the most social thing we have. . . . If [these] deep tensions split my poetic practice, more poems will forge a new one" ("Split, Spark and Space," 252).

Adrienne Rich: "I don't speak these names . . . as a canon: they are voices mingling in a long conversation, a long turbulence, a great, vexed and often maligned tradition, in poetry as in politics. The tradition of radical modernism, which crosses and recrosses the map of poetry. The tradition of those who have written against the silences of their time and location. Without it—in poetry as in politics—our world is unintelligible" (*Poetry and Commitment*, 37).

Mei-mei Berssenbrugge: "The rules do not form a system, and experienced people can apply them" ("Eighty-five Notes," 216).

iii. Rejuvenate: A Creation Myth

with apologies to Alice Notley's *Dr. William's Heiresses*

Hopkins was the first one; he mated with God. His children were Marianne Moore, H.D. & Hart Crane—born out of wedlock. Then H.D. & Marianne Moore conceived—since they were half divine they could do anything they wanted to—& they had 2 children, Robert Duncan and Barbara Guest. Later Moore with W. H. Auden—a mortal 20 years her junior—had a third child, Elizabeth Bishop, who went to Brazil for 15 years but came back heartbroken. From out of the east came the enormous Charles Olson, the son of the man who wrote the 800-page *Cantos*, Olson who maybe rightly thought that he had rewritten the rules of prosody & the history of the United States. Anyway, Charles Olson & Robert Duncan got married: their 2 legitimate children, Ronald Johnson & Robin Blaser, often dressed & acted like their great-great uncles Henry David Thoreau and Ralph Waldo Emerson. However, earlier, before his marriage to Olson, Robert Duncan had a child by the demigod Sigmund Freud. His affair with Freud was long & violent, & his child by Freud was immensely conflicted about his parentage: John

Wieners. Before Wieners's birth, Freud had been having an affair with Duncan's sister, Elizabeth Bishop, & out of that was born Sylvia Plath, of whom no one could say with certainty where she came from, though everyone knew that before her, her half-sister Adrienne Rich was born of Freud's dalliance with Auden, shortly before which Auden & Chester Kallman had adopted fraternal twins from France: John Ashbery & Frank O'Hara. Now Johnson and Blaser were cosmological poets who were both queer and postmodern, as were other of Duncan's children by various gods (such as Thom Gunn) & of Olson & some goddesses, though Freud was too heterosexual & analytical to be as cosmological or queer as he would have liked; thus Robert Lowell, who came from Hart Crane's affair with Freud. & then later, from out of the mating of Viktor Shlovsky & Louis Zukofsky, came Language poetry, whose great aunt was Gertrude Stein, and thus for a generation after Ashbery and Blaser, during the years of the Great Liberation but before the Long Plague, few cosmological or queer postmodern poets were born, though Robert Glück and Bruce Boone and Camille Roy wrote prose like poets did and called themselves New Narrative. Luckily, during the Great Liberation Duncan had an epistolary affair with Baudelaire, & found Aaron Shurin tucked into a perfumed envelope; during the same fortunate years, O'Hara tricked with William Carlos Williams & from this tryst there was born another set of fraternal twins: Eileen Myles and Alice Notley. However, after the years of Great Liberation, after the ascendency of Language poetry & the rule of the president who'd attempted to teach morals to monkeys in *Bedtime for Bonzo*, during the lasting sorrows of the Long Plague, there came to be a generation of poets who looked up & found their fathers & older brothers mostly dead. & when they saw neither fraternity nor paternity in the eyes of the remaining men, they at first became a little lost, many of their mothers & sisters having gone missing, exhausted with grief after all the funerals. As a matter of fact, these poets—who were boys or girls or a mixture of the two—couldn't even believe they even had parents, since, after all, no one had claimed to have fathered or mothered them. How had they been born? After a while, their grief turned to something like freedom. Parentage was more a rumor than a rule—more like gossip than law. & so later on, with the vague fantasy of "tradition" & a sparse fire in their minds, they began to indulge in a speculative kind of ancestor worship—they each fell in love with poets they imagined they recognized as not too distant ancestors. The one named Brian Teare was promiscuous, falling in love again & again, each time as powerfully as the last: first with his great-great grandfather, Gerard Manley Hopkins, and then with a series of poets that created less a tradition than a network of affectionate affinities—Rich & Plath & Moore & H.D. & Bishop & Guest & Notley & Ashbery & Duncan & Blaser & Shurin & Reginald Shepherd, C. D. Wright, Carl Phillips, Mei-mei Berssenbrugge, Nathaniel Mackey, Jean Valentine, D. A. Powell, Susan Howe & Brenda Hillman—each of whose work in some essential way seemed related, though it was in their differing that they became most valuable.

iv. Reject, Rejoice, Rejuvenate

"Improvement," Blake says, "makes strait roads, but the crooked roads without Improvement, are roads of Genius" ("The Marriage of Heaven and Hell," in *The Complete Poetry and Prose of William Blake*, 38).

"Poetic tradition" doesn't exist except in the plural, except insofar as there are *traditions* that each poet makes and/or chooses to participate in, and these traditions are of necessity crooked. As H.D. writes in *Notes on Thought and Vision*, "My sign-posts are not yours, but if I blaze my own trail, it may help to give you confidence and urge you to get out of the murky, dead, old, thousand-times explored old world" (24).

But to claim one's own tradition as the *only right way* to construct the multiple simultaneous histories of poetry is not only an expression of intellectual and aesthetic prejudice; it is to covet the position of the Masters, to willfully enact the malice of History. Didactic patriarchs from Alexander Pope to Ezra Pound to Ron Silliman have attempted to enforce such orthodoxies, but as Thom Gunn reminds us, "You do not have to choose between Bishop and Duncan any more than you have to choose between William Blake and Samuel Johnson" ("The High Road," in *Shelf Life*, 130).

This is what worries me about "gay poetry" as a literary critical term: it too often seems to have made choices for us, preempting our aesthetic freedoms in the name of intellectual shorthand and niche marketing. It not only structures literary criticism and academic discourse but also serves literary publishing, the marketplace, and the libraries that disseminate "gay poetry" into both academic and non-academic communities. I worry that the phrase has made both gay identity and gay poetry too small, like "jumbo shrimp." What I imagine to have begun during Gay Liberation as a proliferation of radical *practices*, expressions of communities claiming new political and sexual freedoms, has devolved into a static category, a narrow one that too often limits aesthetic and intellectual freedoms in the name of solidarity.

Don't misunderstand me: I participate actively in critical discourse and in publishing, and I value the intellectual achievements of individual academics and admire the poetry of my queer colleagues. It's just that I wish each of us would scrutinize the extent of hegemonic power over the way we as individuals structure our discourse with each other and with the wider world: academic legitimacy and publishing in the literary marketplace has too often come at the cost of *self*-definition and of *self*-determined aesthetic practice.

Rather than urge each other on to succeed in the academy and in the literary marketplace on terms dictated by others—terms ratified by our acceptance of them—I wish we would encourage each other to fail to be gay and to be poets in every way except the ways we choose.

I wish we would write as gays and as poets only in ways we embrace in full consciousness of our desires and our actions.

As Gertrude Stein writes in "Patriarchal Poetry": "Reject rejoice rejuvenate rejuvenate rejoice reject rejoice rejuvenate reject rejuvenate reject rejoice" (*The Yale Gertrude Stein*, 111).

I ask us to eschew Power and Progress; I ask us to forget Improvement.

Genius walks the crooked road; Exuberance is beauty.

Sources

Berssenbrugge, Mei-mei. "Eighty-five Notes." In *The Grand Permission: New Writings on Poetics and Motherhood*, edited by Patricia Dienstfrey and Brenda Hillman, 211–16. Middletown, Conn.: Wesleyan University Press, 2003.

Blake, William. *The Complete Poetry and Prose of William Blake*. Newly rev. ed. New York: Anchor Press, 1988.

Bloom, Harold. *The Anxiety of Influence: A Theory of Poetry*. Oxford: Oxford University Press, 1997.

Butler, Judith. *The Psychic Life of Power: Theories in Subjection*. Stanford: Stanford University Press, 1997.

H.D. [Hilda Doolittle]. *Notes on Thought and Vision*. San Francisco: City Lights, 1982.

Duncan, Robert. *A Selected Prose*. New York: New Directions, 1995.

Edelman, Lee. *No Future: Queer Theory and the Death Drive*. Durham, N.C.: Duke University Press, 2004.

Eliot, T. S. *Selected Essays*. New ed. New York: Harcourt, Brace and World, 1960.

Gunn, Thom. *Shelf Life: Essays, Memoirs and an Interview*. London: Faber and Faber, 1993.

Hainsworth, Stuart. "Gramsci's Hegemony Theory and the Ideological Role of the Mass Media." *Mass Media*, May 17, 2000. http://www.cultsock.ndirect.co.uk/MUHome/cshtml/contributions/gramsci.html.

Hillman, Brenda. "Split, Spark and Space: A Poetics of Shared Custody." In *The Grand Permission: New Writings on Poetics and Motherhood*, edited by Patricia Dienstfrey and Brenda Hillman, 245–53. Middletown, Conn.: Wesleyan University Press, 2003.

Howe, Susan. *Europe of Trusts*. Los Angeles: Sun and Moon Press, 1990.

Mackey, Nathaniel. *Discrepant Engagement*. Tuscaloosa: University of Alabama Press, 2000.

Notley, Alice. *Doctor William's Heiresses*. Berkeley: Tuumba Press, 1980.

Rich, Adrienne. *Poetry and Commitment*. New York: W.W. Norton, 2007.

Stein, Gertrude. *The Yale Gertrude Stein*. Edited by Richard Kostelanetz. New Haven, Conn.: Yale University Press, 1980.

Wittig, Monique. *The Straight Mind and Other Essays*. Boston: Beacon Press, 1992.

Romantic

Jeff Mann

I. Daddy

My father turned ninety in March 2011. On the way home from an Appalachian Studies conference in Kentucky, where I'd read some poems and spoken on LGBT life in the Mountain South, my partner John and I swung through Summers County, West Virginia, for an afternoon of birthday celebration at my sister Amy's rural homestead. Outside, the first daffodils gleamed in the chilly afternoon; the vegetable garden lay gray-brown and fallow, soon to be prepared for another season of my father's enthusiastic planting and harvesting. Inside, a wood fire glowed. We drank red-eyes, a West Virginia country concoction of cheap beer and tomato juice (tastier than it sounds, I promise). Amy made a wonderful meal—Swedish meatballs over noodles, broccoli casserole, deviled eggs, and German chocolate cake—supplemented by the bread my father had baked. Daddy gave John and me a loaf to take home; I gave Daddy a big bottle of Bushmill's Irish whiskey as a birthday present.

We're all about good food and drink, my father and I. But we're also devoted to literary pursuits. Daddy and I talked about our recent writing endeavors—he's published another essay on gardening in the

Charleston Gazette; I've published a batch of poems in *The Southern Poetry Anthology*, volume 3, *Contemporary Appalachia*—and our recent reading—he's moving through Mark Twain's voluminous autobiography; I'm perusing a Confederate soldier's memoir, *Detailed Minutiae of Soldier Life in the Army of Northern Virginia, 1861–1865.*

That late-winter afternoon's combination of hillside farm, strong drink, fresh bread, down-home food, and conversations about reading and writing pretty much summarizes my father's legacy. Though we've had our conflicts—both of us possess strong streaks of self-absorption, stubbornness, and selfishness—when it comes to intellect and the creative life, he's been the perfect role model, continuing to educate himself, to read and write, into his tenth decade. I can only hope to emulate him in this regard, and I certainly would never have become a writer without his influence. I would also never have become the kind of writer I am. When I examine my peculiar literary passions and ornery obsessions, I can trace a goodly number of them to those formative years with Daddy, walking the woods with him, reading the books he suggested.

A carping critic once dismissed my poetry as romantic. He meant such an adjective to be derogatory, but I claim the term as a compliment. I can thank my father for this predilection. He brought me up to love nature, imaginative literature, and the past, to read Wordsworth and Keats, to listen to Beethoven, Brahms, Rachmaninoff, and Puccini. Today, browsing the lengthy introduction to romanticism in *The Norton Anthology of English Literature: The Major Authors*, I find myself and my writing effectively summarized: a love of history, the supernatural, and the Gothic; a defiant individualism; a dedication to the natural world; an emphasis on powerful feeling and lyrical autobiography; and a fascination with the local, the rural, the regional, and the commonplace. Such definitions help me make as much sense of my literary influences as my familial ones: Ralph Waldo Emerson, Henry David Thoreau, the English Romantics, Robert Frost, Joni Mitchell, Sylvia Plath, Anne Sexton, Walt Whitman, and assorted gay or Appalachian poets.

II. History and the Gothic

In Covington, Virginia, where I spent my first decade, one of my earliest memories is walking with my father to the public library. There, my initial enthusiasms were King Arthur and his exploits, as well as Greek and Roman mythology, and so I developed a taste for heroic adventure and its depictions in literature. To this day, I'm an occasional reader of the classics in translation—Marcus Aurelius, Ovid, Hesiod, Homer, Sappho—and in the last ten years I've expanded my interests to the mythologies of my bloodlines, Celtic and Germanic. From these readings came my third book of poems, *Ash: Poems from Norse Mythology*, as well as a passion for such tasty video fare as *Gladiator*, *300*, and *Spartacus*.

The supernatural elements of mythology and legend—gods, monsters, enchanters, et al.—also bred in me a fascination with the occult. Watching the supernatural soap opera *Dark Shadows* as a boy only contributed to this. From such influences spring my own enjoyable dabblings in erotic horror: my Appalachian vampire character, Derek Maclaine, has appeared in a novella and several short stories. As an academic, I'm sharply aware of how complete is the dominance of realism in contemporary literary fiction—many of my colleagues regard "genre fiction" such as horror, historical fiction, and literotica as inferior fare— but the achievement of tenure has made me comfortably uncaring of such attitudes.

Romantics also have a fascination with distant places and the past. I'm no different in this regard. One of the few things I'm willing to spend a lot of money on is travel, and writing travel essays is my way of making sense of those wanderings. As for the past, my father attended Washington and Lee for his bachelor's degree in English and later for law school, and so spent time in Lexington, Virginia, where Southern idols Robert E. Lee and Stonewall Jackson lived and are buried. When I visited the campus of W&L to pay my respects at those men's graves in the summer of 2010, I had vivid flashes of memory: being a very young boy there, my father showing me the garage that once had been the stable for Lee's famous horse, Traveller. I could almost hear Daddy's reverent tones again. No surprise, then, that my latest projects all involve the Confederate experience in the "War of Northern Aggression." At the very least, I'll get two novels, a novella, two books of poetry, and a collection of short stories out of my recent readings of Civil War history. From my native region I have also inherited a sense of fatalism and the tragic: as Appomattox proves, a man may fight and fight and sacrifice everything, yet still suffer defeat.

III. Individualism and Nonconformity

Somewhere among the boxes of papers my husband's always after me to sort through and throw out is a mimeographed copy of Ralph Waldo Emerson's essay "Self-Reliance" that my father gave me during my high school years, as well as a paperback copy of *Walden* I devoured during high school study hall. Daddy's love of Emerson and Thoreau he transmitted to me, and their doctrines of individualism and nonconformity have come in hugely handy. From them, I learned to do as I please; to care little for public opinion; to follow my own passions, however eccentric; and to prize solitude and independence. These attitudes have made it easier to take risks in my writing, to deal with topics—adultery, despair, queer lust, BDSM, rage—that I might not otherwise have had the guts to write about, much less publish. My most recent collection of personal essays, *Binding the God*, I find sometimes almost wincingly frank; like myself, it's a crazy amalgam of disparate elements—salaciously detailed erotic memoir, West Virginia folklore, a reverence for the Confederate experience and the Confederate flag, my futile lust for a country music star, my attempt to reconcile pagan mythology with sadomasochism. In other words, it's a collection likely to bemuse or repulse many. It makes me feel uncomfortably exposed. But then I think of my father, who was fired from a high school teaching job for attacking racist policies in Virginia schools in the 1960s. I think of fine queer writers like Dorothy Allison and Patrick Califia, the risks such predecessors have taken; I think of Emerson and Thoreau. And I promise myself to be as defiantly myself as possible.

IV. Nature

All those woodland walks my father and I took have had a great shaping power over my work. One attendee at a poetry reading I once gave claimed that he'd have to study botany to fully enjoy my poems. From Daddy, I learned not only the basics of gardening and wood cutting (both of which this sedentary academic has avoided for years) but also how to identify trees, recognize birds, and read the landscape. An extensive study of Robert Frost's work during my senior year of high school, followed by my undergraduate years at West Virginia

University—devouring Wordsworth's verse in my British literature classes and studying for undergraduate degrees not only in English but in nature interpretation—contributed to these interests.

Rural dwellers are often encouraged to believe that the big city is where all important activities occur—this would be especially true for gays in small towns and the country, many of whom dream of escape to queer-friendly urban areas—but Frost and Wordsworth helped me understand early on that writing poems about sugar maples and milkweed pods is entirely valid. I realize that much gay poetry has focused on city life—Frank O'Hara comes to mind—but that poetics is one I have never shared. As a small-town/country dweller and as a Wiccan (a faith that, like most neo-pagan religions, finds a sense of the divine in nature), I'm not interested in the artificial—and the city is the apotheosis of that—but in the natural. Certainly when I reach for a metaphor, I find it most often in the natural world: tree, bird, sky, rock, stream.

V. Emotion and the "I"

Wordsworth describes poetry as "the spontaneous overflow of powerful feeling." Yes, indeed. Poetry that's distanced and intellectual has never appealed to me a whit. The current popular poetry of ironic wit I find to be tiresome, a waste of time and paper. It seems to me cowardly, as if the poet were afraid of expressing honest emotion for fear of being mocked. The poetry I want to read has a sense of emotional urgency. In such works, it's clear that the poet *needed* to write the poem.

When I discovered Joni Mitchell's album *Hejira* in high school, her lyrical explorations of powerful emotion and of self impressed me tremendously. My ongoing love of her work not only inspired me to teach myself how to play piano, acoustic guitar, and Appalachian dulcimer, but she's also served as a fine role model over the last three and a half decades. Though at present she seems to have retired from the music world (much to my regret), the poetic intensity of her love songs, her risky honesty, as well as her stubborn determination to ignore fad and fashion and create as she pleases have encouraged me to do the same.

So much about romanticism is about intensity, I think: wanting to burn, as often as possible, with Walter Pater's "hard, gemlike flame." During my years at WVU, I found such enviable intensity in the love poems of John Keats and W. B. Yeats, as well as the sonnets of Shake-speare. When I discovered Sylvia Plath's poetry during my senior year, and later, that of Anne Sexton, I found more contemporary models: how to use "powerful feeling," such as despair, desire, loneliness, sorrow, and rage, as fuel for art. The autobiographical nature of such poetry also appealed to me. Though I have since come to appreciate the persona poems of Robert Browning—at this age I'm weary enough of my self and my issues to seek relief from all that by writing poems in others' voices—the verse that feels most authentic to me is personal poetry that speaks, honestly and powerfully, from the revealed self.

I had encountered Walt Whitman's poems here and there in high school and college, but it wasn't until my first year in graduate school at WVU, working for an MA in English, that I read extensive amounts of *Leaves of Grass*. Whitman's use of nature was attractive, true, but it was his attempt to make the personal universal that I found especially inspiring, as well as the frank homoeroticism of the *Calamus* poems. When I read "When I Heard at the Close of the Day," I was astounded. Here was a man in the middle of the nineteenth century describing male love in a natural setting. Here was the kind of life, the kind of love, the kind of poetry I aspired to. I had a similar frisson of excitement encountering Constantine Cavafy's poetry years later, and Hart Crane's work, as well as the homoerotic poems of Ian Young and Gavin Dillard. All of these men showed me that man-on-man love and erotic experience could make for graceful, poignant lyrics.

One note on the risks of autobiographical art. A few years ago, I visited a colleague's creative writing class. The students had read some of my poems; the professor had prompted them to have questions ready. One woman asked me how it felt to publish material that was so utterly, often painfully, personal, how it felt to know that readers knew so much about me: my love life, my erotic eccentricities, my insecurities, resentments, and fears. My first, flip response: "I don't think I *have* that many readers, so it's not really a concern." The real response: that's the kind of candid art that has moved me most deeply as a reader, the kind of art that has deepened my empathy and reduced my isolation, so that's the kind of art I try to create. Being honest about one's life—even during times when autobiographical poetry is out of style—can make one's audience feel less alone. When I receive letters and e-mail messages from readers like me—queers, mountain folks, sufferers from depression or unrequited love—and those folks tell me that reading my work has helped them make sense of themselves, well, I know that, despite the relative lack of critical acclaim, I must be doing something right.

VI. The Commonplace

Finally, romanticism reveres the commonplace and the rustic. It's here that reading other mountain writers has helped me. As Appalachian novelists Denise Giardina and Lee Smith have pointed out, the influence of mass media leads young artists in Appalachia to believe that their lives are not worth the gravity of art. In film and television, mountaineers and Southerners are so often depicted as ridiculous. Who wants to read about hicks?

I was lucky. The first living writer I encountered was an Appalachian poet, a West Virginia poet. Muriel Miller Dressler spoke to my high school when I was in the ninth grade. She read a poem, "Appalachia," that so inspired me that I borrowed my English teacher's mimeograph and copied it by hand. In "Appalachia," Dressler mentions family graveyards: how they are so often located on hilltops. *My* family has a graveyard, on a hilltop in Summers County. By the tenth grade, I was to realize that I was gay and to begin dreaming of a better, a queerer, life, in some distant city, and it was many years before I was to come to terms with my Appalachian identity, many years before I discovered that cities were not for me, but hearing Dressler's poem was the first time I realized that one's local environs, one's region, and all the distinctive commonplaces that come with that place, could be the subject of art.

At WVU, I had no interest in taking the course on Appalachian literature—Appalachia was, for me, a fundamentalist-infested region I wanted to flee as soon as possible—but a West Virginian friend introduced me to the poetry of Maggie Anderson. Anderson was from West Virginia too; she had studied under the same WVU teachers only a decade before me. I bought her first book, *Years That Answer*, and was reminded of what Dressler had shown me before: you can make art from home.

When, after a brief and unsuccessful sojourn in the Washington, D.C., area, I returned to the mountains, determined to somehow claim both gay and Appalachian identities, Anderson's poetry, and later, that of her compatriot Irene McKinney (the late Poet Laureate of West Virginia), showed me how rich Appalachian literary tradition is. Since then, I've taught courses in Appalachian studies and Appalachian literature at Virginia Tech and have encountered—on the page and face to face, at readings and at conferences—a multitude of fine mountain writers. Thus, I've been encouraged to use my own experiences as a mountaineer and a lover of Appalachian folk culture as source material in my writing. At this point, I would be hard pressed to compose something devoid of mountain flora, fauna, cuisine, or custom.

VII. The Individual Talent

I've had several friends over the last thirty years who seem to be exceptional changelings. They are smart, liberal, and creative, yet their kin are average at best; at worst, backwards, plodding, conservative trolls. I look at these friends and wonder how they came to be. They appear to have sprung into the world fully formed, like Athena from Zeus's brow. They are not at all logical products of their environment.

But, oh God, I am very clearly a logical product of mine. This essay has given me a chance to study where I've come from, and there's nary a trace of my hopelessly convoluted personality and literary work that can't be explained by my region, my father's scholarly romanticism, and my early readings. (Well, no one can explain my penchant for leather-sex and my ardor for hairy, butch, bearded men, but Eros is always a mystery, thank the gods.)

I have not mentioned T. S. Eliot yet, and it is with him that I want to end. I loved him in graduate school. I read book-length analyses of *The Waste Land* so as to fully appreciate that long, difficult poem. I savored his despair, imagery, and lyrical music, his echoes of mythology. A pagan, still I relished the exquisite Christian loveliness of *Four Quartets*. A very personal poet, still I found his wide-ranging intelligence downright delectable, despite his attack on personal poetry in "Tradition and the Individual Talent." I hope he would forgive such a queer/autobiographical/ hillbilly poet for quoting from that same essay: "No poet, no artist of any art, has his complete meaning alone. His significance, his appreciation is the appreciation of his relation to the dead poets and

---

artists. You cannot value him alone; you must set him, for contrast and comparison, among the dead."

Well, I am fifty-three. I will be dead soon enough. It is often disheartening to be a writer in the face of the world's vast indifference. It is often hard to continue. Gathering my forerunners about me, even if only in an essay like this, helps considerably. It is as if I were surrounded by warrior-kin. I know beyond a shadow of a doubt that they suffered what I have suffered, that many of my passions have been theirs. If I am to be set anywhere, set me among that family: the mountain regionalists, the nature poets, the love poets, the wild-eyed, self-absorbed, perfervid romantics.

The Tallahatchie Meets the Arve, or Unexpected Gay Confluences in the '70s

Greg Hewett

It was a time before library books had anti-theft magnetic strips, when you showed the librarian your borrower's card, then signed duplicate book cards right below the name of the previous borrower. One card she would place in a pocket pasted inside the back cover of the book, the other she would keep. The point being, it was relatively easy to steal library books back then, but you just wouldn't. You just wouldn't. But I did. At fourteen, I stole a book from our town library, violating the place that had been my refuge from the usual slings and arrows of gay boyhood in America. The hot item was of course a gay book. It was the first I had ever come across, and then only by accident. Though I never became Jean Genet's homosexual-as-thief-as-poet, all these years later I rationalize that I stole it simply because it was 1972, just three years after Stonewall, and I had not heard even the faintest echo of the gay shot heard 'round the world, let alone its message of gay liberation. In fact, I barely knew what the word "gay" meant. It was, for me, the Great Unknown. Yet I *did* know I was ashamed to show the librarian I wanted to read this book bound in lavender, and that she might surmise I was homosexual (because that was the polite word she would have used). I also knew I was scared to have my name appear on the book-card for future borrowers to see, and that they might think I was queer (because that was then a less polite word most other people would have used).

It was also a time before students carried knapsacks, when guys carried books in one arm, hanging at the hip, not in two arms, pressed against the chest, as girls did, or as fairies did. This meant there was no convenient place to stash the stolen book. But I was a scrawny enough teenager and could manage to tuck the 731-page tome in the waistband of my carpenter jeans, and pulled my V-neck sweater over the bulge. I then checked out decoy books that I quite deliberately hung from my hip as I passed through the turnstile into the ungay world with my gay contraband. I felt that I was bringing the Unknown into the Known.

This now long-out-of-print book was *Jonathan to Gide: The Homosexual in History*, a single-volume biographical encyclopedia first published in 1964 by Vantage Press, what was then called a vanity press. Maybe it was self-published because back then no reputable publisher would take on a book like that. The edition I stole—and which still remains in my possession—is from 1969, by Nosbooks, an even more obscure New York imprint that is, as far as I can tell, no longer in existence. At that age, I still thought my public library had every book in the world; in retrospect, I find it amazing that this book of dubious content and provenance was there at all. Maybe there was a gay librarian?

The author-editor of *Jonathan to Gide* is one Noel I. Garde (b. 1925), who at first also seemed to have almost entirely disappeared in the Internet era. I eventually found a pdf for correspondence in the papers of one Edgar H. Leoni, and Noel I. Garde is of course an anagram of, and pseudonym for, Edgar Leoni. Apparently Leoni, who "worked in the insurance industry," is also an expert on Nostradamus, so presumably "Nosbooks" is a contraction of "Nostradamus Books." Crazy as it sounds today (and though I had then never heard of Nostradamus, let alone that his name was a byword for hocus-pocus), I did equate homosexuality with something secret, esoteric, mystical. I was drawn to all that was unknown. Garde/Leoni also wrote for the legendary (and brave), pre-Stonewall, semi-secret gay-rights organization the Mattachine Society, as well as *The Homosexual in Literature* (1959), a copy of which I haven't been able to find.

Among the hundreds of male homosexuals in history contained in *Jonathan to Gide* were the biggest guns, so to speak, including Alexander the Great, Jesus Christ, and George Washington. Alexander, Jesus, and Washington! My whole world *inverted*. And, even more important for a young man with a nebulous notion of becoming a poet, there stood the name of "the poet of them all" (as goes the show-tune I knew as chorus member of a 1971 junior high production of *Kiss Me Kate*): Shakespeare! Too eager, I took every one of Garde's entries at face value. I wasn't skeptical of his methodology, which, when faced with an absence of sound textual evidence, included sketchy psychological profiles that would demonstrate how someone like Jesus, for example, had the proclivity for homosexuality. Also, in an era before "outing" became a pastime, Garde did not include any contemporary figures, with the exception of those, like Gide (who died in 1951), who were "self-proclaimed homosexuals." Longing for some gay identity I'd only vaguely imagined, Garde's list was powerful.

Probably looking a bit hangdog after my crime, I returned to the library to find the authors listed in *Jonathan to Gide*. In those days I could still read innocently, in an ahistorical way. If I found few openly homoerotic voices, or clearly gay characters, I unveiled—or read into— what I thought to be the essence of gay sensibility in their work. I relished holding secret knowledge. These authors were all legitimate enough that I didn't have to steal their books. In particular, I was drawn to the sonnets of Shakespeare and Michelangelo. A certain quatrain by Michelangelo (here translated by Richard Hooker) traced perfectly for me the difficulty—and in my case, the impossibility—of expressing desire between men; it was my unwritten, unspoken, barely thought, high school crushes writ large:

> You know that I know, my lord, that you know
> That I draw close to take pleasure in you,
> And you know that I know that you know who I am;
> So why do you delay our acknowledging each other?

I am still embarrassed to admit to having been a little freaked out by the gay Tweedle Dee and Tweedle Dum of the nineteenth century, Whitman and Wilde. As I didn't really know what gay meant, I don't believe I thought they were "too gay," but Whitman seemed full of hot air and Wilde seemed bitchy (though I would never have used that adjective for a man). Of course a decade later I became devotees of both, after finding their lesser-known, more personal, spiritual, and darker works, *Calamus* and *De Profundis*, respectively. These two writers at last made cameo appearances in a book-length poem I wrote a few years back, *The Eros Conspiracy*.

Andre Gide's *The Counterfeiters* (1925) was the most interesting novel I had ever read. The novel-within-a-novel seemed wonderfully *perverted* (in the etymological sense of "bent") to me, moving me toward experimentation, at least in literature. It also has clearly gay characters who simply happen to be gay. The metaphor of authenticity that played out in the counterfeiting said a lot to me about the problems of gay identity I encountered. How could I know what my real identity—or anybody's—was?

About a year before getting to Gide, I came across Mary Renault's 1972 historical novel *The Persian Boy*. I was babysitting for a couple I thought of as sophisticated. He reminded me of Dick Cavett (who I found sexy), and she was British and resembled, at least to me, Jacqueline Bisset (who was obviously sexy). On their nightstand I found Renault's book. Because it was this particular couple, and the book was in their bedroom, I thought it was illicit. In those days before the Iranian Revolution I don't think I knew exactly what Persian meant, other than maybe exotic, like a carpet, yet the title held an erotic appeal for me anyway. When I saw that it was about Alexander the Great (whose biography I knew well from *Jonathan to Gide*), I devoured it. I had to look up the word "eunuch" to know what the narrator was about. Maybe because I was, like many a closeted high school boy, a metaphorical eunuch, and he was just about my age, I identified with him. However, unlike me, he had a full-blown romantic and erotic life with a man—none other than the Ur-hunk, Alexander. Twisted as it sounds, because Renault was female, and the novel was about one of the great figures in history, it seemed to me somehow more "objective," thereby lending legitimacy to homosexuality in literature, making it less of what I'd come to see as a personal problem of mine.

All of my influences were not, however, literary or historical. In the same year I stole *Jonathan to Gide*, ABC TV's Movie of the Week presented *That Certain Summer*, one of the first portrayals of gay life on television, and still one of the most compelling. I had no idea what was coming on the night it was aired—my family just had a habit of tuning

Greg Hewett

in to the Movie of the Week—or that my life would be altered. I sat in our wood-paneled basement family room, "hot with shame" and "feverish with excitement" (idioms I stole from God-knows-where for my diary) as it became clear what the movie was about. Shame, because the year before I recalled sitting on the same couch watching a new crime show, *McMillan and Wife*, and my mother muttering, "I used to like Rock Hudson, until I heard he was queer." Excitement, because here were two men—from the same middle class I came from—in love, and living together. Plus, they were played by two prominent and attractive actors: Hal Holbrook and Martin Sheen (can you see Charlie tackling such a role?). Weirdly, I identified less with the gay men than with the straight son of Holbrook's character, who, on a custody visit, discovers his father's relationship and is filled with shame. The son, played by cute and intense Scott Jacoby (who was just two years older than me), eventually comes to a partial understanding of his father's life, but in the end remains realistically ambivalent.

Four years later, I confronted a contemporary gay character of around my age for the first time. It was in the movie *Ode to Billy Joe*, based on Bobbie Gentry's 1967 hit-song, "Ode to Billie Joe" (with an "-ie" ending). The title character was played by Robby Benson, who, like Jacoby, was two years older than me. The reasons for Billy/Billie Joe jumping off the Tallahatchie Bridge, which had in the Southern Gothic narrative of the song remained mysterious, became an explicit gay melodrama in the movie. Depressing and melodramatic as it was, it still had a gay character, and one with great eyes and great lips. *That Certain Summer* and *Ode to Billy Joe* showed me contemporary gay life, and somewhere deep inside I felt I could someday use similar material. What had been my secret, and unknown to the culture at large, was fast becoming known.

I'm going to stay with my influences in those years when gay life was just becoming known to American culture at large, more precisely 1970–76, which also happens to be the time of my adolescence. This is also when my *sense* of literature and being a writer were formed, before I got too *analytical* in college.

Influences are of course not simply a list of books read, but, as the word suggests, a flowing into. In this case it might be a rambling, a series of confluences. Although the particular confluence of streams and rivers—some underground—mapped here may be unique to me, the great watershed of culture is obviously something I share with all writers. In this way, each of us, at least in part, is representative. And maybe it's a case of denial or arrested development, but I never felt the infamously Oedipal anxiety of influence, never felt ol' Daddy Shagspear, or the Great Gray Poet, or anybody else, was going to castrate me. I always felt a brotherly love, or friendly lust, toward writers I wanted to flow into me, as it were.

When I was sixteen, my thoughtful father, seeing I had a budding interest in poetry (though having no interest himself), bought me three anthologies that influenced me broadly: the 1970 shorter edition of *The Norton Anthology of Poetry*; the now-famous 1976 *Norton Modern Poems*, edited by Richard Ellmann and Robert O'Clair; and the groundbreaking 1966 *Modern European Poetry*, edited by Willis Barnstone. Clearly, there are many unavoidable influences in comprehensive collections such as these, so I will gloss just the ones that were most important to me.

I had read Lord Byron after finding him in *Jonathan to Gide*, and while I, like legions of men and women over generations, fell in love with portraits of him, and was titillated by his scandalous bisexual appetite, at the time I didn't really like his poetry. The neoclassical wit made this prototype of the Romantic Hero seem, ironically, not quite romantic enough for me. However, in *The Norton* I found his dashing sidekick, Percy Bysshe Shelley, and though the name came off as a bit femmy to my internal homophobe, I fell for his poetry. He was a notorious womanizer, but, superficial as it sounds, because he had such an intense relationship with a known bisexual, and wrote essays on free love and atheism, I took him on as a literary love, and he became a potent influence. He, like so many figures I was drawn to, was more of a brotherly than a fatherly figure. If I had to pick a single poem as the one that has influenced me most, it would be Shelley's "Mont Blanc." The closing lines of this poem addressed to a mountain seemed to me exactly what not only poetry, but existence, was about:

> And what were thou, and earth, and stars, and sea,
> if to the human mind's imaginings
> Silence and solitude were vacancy?

"Mont Blanc" of course has no gay voice, characters, or theme, but something about the Unknown it both enacts and tries to define allowed me, living in the closeted world of middle-class America, to grossly misread it (albeit at an almost subconscious level) as gay. As absurdly Romantic as it sounds, I reveled in the idea that I was—that gay people were—what was the Unknown to the Straight World, just as a Gay World beyond the Straight World was the Unknown to me.

Reading *Modern European Poetry*, I thought Constantine Cavafy was my discovery. I had no idea he had already influenced two generations of gay poets. It was not one of his overtly homoerotic poems that struck me first, but "Ithaka," probably for the simple reason that I came from another Ithaca. The poem became a credo for me. Although I had not set out from my upstate New York Ithaca yet, and had precious little experience of any kind in the world, the closing lines nevertheless spoke to me, or some future me, about who I was in relation to where I came from:

> And if you find her poor, Ithaka won't have fooled you.
> Wise as you will have become, so full of experience,
> you will have understood by then what these Ithakas mean.
>
> (Trans. Edmund Keeley/Philip Sherrard)

Cavafy made the unknown future knowable to me. Furthermore, Cavafy's understated, sadly ironic poems of cheap cafes, backstreets, and backrooms—places then completely unknown to me—also influenced me. He was writing poetry about his contemporary gay subculture, and I wanted to write about mine.

In *Modern Poems* I found my most important twentieth-century influence, my literary gal-pal, H.D. I recalled having seen her poems a few years before, at my great-aunt Leocadia's apartment in New York City. Aunt Leocadia *adored* poetry. Leafing through the thin volumes lining her shelves, I was drawn to the title *Sea Garden*. I opened to "Sea Rose":

> Rose, harsh rose,
> marred and with stint of petals,
> meagre flower, thin,
> sparse of leaf . . .

I knew that this was what I wanted in a modern poem, in a modern poet, in *me*. I didn't know then what modernism was, and didn't think of the stanzas as "Imagistic" or "crystalline." As hopelessly un-modernist as it sounds, I simply felt fierce emotion and a connection with this other soul. In short, I lusted. Her sounds, her rhythm, and her imagery made me want to roam the shore with her voice in my head—or better, I wanted to run with this poet who could call a rose "harsh," wanted to be "flung on the sand" with that rose. How, in a world where love and sex were defined by *Charlie's Angels* and *Last Tango in Paris*, the Carpenters and Janis Joplin, *Love Story* and *Fear of Flying*, did a teenage boy get nailed by H.D.? Maybe it was because her pantheistic passion was virtually *unknown* to the rampantly heterosexual culture in which I lived? In my last year of high school her spirit inhabited mine. I read her out loud to myself sprawled on the black beanbag chair in my room, heels dug into the deep, orange shag carpeting. Though I didn't then know what a drama queen was, my inner drama queen begged to echo her Eurydice's defiant cry to the world:

> Before I am lost,
> hell must open like a red rose
> for the dead to pass.

H.D. led me to Robert Duncan in my last year of high school. While reading his "The Torso, Passages 18" in a bookstore, I felt the bodily experience in the poem: "His hands unlocking chambers of my male body . . ." When the word ". . . homosexual?" appeared a few lines later—on a line all by itself, preceded by ellipses and followed by a question-mark—I replaced the book (*Bending the Bow*) on the shelf and practically slunk out of the bookstore. I was a closeted teenager and my physical reaction was that strong. Duncan's poetry combined the open homosexuality of Cavafy with the Unknown I'd found in Shelley and H.D. The mystical–spiritual bent in poetry I still, in some willfully ignorant place inside me, associate in a positive way with homosexuality.

Part of what made my experiences with Shelley, H.D., and Duncan so raw and charged is that I misread their mythic and sometimes mystical poetry as confessional. And not just as their confessions, but mine too. By way of allusion and imagery, "The Torso" told the story of the loves I had found in that stolen library book—back to Edward II, and even farther, to Alexander, to Jonathan and David. Of course there really is no confession in Shelley, H.D., or Duncan. What happens—or at least what happened to me—is that in their words, and in the very breath of their lines, myth flows into the psyche. The Unknown doesn't become the Known, but Ways of Knowing. And into this yin-yang of Knowing and Not-Knowing, I wanted to more directly confront my contemporary culture than they had theirs. I wanted to overlay the America that was finally being imagined and seen in *That Certain Summer* and *Ode to Billy Joe* with H.D.'s seemingly timeless and symbolic beach and underworld, and with the universal and metaphysical River Arve from where Shelley confronted Mont Blanc. It is the whitewater created by the flowing together of ever-diverging, contradictory, and paradoxical influences that has rushed me from Ithaca in the '70s to where I am now. Though hardly an Odysseus, the next time I voyage back to Ithaca I will pay tribute to Influence by returning *Jonathan to Gide* to the library, along with this essay as explanation, as words of contrition and gratitude, and pay a very late late-fee. To paraphrase Cavafy, with so much experience, I must already have understood by now what these Ithacas mean.

How I Learned to Drive

The Education
of a Gay Disabled Writer

Kenny Fries

When I was in high school, all of my friends took driver's education. It was 1976, fourteen years before the Americans with Disabilities Act (ADA) would require public schools to provide full access to disabled and nondisabled alike. I was sixteen, many years before my awareness of myself as a disabled person would begin to blossom. I sat out driver's ed during my high school years.

Besides Mrs. Green, my elderly next-door neighbor who had polio when she was a child, I did not know anyone who was disabled. And all I knew about Mrs. Green's disability history was that when she was much younger she had rigged up a system of blocks and pulleys, her own primitive version of hand-controls, which enabled her to drive.

Four years later, at the beginning of my senior year at Brandeis, I was having trouble with my right knee; I knew it was time to learn to drive. I located a driving school in nearby Brookline that gave driving lessons on hand-controlled cars. When I went into Boston to take my driver's permit written test, I sat in a McDonald's across from the old Boston Garden, waiting for the test to begin.

In that McDonald's on that October day over thirty-four years ago, I was reading Adrienne Rich's *Diving into the Wreck*. Reading the title poem, I halted at its last line, in which the poet/speaker states that in her metaphorical underwater exploration she carries with her "a book of myths / in which / our names do not appear." I had begun to write seriously, or what I then thought of as seriously, the year before, during my year studying abroad in London and Cambridge. Reading these words, as well as the other poems in Rich's book, would be the catalytic event that moved my writing closer to what I wanted to write: a book in which my name, my experience, did appear.

I attended a reading Rich gave at Brandeis later that fall. After the reading, I lined up and waited to have her sign my copy of *Diving into the Wreck*. When it was my turn, I shyly handed the book to Rich. Softly I told her, "You're my inspiration."

It took me another nine years to write my first successful poems about disability and my disability experience. Those words at the end of "Diving into the Wreck," that "book in which our names do not appear," kept me at it.

From the time I read Rich's work in that Boston McDonald's until I began writing the poems that would eventually become *Anesthesia*, my first full-length book of poems, my identity as a writer leaned more toward another aspect of my experience that differentiated me from most of my peers. In my writing I was exploring my experience as a gay man, and in those days my kinship with the lesbian Rich had more to do with our both being homosexual.

By 1986 I was living in San Francisco. MFA in hand, I was entrenched in the growing gay and lesbian community of writers. That year, Rich's *Your Native Land, Your Life* was published. In her "Contradiction: Tracking Poems," I noticed Rich was writing poems about "physical pain." At the time, I thought these poems only metaphorically alluded to a physical disability. But attending a Rich reading in the Bay Area, I noticed the presence of her plain Lucite cane. I learned that Rich was, in fact, disabled, due to severe arthritis.

For an epigraph to *Diving into the Wreck*, Rich had quoted George Eliot: "there is no private life which is not determined by a wider public life." Now, not only was Rich writing about a familiar place I had yet to name for myself, that place where the personal cannot be distinguished from the social, where the cultural becomes the political, but also what had always spoken clearly to me in a homosexual context now began to resonate regarding disability.

As I was exploring my disability experience in my work, I was also beginning to meet and become friends with other people who lived with physical disabilities. As fate would have it, I was living in the Bay Area, so my new friends just happened to be leaders of the disability rights movement. Slowly, I began to become aware of other writers, such as Anne Finger, who were writing with disability as the focus of their work, as well as some nondisabled writers who, like Katherine Dunn in her novel *Geek Love*, turned the world upside down, making disability the norm, or counterbalanced the preponderance of negative stereotypes of people with disabilities.

But it wasn't until 1994, when I was invited to participate in the historic chautauqua on disability and performance, organized by Vicki Lewis at the Mark Taper Forum in Los Angeles, that I was confronted with the collective force of what is now called "disability culture." It was at the chautauqua that I finally met Anne Finger (we had previously talked on the phone), Susan Nussbaum, Katinka Neuhof, and others who would eventually form the core of *Staring Back: The Disability Experience from the Inside Out*, the anthology of writers with disabilities I edited.

Staring Back was published in 1997. In the anthology, I included four sections of "Contradictions: Tracking Poems" by Adrienne Rich. Lines from these poems seemed to state the intention of *Staring Back* so clearly:

> The problem, unstated till now, is how
> to live in a damaged body
> in a world where pain is meant to be gagged
> uncured un-grieved-over. The problem is
> to connect, without hysteria, the pain
> of any one's body with the pain of the body's world

In order to obtain permission to include her poems, Rich's publisher asked me to provide the introduction and table of contents for the anthology. I dutifully sent along the table of contents. But I had yet to write the introduction. In its place I sent reviews of Rich's work that I had published over the years. In less than a month, I received a postcard from Rich telling me she would be granting the permission for her poems to be included in *Staring Back*.

As a thank you, I sent her a copy of *Anesthesia*, as well as my memoir, *Body, Remember*, both of which had recently been published. When Rich read at a local university (by then I was living in Northampton, Massachusetts) I introduced myself to her. She knew who I was. Graciously, she told me that, having read my books, she truly owed me a letter.

A few years later, about to publish *Desert Walking*, my second book of poems, I wrote to Rich to ask permission to use a line from one her poems as the book's epigraph. Quickly, I received word from her granting the permission. In her letter, she wrote about just being in New Mexico, so the title of my book, as well as the line from her work I wanted to use, seemed like a continuation of her time in New Mexico.

Recently, I had taken a rafting trip down the Grand Canyon with a group of disabled people. When I wrote to Rich, I had told her about the trip. In her letter, she told me she envied and admired my travels. She wanted to know more about the trip. She also mentioned wanting to take a trip to see the cave paintings at Lascaux, a trip she was told she could physically manage.

I wrote back with details of the Grand Canyon trip. I also included a copy of *Desert Walking*. It took a while to hear back from her. When I did hear from her it was through e-mail, a surprise since she hadn't had e-mail up to this time in our correspondence. In her e-mail she mentioned she had been traveling and her mother had died. She was using e-mail because she didn't want to further delay her response. Rich kindly told me she admired *Desert Walking*: "it is honest and courageous and all that I associate with you; but the poems are also, and most importantly, very beautiful. I am honored that my words are part of this." The impact of her saying this, coming from the writer who had inspired me to write when I was an undergraduate, has never lessened.

In 2005, after time on a grant in Japan, I was living in New York City. A friend and I went to hear Rich read at the 92nd Street Y. When she entered the stage, I noticed she was moving much more slowly than I remembered. I was just as taken by her reading as I had been when first hearing her read at Brandeis.

After the reading, my friend and I lined up. I wanted to speak to Rich, if only briefly. After our long wait, we finally reached where Rich sat signing books. Seeing me, she stood up. She took my hand in hers.

"How are you?" I asked.

"As you could see, I'm not moving as well as I used to. But, I'm okay. In this, you are my inspiration."

I was glad my friend was with me as witness. I could not believe what I had just heard. The writer who I most admired had just said to me the same words as I had said to her over twenty years ago. Somehow, over the years, my brief exchanges with Adrienne Rich had come full circle.

A few more years passed. When my next book, *The History of My Shoes and the Evolution of Darwin's Theory*, was published, I sent Rich a letter and a copy of the book. In a matter of weeks, she replied, once again with praise for the book, telling me how much she learned from it. By now, not only was it clear that, years ago, it was by reading *Diving into the Wreck* in that Boston McDonald's before taking my permit test, I had truly learned to drive. More importantly, I now had created a body of work, a book of myths in which my name, finally, does appear.

How to Skin a Deer

Martin Hyatt

I usually don't admit it. But sometimes I miss him. Sometimes I really miss my father. I don't know why I feel embarrassed to say that. Maybe because I've always pretended that it has not mattered to me that I didn't have him for long. And that it never mattered to me that even when he was here, he was only half here.

On the October day he died, he was helping build a house for one of Huey Long's former bodyguards. My mother was in the kitchen shredding lettuce for roast beef po' boys when we got the call. Until the call, it was just another day, around four o'clock after school. Apparently a short while earlier, he had said, "Oh, God, here it comes," and dropped dead of a heart attack.

I was eleven.

⁓

I spent many of the summers after my father died flying through the woods on three-wheelers with my cousin Terry. We would spend the days riding and sweating through the Louisiana heat. And we would cool off in the pond. I never was much of a swimmer, but I liked being in the water. We stayed out late at night, sneaking out and roaming the gravel and dirt roads and open fields of Uncle Hezzy's nursery.

On those nights, sometimes with other friends, we would lie out on the flatbeds of trucks and stare at the moon, talking about girls and escaping in eighteen-wheelers or airplanes. Several summers later, I would get braver and get on a bus headed west. But at that time, I was content just to dream of breaking free.

One day, while we were speeding on a three-wheeler, we came across some of Terry's uncles. I could smell it before I saw it. There was a huge deer hanging from a tree. And they were cleaning it. The deer was sort of all over the ground and weighing down the tree at the same time. I had never seen anything like it. I had never seen a deer so big or an animal so dead. And I had never seen men and boys connect the way those guys were connected. Even though there was tension in that family, the same way there is in most, in that moment they seemed so united. There was peace.

And I didn't understand exactly what was happening, why they would kill such a beautiful deer, why they had to rip it more apart afterward, why I couldn't truly be part of this group. And it made me angry at my father, that he hadn't taught me about all of this, about any of this. That he hadn't taught me how to hunt. How my uncle Raymond had to be the one to teach me how to fish and how to trawl for shrimp. How my shop teacher had to teach me how to use a saw even though my father was a carpenter. I couldn't understand why he had not taught me how to skin a deer.

_c›_

When I was nine and ten years old, my father bought me a typewriter. He bought me a different one two years in a row. Those were big Christmases because he was actually working or had gotten some money from the VA. Those years, besides the Sears typewriter, I got a pinball machine and a handheld electronic NFL football game too.

The kitchen table was where everything happened in our house: food, poker games, fights, laughter, sadness. And my father would play Porter Wagoner and Lefty Frizzell. And as "A Satisfied Mind" poured out of the speakers, I would sit in one of the chairs at the table and type away. I would create and re-create stories. I would write story sequels to The Movie Channel movies I had just seen on our new cable television.

I wrote a continuation of *Rock 'n' Roll High School* where Riff Randall and the Ramones ended up in a detention center.

My father would sing along to the music, and sometimes he would play his Dobro guitar or fiddle. And I would sit, feeling as safe as I ever would with him. There were other times when he wasn't playing the guitar, when we weren't listening to music. In fact, much of the time, he was sitting there staring off into space, sad, broken hearted about the way his life had turned out. About not being a performer on the Grand Ole Opry. He was full of dead dreams and guilt about not being able to take proper care of his family. Maybe he needed a typewriter too.

And he would ask me to spell words. I could spell anything he asked me to. My father was the most happy when I spelled words correctly. When I spelled words that he could not. He really liked me then. He loved me then. And he would tell me stories about World War II and how Uncle Denman was so disturbed because he helped to liberate Buchenwald. He told me how Uncle Woody landed on the beaches of Normandy. He would tell me stories about his days as a taxi driver when he drove Minnie Pearl around. He told me about how Hank Williams and Patsy Cline died.

One night at that kitchen table, he promised that he would show me how to build a wooden toolbox for the 4-H parish fair competition. "Tomorrow," he said. "Tomorrow after school we'll work on it." I thought maybe building things like the objects he built as a carpenter would be as fun as having the typewriter. Two days later, I returned home from school and I saw the toolbox sitting there. Shiny and varnished and perfect. He had built it without me. When it won a third-place ribbon from the judges, I felt like I had just actually lost in the competition.

So I had to hold onto my exchanges with him those nights at the kitchen table. That's what he knew how to do. How to watch me write. But I never forgave him for that wooden box that he made for me instead of with me. At that point, it was like he was already gone.

—◦—

I used to have dreams that he would come back. I used to dream that he was just kidding and returned. I never could remember the strange explanations about why he had faked his own death, but in my dreams, they made perfect sense. He was always smiling in the dreams. My father had a great smile.

In the days that followed his death, there was shock. My relatives came from Belle Chasse to help out. My cousins were all around. My aunt Jean came from Grand Bay, Alabama, to stay with us. She was very round by then, about a hundred pounds overweight. She had once been a great beauty. Once being only twenty years earlier. She kept us awake at night coughing what sounded like the cough of death. I guess it was. She, too, was gone within a few weeks, just before Thanksgiving. Dead at the age of thirty-nine. She went away while spitting up red pills in a run-down house trailer.

There were lots of funerals those couple of years. They culminated in the one for my aunt Marie, who also died at the age of thirty-nine. Her liver disappeared with every vodka and orange juice she drank. Just after Christmas, Aunt Marie showed up drunk at my grandma Mayford's funeral. And after that drunken scene, Aunt Marie was the next one to go. Where I come from, there is a lot of dying like that.

Everyone wondered what was going to happen to us. How would my mother survive? How would she take care of us? How tragic it must be with James, my mentally retarded brother, to care for, as well as me and my sister. I think people underestimated her.

And I could tell, by things that people said and did, that they thought I needed a father. "A boy needs a father figure, a role model," they would say. So people tried to step in. For the first time in my life, they would take me out to play baseball or go for bike rides. It was always so obvious that they'd had a conversation about how, for example, older cousin Michael was going to teach me how to throw, or how older cousin Ray was going to go bike riding with me. It was all so forced.

I did want a father, a dad, but I didn't want any of them to be him. I didn't like the way it all felt so planned, so unnatural the way that they orchestrated doing things with me. The only one of them I wanted to be around was my uncle Raymond. And it was great to go out on the boat with him. I loved it when we would pull in the nets so full of shrimp on those early lake mornings. When I would get a bite on my fishing line, I would hope I was strong enough to reel it in. But even if it got away, Uncle Raymond made me feel like a champion. I was never a great fisherman, but on that boat with my uncle, I felt like one. Later in the day, we'd all sit around big folding tables, the whole family cleaning the fish and shrimp, freeze-bagging everything for leaner days.

A few years on, in my late teens, when Uncle Raymond and my aunt Mildred started to suspect I was gay, things got tense. I grew away from them. When my flamboyant friend, Vincent, became a hair stylist, they said, "Be careful around him. Don't let him put his hands on you. Don't let him cut your hair. Don't let him touch you." Their words actually made me afraid of them, not of Vincent. I went away to college, and they died one right after the other. I don't think Uncle Raymond ever knew how much I appreciated those mornings on the boat with him. Because I wasn't great at fishing, I don't think he ever knew how much it meant to me. Or how much I loved him.

_ɔ_

Besides my Uncle Raymond, the only other people who I wanted to be my father never could be. Never. That is because they only lived inside of my television. Jimmy Connors was one of them. He was the reason that I got a cheap Wilson tennis racket and a practice contraption from the Fingerhut catalog. It was a tennis ball attached to a string attached to a mound. I would play on the concrete slab Uncle Denman had poured out back. Around there, tennis was a country club sport, so I couldn't really play like I wanted to. But in the backyard, while our alcoholic neighbors fought and screamed in the shotgun shack next door, I'd spend hours hitting, playing tennis with myself. I wanted to know how to play better, to really play instead of fake playing like I was doing. I wanted Jimmy Connors to show up and teach me how. I used to fantasize that he would help me play the right way so that one day I could go to Wimbledon or to the U.S. Open. He'd show me all his tricks and how to be a fighter like he was on the court. I'd spend summers glued to the TV watching him slug it out with McEnroe in all the big tournaments. I knew he wouldn't really show up, couldn't really show up, couldn't really teach me how to play.

I also knew that Morten Anderson couldn't take time off from playing with the Saints to teach me how to kick like he did. For me, he was the best Saint. I idolized him. I knew that I was underweight, all skinny arms and legs, and that I didn't have the strength or power for football. But I thought that maybe I could be a kicker. I thought that Morten Anderson could just take some time off and walk off the field of the Superdome and come across Lake Ponchartrain. I could imagine him walking on the water, all twenty-four miles of it, just walking and kicking perfect, long field goals across the lake until he got to the north shore. And once he was there, he would come to my house and show me how to kick like him. To kick like it was the most important thing, like it was saving the world.

And if neither one of them would show up to teach me how to play sports the way I wanted to, I'd imagine that Dean Martin would come for me. In the '70s, I'd become fascinated with him on the celebrity roasts. He seemed so kind, so cool, so laid back. He seemed like a man who wouldn't just build a toolbox for his son without teaching him how. He seemed strong to me, like he wouldn't leave. Like he wouldn't die. I'd imagine that he'd come and adopt me, and take me to California and teach me how to swim in the pool at the Beverly Hills hotel. And at night, I could fall asleep in booths of Las Vegas hotels and casinos while he was singing "Everybody Loves Somebody."

_෴_

I spent too much of my adult life trying to find a father. I roamed the country and beyond looking for him. From Santa Monica to New York to Italy to France. I spent too many years trying to fill that 1981 void, trying to find what I had lost when I was eleven. I searched for my father in the darkest of nights, in the broadness of daylight, in a bottle of Jack Daniels, in a bag of dope. And I never found him.

I wanted him to come back. But now I feel old and tired, and have finally stopped looking. But if I could still have him come back, I would. I would have him here with me. And I wouldn't have to make him do things with me. If I had my way, he would come back, and he would want to teach me everything that he had not. He would teach me how to change my grip for a one-handed backhand, and how to kick a field goal. He would teach me how to build a shelf, how to get a close shave, and how to drive a truck. He'd show me how to climb a mountain, how to swim in the ocean, how to scale a fish. How to skin a deer.

I realize now that it is a waste of time trying to find something that I already had. Only recently did I realize that I did have him. For a while, I had a father. Had a dad. And he taught me how to sit at the kitchen table and spell words better than him and to know more words than he would ever know. He taught me to how to daydream to Merle Haggard and Bill Monroe. He taught me how music and words could mean everything, just like kicking a field goal or hitting a one-handed backhand can. And he taught me how to plant my fingers on the keyboard and watch the impressions of the letters and words appear on the paper. And how one word beside another word beside another word fit with the music from the stereo. And how those words and my dreams could create something new. Just like building a house or a wooden box for 4-H.

He taught me how to do this. How to be a writer. These days, I still find myself sitting at kitchen tables at night, with music playing and my fingers on a keyboard. My father was not a writer, but he made me one. He taught me how to be a dreamer, how to tell stories, and how to live a life that he was never able to live. And sometimes that is the best thing a father can ever give a son.

The Little Girls
with Penises

Jim Elledge

Years ago, I had coffee with a friend of mine who, during our chit-chat, mentioned an exhibit he'd attended a few days earlier at the American Folk Art Museum, a major show by Henry Darger (1892–1973). I'd never heard of Darger, but my friend piqued my interest when he mentioned that Darger painted thousands of naked little girls and added penises to them. Penises on little girls! How weird is that?

How wonderful is that?

The following weekend, there I was at the exhibit, making my way up and down the aisles of Darger's paintings. Most were very long. Many were peopled with his little girls with penises. Some of the little girls were running from adults. Some were being eviscerated by adults. Others were simply hanging out in an Edenic garden—with other little girls with penises who also had rams' horns protruding from the sides of their heads.

As it turned out, some of the children on those canvasses were naked little girls without penises, and others were little boys with penises.

Hmmmmmmmmmmm.

﹏☙

A few months before that Saturday in April 2002, had anyone asked me about my literary lineage, I would have rattled off the far-from-holy trinity of my daddies: James Dickey, W. H. Auden, and Frank O'Hara. Dickey's willingness to transform himself into a half-sheep, half-human child on display in a museum, a creature who mumbles his story from the jar of formaldehyde in which he's been preserved, unlocked a huge door for me. With his experiments with form, his inventiveness and fearlessness, Auden invited me to push that door open and step beyond the limits circumstances had imposed on me. And O'Hara, who was standing on the other side of the door naked as a jaybird, whispered in my ear that any ol' doodad is as valuable as Elizabeth Taylor's—God love her—diamonds.

I tried to ignore his hard-on.

—๑

Right after seeing the Darger exhibit, I began reading everything I could about him, beginning with the *Village Voice* piece that had appeared the same week that I went to the exhibit. It was a review of John MacGregor's book-length study of Darger, which I then bought—at a hefty $85.00— and devoured. In his bibliography and with Google searches, I found other work about Darger. Ultimately, they all said the same thing. The hermit-like painter was mentally unhinged, had been locked up in an asylum when he was a child, and was quite possibly (some claimed *probably*) a pedophile, sadist, and/or serial killer. According to them, the little girls with penises revealed his pedophilic inclination and the eviscerated little girls with penises revealed his sadistic and murderous obsession. I knew in my gut that they were right about one, but only one, thing. The little girls with penises were key to understanding Darger. What I disagreed with was their far-from-logical conclusions that made them seem as twisted as they claimed Darger had been.

As I read one then another writer's opinions about Darger, and after I found and read the authors that each writer had quoted in his or her piece, it became obvious to me that almost everything any person wrote about Darger could be traced back to one or two of the early reviewers of his exhibits. They knew that he had been institutionalized in the

Illinois Asylum for Feeble-Minded Children, something that Nathan Lerner knew and mentioned to others. A well-known Chicago artist in his own right, Lerner was Darger's landlord, had preserved Darger's treasure trove of paintings, and had overseen their first exhibit. Reviewers assumed that, because Darger had been institutionalized, someone must have diagnosed him with a mental illness, and they began the practice of looking at his life and his paintings through a medical lens, a precedent that all of those who followed thoughtlessly continued to do. I say *thoughtlessly* because, for decades, no one bothered to find out what that diagnosis was.

MacGregor solved the mystery. By the time he was twelve years old, Darger had a six-year history of masturbation, or "self-abuse" as it was then usually called. He'd also had a record of run-ins with the police. Alcoholic, lame, ill, and dirt-poor, Henry's father was sixty-six and had had enough of the boy's shenanigans, which he had tried his best to ignore. He used the boy's history of self-abuse as an excuse to ship Darger off to a "children's nut house," as Darger once called it, in Lincoln, Illinois. Darger hadn't been diagnosed with anything but having a normal boy's libido. Despite knowing the ludicrous diagnosis, MacGregor ignored Darger's normalcy, preferring to focus on his non-existent "feeble-mindedness."

MacGregor's book certainly brought much-needed attention to Darger, stirring up interest in his art and nearly single-handedly making him the darling of the gurus of outsider art, but at the same time, he intensified the gibberish that had surrounded Darger for decades. As wonderful as Jennifer Yu's documentary film (*In the Realms of the Unreal: The Mystery of Henry Darger*) is, and despite the fact that she single-handedly brought a popular, national attention to Darger and his work, she basically parroted MacGregor. Even bloggers have jumped onto the Darger-as-loony bandwagon, following MacGregor's lead.

⸻

Within a couple of months after seeing the Darger exhibit and reading about him, I realized that there was a decidedly different narrative for his life than MacGregor offered, one that didn't have to stare at him through a medical lens, and I set out to write a book that would do just that. Ten years later, I'm now 453 pages into my biography of Henry Darger with another 60 or so pages to go. At the same time that I was reading voraciously about Darger and anything that I thought might help me understand him—including histories of Chicago from the late 1800s into the Roaring Twenties, a thousand-plus-page report from the investigation into the goings-on in the asylum in which he had been incarcerated when he was twelve, and the autobiography that he had begun writing in 1968, when he was seventy-six—I also suddenly and unexpectedly began writing prose poems about him.

—⁓—

At first, I thought it would be simply a few pieces, but they appeared quickly and in herds. The information that I was digging up about him and his times began to flood my subconscious and then bubble to the surface of my consciousness as prose poems. To say that I had begun to understand him and his various predicaments is to put it mildly. Our lives paralleled, even intersected, one another's in some important and offbeat ways. It wasn't simply that we were both born in Illinois or that we had lived in Chicago, but that, during the last year or so of his life, we lived only two blocks from each other. I knew one of the kids in the neighborhood who, as it turned out, had been an altar boy at the church Darger obsessively attended, Saint Vincent DePaul's. I vaguely remember seeing Nathan Lerner's wife, Kiyoko, around 851 Webster, where Darger lived from 1932 to 1972. Unfortunately, I don't recall ever seeing Darger, although he was on the street a great deal of the time after he retired in 1963, and I knew several of what we then called "street people" who lived in the neighborhood, chiefly under the "L" tracks at the Armitage stop. But I had much more of a connection to him than that.

Before his eighth birthday, he physically abused children younger than he. He was an arsonist, setting fire to a neighbor's property to get back at the man who'd accused him of stealing. He slashed his teacher in the classroom because she had punished him for some infraction and cut her so badly that she needed medical attention. He threw soot into the eyes of a neighbor girl, who also needed medical attention. He sneaked out of his apartment late at night to visit a man who worked as a night watchman in a factory near his home.

In the summer of 1900, his father dumped the eight-year-old at the Mission of Our Lady of Mercy, where he hoped the priests who ran the mission would have a positive effect on his boy.

The priests failed miserably. Shortly after school began that fall, he was expelled for cutting up in class. Trying to fit in, he became the class clown, making silly noises at school not once, not twice, but many, many times and after he'd been warned over and over again to keep quiet. He earned a nickname, "Crazy," because of the noises he had made, and the other kids taunted him with it. Always small for his age, he was the target of most of the other boys who lived at the mission and of men and boys who lived in the neighborhood, one of Chicago's notorious "vice districts," called West Madison Street after its chief thoroughfare. Then he got caught up in some sort of sexual escapade with three other boys at the mission, and the priests demanded that his father do something about his incorrigible son. He did. He got a doctor to examine the boy several times and then to fill out the application that would allow him to ship Darger off to the "children's nut house" in Lincoln. He arrived at the asylum by train on Thanksgiving Day 1904. The twelve-year-old would never lay eyes on his father again.

Those are the things that Darger admits to in his autobiography, but they were only the tip of the iceberg. Everything that he experienced can be traced back to his being abandoned—thrown away, actually—by just about every adult in his life. Without going into detail, abandonment—being tossed out without a thought—and its various negative effects on a child was something that I understood all too well.

_⌒_

I don't remember which of the prose poems that I began writing about Darger was first, but they arrived virtually effortlessly, one after another, several each month for a couple of years. I began submitting them to journals right away. Brian Teare, who was then involved with *Five Fingers Review*, a journal I had long admired, took some. Other editors to whom I submitted some over the transom kindly accepted them: *Hotel Amerika, Court Green, Drunken Boat*, and others.

At the time, I thought the prose poems would form a sequence of twenty or so, a chapbook-size group, but as the years passed and I continued to write them, their number grew: ten, twenty-five, thirty-seven, fifty-three . . . Suddenly, I had a full-length collection. Initially, I planned to call it *The Book of the Heart Taken by Love*, and I did use that title for the chapbook that included nineteen of them, but Peter Covino suggested *H* for its title (and a few changes with the manuscript itself), which I was happy to use, and thanks to Charlie Jensen, *H* was published by Lethe Press in 2012.

H is what I think of as an *impressionistic* biography of Darger. Like snapshots from Darger's life, its individual pieces are, in many ways, as "invented" as anything that earlier writers have created about him. Unlike previous writers' works, the prose poems point to the same decidedly different possible interpretation of his life that my "real" biography about him does. The two projects—the prose poems, the biography—fed into one another, wrapped around one another, infused each other with . . . what? Blood? Spirit? I don't know, but I know they did.

So for nearly ten years, all of my scholarly energy and all of my creativity have been focused on Henry Darger, a painter and novelist whose life has been as misunderstood as any medieval saint's. He has also become a completely unexpected . . . I almost typed "influence on my career . . . ," but he's been far more concrete than *influence* suggests. He's been the bull's eye of my career for a decade.

In the same way, Brian, Peter, and Charlie—who play an extremely important role in the evolution of my prose poems about Darger—are more concrete, more real than influence suggests. In their own distinct ways, Brian, Peter, and Charlie—although much younger than I—are just as much my daddies as Dickey, Auden, and O'Hara are. Brian, Peter, and Charlie have given support and offered direction through the evolution of the individual prose poems into a book. *H* exists because they do.

A daddy's relationship to a writer is very complicated, as I've learned. He may crack the whip from a distance of many decades (if not centuries) or take charge personal and up close, only yesterday or tomorrow. I'm lucky to have had both—an older generation and a younger. I'm lucky to have gone to the exhibit of Darger's work at the American Folk Art Museum and to have marveled at the little girls with penises.

Can little girls with penises be daddies?

Hmmmmmmmmmmm.

Oubloir

David McConnell

My father died when I was a teenager, and still pretty kidlike at that. I went to sleep for days. The sleep of grief resembled ordinary adolescent sleep, luxuriously prolonged, almost malingering, so deeply groggy that thought stuck to flesh and rumpled sheets printed red runes on my cheek. When I finally woke up, I had to go home and endure all the funereal routines in a pulpy state that soaked up detailed memories like a sponge.

Decades passed. My mom soldiered on as living particulars of my father were gradually expunged (magazine subscriptions dropped), and she became a different person than she'd been when my father was around. I suppose I did too. I was too old to be "fatherless" but too young not to have a father. I'd already left home, so an absent parent looked perfectly natural. No one asked whether my father were still alive, and if it happened to come up that he wasn't, I'd ward off untimely sympathy as quickly as returning a tennis ball: "Oh, it's no big deal. It was a really long time ago." My father grew into the negative version of himself I've lived with most of my life: a man from whom talk quickly passes to something else, even among family, someone who does not arouse strong emotions, someone who may be in the long, silent, purely interior process of being elided, edited, even forgotten. Who was he? A lawyer, a banker. Short and sweet.

Unlike the living but "absent" fathers so common among upper-middle-class men of my dad's generation—absentees who give off a famously crippling hint of cruelty or at least uninterest—my father since his death is innocent and very much under my control. I can think about him or not. One year, I felt a need to undo his absence completely, to get to know him, and luckily boxes of documents remained: years and years of diaries, school themes and essays, even short stories and an unpublished novel. I read it all. While the man who emerged resembled my father—an aspiring writer, dry, intelligent, amused, social, finicky, ethical, dutiful, precise, well behaved—he wasn't exactly the same man, because, except for a few literary creepers, all the documents ended with his marriage and the start of our family. So the picture didn't exactly match the father of my memory. Even less did it resemble the vanished father I've spent my life with. I'd call him a kind of ghost, but that sounds supernatural. My vanished father is a real, completely natural prodigy.

The easy thing is to say he's my invention. That's a psychological take and can't be argued against as far as it goes. The door to his memory is elaborately decorated with my stock of symbols for him. These used to be memories themselves, but now they're too worn: the fluttering kiss that adjusted his lips against his teeth, the martini/tobacco/stubble of an actual kiss, his full head of hair the color of cooked egg white glazed with butter, the tinkling of ice cubes, the huge glossy biography or atlas open on his lap. The convenience of these tokens is that I can think about my father without actually opening the door to his memory. In fact, I doubt I've opened the door in years. That begs a psychological explanation.

Instead, I allow myself a fantasy about time. Namely, that every moment is eternal, though none can ever be changed or recaptured. My justification for this fantasy is the well-known fact that the light of distant stars is old, from the sun's minutes to millions and billions of years old. Astronomers are in the habit of amazing us by explaining that the star you see tonight may no longer exist *now*. I extend this idea by imagining an infinitely powerful telescope and, say, an old-fashioned car trumpet the size of a planetary nebula. With these and other fantastic tools an astronomer on the far side of the galaxy (actually, not even that far) could look back at earth and see and eavesdrop on my father *now* living some bland sequence of his long-ended life in "real time." The joke used to be that old *I Love Lucy* shows traveled through space forever, but, given the proper instruments to read it all, everything that ever happened on earth can be accessed. Every instant is eternal.

So my father—though this sounds like a kid's absurd boast and no job could be less suited to him—is an astronaut. The film of his life spirals out into the universe from our local revolutions and orbits in a vast tangle. Yet somehow space-time maintains a perfect record of him compared to which my memory is a joke. This fantasy means I don't really have to remember him myself. The job's been done impeccably. His book is written.

But I can't unremember him. I keep the door of memory closed because a room is there. This idea is a little uncomfortable, creepy even. I once heard about an old woman whose husband died in bed. She was so crushed, rendered so incapable and confused by emotion, that she couldn't rouse herself and slept alone with the body for a day or two. In even more unsettling stories a state of mind like that drags on for years. The body sits in a closet or a car and mummifies naturally. Maybe my father is more like that. I've visited his grave and felt not the slightest frisson of anything, as if I know he isn't there. He's in his room.

Even as a child I think I preferred it when my father wasn't there. Then I could go through his stuff, which was fascinating. The drawer of his bedside table was full of partly crumpled soft packs of Kent, one or two cigarettes remaining in most, and so many books of matches that the drawer smelled of match heads, red phosphorous, sulfur, and paraffin, more than tobacco. That pungent, explosive-smelling drawer seemed to contain every danger. Then there was the drawer of his desk. It held whole phylogeny of defunct pens and pencils, including a fat fountain pen with a tiny golden pump arm and a joke pencil with a rubber shaft. Inside were also financial scrawls in his minute hand, coins from all over the world, and box of odd pencil shavings I determined must be snuff! The snuff could only date from his father's time. My dad wasn't especially old-fashioned, and I'm certain he never used snuff. I tried it. I also tried drinking like my father, though not gin, which I knew I loathed.

Late at night I'd pour crème de menthe, the only alcohol I could bear, into a tiny liqueur glass. Up in the attic I'd sip it and mess around with files of old bank statements, as if high finance were all about papers and attitude, not math and money, neither of which I particularly liked. "Take care of that for me, will you?" I'd order some imaginary peon.

I started taking a gentle, fatherly interest in my friends, though it made me the butt of teasing. I didn't care. My imperturbability disarmed them. I didn't realize until many years later how much my friends adored the way I listened to their problems, acknowledged their tough situations, weighed courses of action with them. From what they said I learned that most parents were horrible.

I wrote for years before I grasped the "i before e except after c" rule. In other words, for me it really was that lifetime calling people talk about, reverential hokum I've always denied or squinted at in discomfort. One thing about writing I liked from the start was the solitude, so it came as quite a surprise to learn that my dad had also been or had tried to be a writer (those stories and the novel I later read). For a long time I thought this made for a neat psychological design—like the twining ornamentation of the Lindisfarne Gospel. I imagined I was living, moment by moment, my father's life for him—but the way it ought to have been lived, simply because I was, as he admitted in his last ill and feeble openness, "stronger" than he was. To this day I smoke and drink in a way that has more to do with his era, the '30s, '40s, and '50s, than the new century.

In my very unwriterly don't-ask attitude about the past, I occasionally choose a visionary way of thinking, wild and absurd, over memory, which is so likely to be small and hurtful. For example, I've made my friends laugh by insisting, seriously, that I want my body flash-frozen after my own death and ejected into space. Real interstellar space, I mean—no decaying orbit into the sun! No one will lie next to me in pulpy sleep. This vision of airless and eternal solitude strikes me as heavenly. After all, something *might* happen. Or I imagine myself to be a great heartless machine, a robot as looming, mute, and immoveable as the Colossus of Rhodes. If there's a door of memory, it would be, as is always the case with hollow-gutted robots, in my brazen chest. I'm vast and metallic enough not to care, so   here—let me reach down for the door and open it. Its hinges make a bit of a squeal.

Behold, my dad is inside me like Baudelaire in his mansard! An under-furnished room with a threadbare rug is open to the night sky. Only a wrought-iron balcony separates it from the metal precipice of my belly. Wearing a claret dressing gown—OK, bathrobe, but you should have seen the way he wore it!—he shuffles to the balcony, never suspecting where he really is. He doesn't look up but out as I peer down over bronze cheeks. Behind him I can make out a desk. So! Just like Baudelaire, he's been writing. He leans on the balcony and kisses the night air, a fretful motion of the lips belying his obvious serenity. He seems terribly alone yet wonderfully content as he conjures whatever gardens and fountains he's conjuring with his imagination. He hardly seems to notice the stars looking back at him. The fresh air must feel marvelous. I know the atmosphere in that tiny room smells of match heads. Later, when he goes back to work, the scritch-scratch of his pen is liable to ignite in that sulfurous air. The letters of his manuscript will burst into vivid flame. The pages, more legible than ever, will burn and levitate as he sits back in his chair in surprise and delight. But for now he leans on the balcony, sentences tumbling into his head like a tangle of golden threads from heaven.

Beloved *Jotoranos*

Rigoberto González

I will refer to my literary forefathers as *antepasados*, acknowledging the cultural connection of our shared Mexican (south of the border) and Chicano (north of the border) heritage. But I'd like to take it a step further, and recognize another important commonality: our queer identity. I will refer to my literary forefathers, then, as *jotoranos*—my veteran gay godparents. These are the people who came before and who fought first, who braved the public stages and weathered the stormy audiences so that my own journey would be a little less terrifying and a lot more rewarding.

In the era where terms such as "post-racial" and "post-gay" are erasing and disrespecting the scars and stretch marks of our ancestors' pasts, I felt especially compelled to thank these incredible teachers, mentors, and role models, through the act of love I learned from them.

The seven thumbnail portraits that follow are only glimpses into the queer Chicano consciousness that has fueled my passion for the artistry and activism of language. Without it, there would be no me. Or rather, there would be a different me, less fulfilled and less skilled than the person who, through the works of these beloved *jotoranos*, has learned the pain of remembering, the pleasure of reading, and the responsibility of writing.

Arturo Islas

Arturo Islas died one day after Valentine's Day in 1991, almost a year after the release of his second novel, *Migrant Souls*. News of his death was a particularly disappointing moment for me because I had resolved to attend Stanford University's graduate program just to work with him. I was only a junior at the University of California, Riverside, but I already had aspirations to become a writer. I had been reading Chicano literature voraciously, and one of the books that had moved me had been *The Rain God* (1984). The sequel to the Angel family saga, it had just been released to wide acclaim, and I spent the next twelve months fantasizing about telling Islas all about me. You see, the other thing I knew about him was that he was gay. A gay Chicano writer. Who knew there were two of us?

Miguel Chico, the college student who was hiding from his family by moving away, was someone I could relate to. I understood his bitterness over his invisibility, his dismay with the family dramas, and his heartbreak at the death of Uncle Felix, a cautionary tale of the dangers of homosexuality. And though Miguel Chico took a step back from the primary plot lines of *Migrant Souls*, he was still there, observing from a distance and trying to find a purpose for all of the knowledge he had acquired in school. I knew Miguel Chico's affliction, a melancholy that comes from loneliness and isolation, from breathing the same stale air inside the closet.

When I found out that Islas had died from complications related to AIDS I was devastated. This was not the narrative I wanted to follow—defeated by the very sexuality that was already making us foreigners in our communities. This was not supposed to be Miguel Chico's fate. Certainly not mine. But I accepted it as a reality of the times. It was a possibility that even literary icons could succumb to.

Suspending Miguel Chico at book 2 of a projected trilogy became a difficult state of incompleteness to inhabit. I wanted to find a light in his life that I could no longer see in Islas. I didn't know his happier memories because I never got to meet him. All I could do was piece together a fragmented portrait through his novels and through the snippets of information from his obituary.

But then came the posthumous novel *La Mollie and the King of Tears* (1996), which wasn't exactly the third book I had been pining for, but it did offer something else: a glimpse into Islas himself. The cool cat Shakespeare Louie, the protagonist of the novel, had a nutty teacher, Mr. Angel, who had a limp and a colostomy, just like Islas had. During one of his unconventional lessons, Mr. Angel comes to class wearing a woman's slip—his attempt at personifying a concept: a Freudian slip. Shakespeare Louie, jazz musician and lovesick *vato* from *el barrio*, actually becomes aroused watching Mr. Angel in drag. I was floored by this admission. Islas had somehow sexualized himself through his own characters by giving one of them permission to see past physical disability and to cross the border between gay and straight—transgressions without tragic consequences.

I felt that Islas had winked at me from the page, letting me know that it was going to be all right. That Miguel Chico, whether he had found happiness or not, had lived, loved and been loved, and that was the important part of the story.

John Rechy

As a gay boy living in the pre-Internet era, I had absolutely no access to gay pornography. In fact, I didn't even have a home computer until I was twenty-eight years old. So before then, there was straight porn (magazines I could dig out from beneath the mattresses of any of the beds in the house) and the skin flicks of my mind—my adolescent fantasies. Thankfully, in college, there was a third option: John Rechy.

I first heard of Rechy while I was on a summer scholarship as research assistant for an out-professor in the English Department, Gregory Bredbeck. At nineteen, I wasn't out of the closet on campus, but I suspected he knew and wanted me to know more. We were matched by accident and this turned out to be the best summer school I ever had.

My assignment was to seek out information for two of his projects. The first had me reading Elizabethan poetry with homoerotic overtones, like the pastorals of Richard Barnfield, whose celebrated "Affectionate Shepherd" had me spinning since I knew what little pain and little joy doth awaited that shepherd boy! This material fed into Professor

Bredbeck's scandalous book, *Sodomy and Interpretation from Marlowe to Milton* (1991). The second project was a study on more contemporary homoerotic literature, so he thought it would be a great idea if I looked at John Rechy.

I was stunned by the gorgeous photographs I found, many highlighting Rechy's trim and toned physique. I was intrigued by his middle name, Francisco, and that he had been born in El Paso, Texas. I was shocked by the details of his early life as a hustler—a fact that funneled a startling authenticity to his works. But his vanity, his literary bravado, and even his name (his father was of Irish ancestry) are why he's been excluded from most Chicano or Latino literary canons.

Prof. Bredbeck gave me a copy of *Bodies & Souls* (1983), which became my naughty companion throughout many of my lonely nights in college. Eventually I read Rechy's classic *City of Night* (1963) and *Numbers* (1967)—amused by how many Chicano professors dismissed his work as pornography, and how I was employing the sex scenes as such, even as I objected to this unfair characterization.

I continued to read Rechy's works, especially after I became a book reviewer for the *El Paso Times*, which clamored for reviews of Rechy's books since he was a native son and, coincidentally, the only other book columnist that newspaper ever had. I reviewed (favorably) *The Life and Adventures of Lyle Clemens* (2003) and *Beneath the Skin* (2004), a collection of essays that gave me new insights into Rechy's politics and pride. He was a man of convictions—he despised the word "queer," he celebrated his Mexican ancestry, he wasn't ashamed of his past, of how he continued to hustle even as he taught writing classes in the daytime. Once he was standing, nice and oiled on a street corner, when a group of his students passed by in a car and yelled out, "Hey, professor, do you need a ride?" Such multilayered ironies were never lost on him.

Now in his late seventies, Rechy's still kicking. And I had a chance to meet him finally in 2008, when I was a faculty member for the Lambda Literary Foundation Queer Writers Conference. He showed up in a snazzy silver sports car, and I was in charge of escorting him to the auditorium where he was going to give a talk. He chose the elevator because of his bad knees. And in that elevator I introduced myself again as the book reviewer for the *El Paso Times*. "Yes, yes, of course, I know you, Rigoberto!" he declared, and I beamed. At the end of his presentation, I rushed the stage to get my book signed first. I handed him a new edition of *City of Night* and a pen. He looked up at me, smiled, and asked, "What is your name, young man?"

I'm fine if Mr. Rechy forgets who I am. What's important is all the literary and masturbatory pleasure he gave to me. And Professor Bredbeck (who died in 2007 of AIDS at the tender age of forty-four) I will always remember.

Michael Nava

The name Michael Nava is inextricably bound to Henry Ríos. For the longest time I wasn't compelled to read his books, because they were murder mysteries—a genre I loved but had outgrown by the time I started college. In my Chicano studies classes his name wasn't mentioned, even though he published five of his seven titles while I was earning my three degrees. My queer Chicano friends did know about him, though, and kept bringing up how cute he was and how charming that he was an activist lawyer who wrote books. I went out to the local used bookstore and bought the book with the best author photo, a hardcover edition of *The Burning Plain* (1997). I also snatched up two paperback editions of *The Little Death* (1986) and *Goldenboy* (1988).

Before I made the big move to New York City in 1998, I drove my two cats and boxes of books across the California border to my brother's house. And thereafter, every time I visited, I picked up a book or two to read on his lawn. On one occasion I devoured the Henry Ríos paperbacks, enthralled by plots certainly, but also by the moral struggles of this regular gay guy who just wants to do what's right. It seemed unfair suddenly that Nava had been excluded from the reading lists of my education—my queer education. Here, finally, was a complex representation of a man whose inner demons had less to do with his sexuality than with the social fabric of truth and justice. But most importantly, Henry Ríos didn't define himself strictly through a single cultural lens—as either gay or Chicano—he was both. And he didn't qualify his profession through either identity because he was both.

It's important to note however that Nava is celebrated primarily by the queer literary community—the Chicano/Latino literary establishment has yet to catch up. I recall that back in 1997, while I was an artist-in-residence in celebrated Chicano writer Rudolfo Anaya's La Casita in Jemez Springs, New Mexico, my host was telling me he was going to establish a Chicano Mystery Writers Union because they were growing (he was two titles into his Sonny Baca series). When I asked him who would be invited, he listed Manuel Ramos, Rolando Hinojosa-Smith, and Lucha Corpi.

"That's four of us," he declared.

"What about Michael Nava?" I suggested. He looked at me blankly.

I'm happy to report, however, that in 2005 a teacher-scholar from Tucson, Arizona, wrote *Chicano Detective Fiction: A Critical Study of Five Novelists*. Without Nava's seven queer murder mysteries, Susan Baker Sotelo's analysis of Chicano literature's "21 whodunits" would be sadly lacking in scope and complexity. That same year, Brown University scholar Ralph E. Rodriguez released *Brown Gumshoes: Detective Fiction and the Search for Chicana/o Identity*, in which the works of the same five novelists (Nava, along with Rudolfo Anaya, Lucha Corpi, Rolando Hinojosa, and Manuel Ramos) are profiled.

Michael Nava and I had the opportunity to discuss these matters when we crossed paths three times within the same year in 2010—at the Association of Writers and Writing Programs Annual Conference in Denver, at the Saints and Sinners Literary Festival in New Orleans, and at the National Association of Chicano Studies' Queer Conference (where I picked up the term "jotoranos" from the hip queer Xicano kids) in Eugene, Oregon, where he presented the keynote address, taking time out of his campaign to be the first gay Latino judge in San Francisco. I congratulated him on all counts, reminding him that we needed him much more than he needed us.

Richard Rodriguez

I'm detecting a pattern: why are the queer writers not invited to the Chicano party? Of the four mentioned so far, Richard Rodriguez is probably the most embattled. To summarize: there was always a quiet politeness about Islas's sexuality—a don't ask, don't tell approach that basically closeted him all over again; Rechy was too "out there" for the curriculum reading lists, and Nava was never there. But Rodriguez continues to be Chicano literature's black sheep, who betrayed *la raza* with his pen.

The book in question is *Hunger of Memory: The Education of Richard Rodriguez* (1982). Though this is an autobiographical account of one person's cultural displacement—surviving in an English-speaking world while living in a Spanish-speaking household—it has been held up as a go-to text that fortifies arguments against bilingual education or Affirmative Action. (Which is why Chicanos in particular—pro–bilingual education and pro–Affirmative Action—despise the book.)

In reality, the book is much more complex: it is about the negative conditioning and positive discipline that comes from being raised a Catholic; it is about the emotional and geographical distancing that occurs when a young man pursues a formal education and learns an academic language foreign to his parents, away from his parents; it is about loneliness. Sadly, both the pro- and anti-Rodriguez camps have pared down the text—a stylistically rich narrative—to a few vulgar catchphrases.

The newer generations are not as invested in the fight. Partly because Rodriguez has since published two more books, *Days of Obligation: An Argument with My Mexican Father* (1992) and *Brown: The Last Discovery of America* (2002). In the pages of these books he softens his positions on language and identity because he has moved forward with the changes in society, such as the growth in visibility of Latinos in the mainstream media and culture, and the awareness of the outspoken complex articulations against labels springing up from the postmodern Generación Ñ, which reconciles with language and heritage on its own terms. He's also become invested as a world citizen, bringing attention to the travesties of war as an appeal to U.S. empathy and political responsibility through his journalistic profiles on *The McNeil/Lehrer NewsHour*.

Unfortunately, he has not been forgiven or forgotten, and his name opens deep-seated wounds in the battle between assimilation and acculturation. I had the opportunity, over a period of two years (2002–4), to converse with Richard about these and other matters. I didn't find the monster I was taught by my Chicano instructors to see. This had everything to do with the connection Richard and I had between us as gay men.

When *Hunger of Memory* was released, there were few clues about Richard's homosexuality. So when he was finally outed, Chicano scholars unfairly assessed what they called his "self-loathing" as the social anxiety of a closeted narrative. It became an easy way to explain away his conservative views and to alienate him—and his books—even further. Richard eventually comes out in his work, when he writes in "The Late Victorians" chapter of *Day of Obligation* about his loneliness as a gay man of color living in the Castro District of San Francisco. In Brown he goes a step further, writing deprecatingly about himself as an "old queen."

Our identities as gay men of color helped us reach past our differences and to interact as intellectuals and as political beings. Richard was always flirty and witty (something I would have never guessed) but it was clear that he was still—despite all the success and attention—lonely.

I remember at one point we were walking down Madison Avenue, and the older Upper East Side crowd kept looking at us—at Richard. At first I took offense, but Richard simply shook his head and said, "These people don't know me. They've never read my books. They just recognize me from TV." A few seconds later, they all turned their attention to an even bigger celebrity: Sean Connery.

Richard and I exchanged a number of e-mails and phone calls during those two years, our gay repartee coloring the language a rosy pink. I was his Butterfly Boy and he was my Beloved Richard—we became a support group with its two members on different coasts. I called him when I entered rehab; he called me after his mother's funeral; I wrote to him after each break-up and heartbreak; he wrote to me after every trip abroad.

And just as suddenly as he appeared in my life he disappeared. This wasn't entirely unexpected. Richard is larger-than-life, a man of the world who travels solo because he carries a painful burden on his shoulders already. Even the weight of one butterfly coming to rest on him would be too much to bear.

Salvador Novo

This story comes with a bit of drama. Back in 2002 I had an affair with a historian whose specialization was nineteenth-century Mexico. We'll call him Víctor. Ours was an uneasy courtship, because I tended to seek him out when he wasn't single, and he did the same with me. And on one of these ventures we met up in Mexico City, where we had a marvelous time exploring a number of historically significant sites. It was like sleeping with the city's most learned tour guide. Our bickering, however, was just as passionate as our lovemaking, and that particular rendezvous ended with Víctor dragging my suitcase out into the street, flinging it into the trunk of a cab, and slamming the taxi door in my face.

Such a backstory would have amused Salvador Novo without a doubt. In fact, he was the excuse we'd used to meet up in Mexico City. Víctor had been wanting to translate the works of Novo, especially his poetry, for some time. But he was not a poet, so he needed a bilingual one to move this project along.

I knew little of Novo except for what Víctor told me: that Novo was a flaming, privileged dandy à la Oscar Wilde, who was unafraid to write naughty poems about his fellow bon vivants; that he could write anything—plays, criticism, essays, memoir (he wrote the first gay memoir in Latin America in 1945)—and was considered to be the official chronicler of Mexico City (in 1967 he published a comprehensive study of Mexico City's culinary art). He died in 1974 at the age of seventy, and he had mentored, among others, Mexico's leading gay intellectual Carlos Monsiváis.

Víctor and I scheduled a meeting with Monsiváis (or Monsi, as he was affectionately called) to discuss how to proceed. I had already been taking a crack at translating a few of the poems and an essay, and Novo's work delighted me. It was so—for lack of a better word—fey. Novo loved beauty and luxury and wasn't afraid to appreciate it on the page without apology. He would write bold statements like "There have always been queers in Mexico" and backhanded verses like this poem dated October 2, 1915, which I translated. It is simply titled "For Salvador Guerrero":

> Oh, Salvador, you're so vindictive!
> And always so presumptive,
> that this morning, while I read,
> and while I schemed in bed,

you, remembering my past offense,
accused me to our Lord; I, left reprimanded
and bereft, but won't expect to be avenged
for vengeance, I hear,
is the vilest of weapons and for villains,
and double-edged, a spear
that wounds the avenger and not the object of revenge.
A single forgiveness, and a thousand reprisals we avoid
and that is why I don't remain annoyed
with you. As proof of that I offer you my pardon.

Such fierceness strengthened my own resolve to introduce this incredible writer to English-reading audiences, especially my fellow queers. I was shocked that such a find, such a voice, had never been translated before.

After visiting with Monsi, we found out why Novo had never been allowed to leave the country: it turns out that he had a dozen or so possessive relatives who refuse to grant anyone the right to translate without a generous compensation. And what's more, none of these relatives (none of them his direct descendants since Novo never had children) even speak to one another. So whoever deals with him has to deal with each interested party's individual attorney.

Now, even Monsi is dead. And still Novo hasn't crossed the border. As for Víctor, I am happy to report that he has found a partner worthy of monogamy.

Francisco X. Alarcón

I have written about Francisco a few times before, but I didn't want to leave him out. Besides, I don't tire of it. Each time I sit down to write I think of something else worth remembering. On this occasion I would like to celebrate his untiring devotion to activism through poetry.

When I was his student at UC–Davis, back in 1993, he asked the class if anyone of us wrote poetry. A few shy hands went up, including mine, although I was there to earn an MA degree in creative writing. He suggested that we get together once in a while to exchange poems and to learn from one another. I was so taken by the gesture that I began to think of these meetings as an important supplement to my graduate poetry workshops. Francisco always showed up smiling and he guided discussion so earnestly because he believed in us as poets.

One day he surprised us by inviting us to hear another group of students read poetry, and that night we drove to nearby Sacramento where, unbeknownst to us, Francisco had been teaching a night class to a group of older folks. Gray-haired and wrinkled, their energy and love for the poem energized us. They invited us to read our own poems, and some of us did. And then the audience clamored for Francisco to read one or two of his poems, and he complied without hesitation. That's another thing I always admired about him: when he reads his work—columns in Spanish and English of two- or three-word lines that controlled his breathing all the way to the bottom of the page—it's always in the spirit of sharing, not showboating.

I kept in touch with Francisco only through an occasional e-mail. He was gracious enough when he found out that my first column with the *El Paso Times* was a review of his book *Del otro lado de la noche / From the Other Side of Night* (2002), which included a number of homo-erotic verses.

We ran into each other on the conference circuit. And in between those chance meetings I would hear reports that he was still fighting the good fight. I got to see another glimpse of that when he established a Facebook page in response to SB 1070, the Arizona law that basically allows racial profiling and the persecution of any person who looks Mexican. Francisco posts protest poetry submitted by anyone who is moved into activist verse. As a global forum it is attracting a sizable following. None of this surprises me. If any poet will make this a better world it will be Francisco X. Alarcón, he of the contagious laugh and glorious ponytail, and a spirit with the scent of sage and copal. ¡Tahui!

Gloria Anzaldúa

La mujer always has the last word.

On May 15, 2004, the day of Gloria's death, I lit a candle at my altar in my Upper East Side apartment and I read a few paragraphs of Chicano literature's most important book, *Borderlands / La Frontera: The New Mestiza* (1987). The wisdom of this woman's vision allowed many of us to find a place in our community—to reconcile our sense of disorientation with and our affection for our very own tormentors—our families. Before Gloria, the intersection of ethnicity and sexuality, of Chicanismo + queerness = jotería, had yet to take shape as a theoretical framework. We lived it but we couldn't quite articulate it within the lines of our poetry, the plots in our stories, the strokes of our paintings. She gave order to the chaos of our multiple planes of existence.

I left the candle burning and then stepped out to grab a sandwich from the deli across the street. And during those brief fifteen minutes away something—I have to say it—magical happened to that candle. I came home to discover that the wax had splattered all over the wall as if someone had blown out the flame with an unrestrained force.

"Only Gloria," I muttered. Even her ghost was an untamed tongue.

I never had a chance to meet Gloria Anzaldúa, though I did have the opportunity to leave a sugar skull on her grave on the Day of the Dead.

November 2008. I was flying down to McAllen, Texas, to attend the wedding of a young Chicano poet, John Olivares Espinoza. I invited another Chicana poet, Emmy Pérez, to be my date since I was staying with her. It was she who suggested we make this pilgrimage to Gloria's grave. But first we decided to cross the Mexican border into Reynosa, where the Day of Dead spirit was in full swing. The large sugar skull called to me, and I thought it would be an appropriate gift for the woman who gave us borderland theory.

As I was walking back into Texas through customs, I didn't give the skull in my hand much thought, though this strange item did give the customs official, a young man in the trademark forest green migra uniform, pause.

"Excuse me, sir," he said. "What is that?"

I raised my eyebrows. "You're kidding, right?" I said.

The customs official was startled by my casual tone, though I really did think he was joking.

"I ask the questions around here," he said, scowling. "What's that made of?"

My jaw dropped. "Sugar," I said simply.

He was obviously Latino, his name tag confirmed it, and he worked here, on the border between the Day of the Dead and Halloween of all places; why wouldn't he recognize a symbol from either holiday? Additionally, my gaydar suddenly perked up, and though there really wasn't any way to confirm it I suspected that, surely, most probably, the dude was also queer. What was this show of power about?

And then I remembered Gloria. In fact, just like the candle wax blowing all over the wall, this had to be a message. No, the struggle is not over; yes, every minute means one more person to educate—especially, our own kind.

I stared at the customs official, and though his face didn't change his eyes did. He was performing on many levels—as a border keeper, as a Homeland Security authority, as a human resisting the tugs of his private identities. Since this was his turf he's the one who broke the spell. He waved me through and focused his attention on the person behind me.

When I stood over Gloria's grave I didn't have to recount the story, it was all packed and pasted to the skull like the colorful swirls around the sockets. I placed the sugar skull on one corner of the large marble and granite tombstone—the largest in the small and humble cemetery of Hargill, Texas, where Gloria was also born. Snakes had been carved into the face of the stone, and snake holes surrounded the grave.

My friend Emmy stepped away to let me spend some time with Gloria alone, and all I could think to say was, "I didn't get my entire deposit back when I vacated that apartment in the Upper East Side, pinche. You left a permanent mark." I giggled and then I wept in gratitude.

Leaving Berlin

Ellery Washington

I was still living in Berlin then, in the midst of a bad run of events, when I got the news that my friend Joyce was dead—killed in a head-on collision with a semitrailer rig, a hundred or so miles east of Albuquerque.

It was an unusually bright day for September, five years ago, and I had spent the hours before hearing about Joyce on the terrace at Café Einstein in Mitte, lounging beneath the yellow-leaved linden trees and gossiping with Felix. Felix had a nose for misfortune, and that afternoon it must have seemed to him like I was rife with it. As hard as I tried to steer the conversation toward our friend Amir's handsome new boyfriend, or Thomas's hip new club on Invalidenstrasse, or the rigidly poised newscaster whom Bernd had spotted Friday night at a sex party near Nollendorfplatz, Felix kept bringing it back to me. "You simply can't shake it," he said, referring to my recent spate of bad luck. "Maybe you need a change."

There was no arguing the point. In the past six weeks I'd been hospitalized twice, once following a nasty fall on my bike, and a second time to treat a mysterious infection in my left thigh. Meanwhile, the American film producer I was working for had skipped town, stiffing me the payment for almost a year's worth of work, and the German immigration board was threatening to suspend my visa if they didn't receive tax documents I had requested from France months earlier. France was the country where I had already established European residency, and it was becoming clear I'd have to go back and request the absent paperwork in person.

What's more, I felt completely uninspired. I hadn't even looked at the novel I'd started or worked on a story of my own in over two years. Not since I arrived in Berlin.

"You will never see that money," Felix said, frankly, his voice as flat and deep and earnest as always. I had just given him the latest news on the AWOL film producer: he was back in New York, still being sued for embezzling funds in Berlin, and still dodging my calls. Felix and I were on our third set of double espressos now, the sun rapidly going down. Light streaks of sapphire and orange stroked the lindens from an angle that hadn't been possible only moments before. Felix fixed his steel blue eyes on me and gripped my arm. "No matter," he said, nodding his head with certainty. "Something else will work."

I couldn't say for sure: maybe it was the sudden brilliance of the linden leaves, or the thought of spending a week in Paris—of catching up with old friends over coffee at L'Etoile Manquante and ordering *confie de canard* at Au Pere Feuittard. *A change of scenery.* Or perhaps it was simply the episodic crush I had on Felix. Whatever the cause, I was momentarily struck by the feeling that my luck was about to change. After all, life in Berlin hadn't always been so tough. My first year there had passed in a fantastic blur of increasingly stimulating work, multi-city film festivals, late-night dinner parties, and early morning cocktails. So now I thought, just as Felix had suggested, something was bound to work. Leaning on his encouragement, I ended the conversation by laughing at my own temporary setbacks, by telling Felix about a lucrative project I was hoping to pick up with a young German filmmaker, a recent winner in the Best Foreign Film category at the Academy Awards, and I vowed to set aside time to indulge my own work, regardless of whether or not I had a paying project waiting for me when I returned from Paris.

I left Café Einstein, then, and strolled down Friedrichstrasse with a renewed sense of possibility, a lightheartedness that stayed with me even as I reached the front door of my apartment, stuck the key in the lock, and caught the first glimpse of the red message light blinking on my answering machine.

⟵꙳

"She died instantly," Julie was saying, the strain in her voice nearly stifling the words. I had listened to her message—*"There's been an accident . . . Joyce is dead"*—half a dozen times before I finally found the courage to call her back. "The police report said the passenger car didn't stop. It must have been dusk. And they didn't see the red light, and— *well*—a couple of witnesses saw them hit the truck."

Julie was an old friend of Joyce's, an even older friend of mine. Julie and I had gone to grade school and high school together. We had managed to keep in touch throughout college and early adulthood and newborns (hers), a life-threatening illness (mine), and even after I had moved to Paris and she to the suburbs of Washington, D.C. She had gotten the details regarding the accident from her husband, Curt, who had gotten them from Joyce's husband, John. As she understood it, Joyce wasn't the one driving the car. She and her closest friend, Alice Brice, an ex-colleague from La Cueva High—another retired schoolteacher— were returning home to Albuquerque from Clovis, on US 60, after a bookselling trip in eastern New Mexico. Apparently Alice was driving. "The force of the collision caused a big explosion," Julie went on. "Which is why even the police said they probably died instantly." She took a deep breath, then, "Yes," she said. "I'm sure she died instantly."

We were both silent a long while, before, finally, she asked, "Are you all right?"

I could feel the tears streaming down my face, but my throat was completely dry, and I had no idea what sounds, if any, had already escaped my mouth. Suddenly, I felt the need to apologize. "I'm sorry," I said. I couldn't stop crying. "I'll call you back tomorrow."

⟵꙳

I met Joyce in the fall of 1979, in Albuquerque, my freshman year at Manzano High. I was only fourteen, and she was Ms. Briscoe, my English teacher. "*Ms.*," she explained, the first day of class, "because unlike Miss or Mrs., Ms. represents a *titled* form of gender equality. Miss or Mrs. defines a woman by her relationship—or lack thereof—to a man, whereas Ms. is neutral, as equally independent from anyone else as its male counterpart, Mr."

Ms. Briscoe was in her late twenties, wiry and pale—a bright redhead—prone to rapid hand gestures, spurts of laughter, and, when required, controlled consternation. She had a steady gaze, a way of focusing solely on the moment at hand. She talked to students, conducted lessons in grammar, and, most importantly, lectured on the books we were required to read with an enthusiasm that rivaled my father's zeal for sports. From the first day of class she had my full attention: I took copious notes, listening closely as she spoke about Nick Carraway as a nonintrusive first-person narrator in *The Great Gatsby*, the theme of alienation in *The Catcher in the Rye*, the nature of evil explored in *East of Eden*. And still nothing she said in class or assigned for us to read at home prepared me for *Moby-Dick*.

— *Oh Queequeg!*

For weeks Ms. Briscoe used Melville to delve into notions of story, metaphor, history and myth, religion, and philosophy as they related to an author's intent. There was a lot of talk about Freewill vs. Determinism, about a God made deaf by the sound of his own fate-weaving machine—the Warp and Woof of Destiny—about the various symbols embedded in the image of the Great White Whale and Captain Ahab's quest to conquer him. Every day Ms. Briscoe led us deeper and deeper beneath the surface of Melville's text. And yet, beyond all of this, there was Queequeg:

> Savage though he was, and hideously marred about the face—at least to my taste—his countenance yet had a something in it which was by no means disagreeable. You cannot hide the soul. Through all his unearthly tattooings, I thought I saw the traces of a simple honest heart; and in his large, deep eyes, fiery black and bold, there seemed tokens of a spirit that would dare a thousand devils.

Queequeg, the harpooner, the cannibal, the noble heathen from Kokovo, a Polynesian island not located on any map (drawing Ms. Briscoe back to a discussion on Romanticism), enters the story in chapter 2, in the middle of the night, literally by climbing into the protagonist's, Ishmael's, bed. With his exotic origins, his dark skin and impressive harpoon, Queequeg brings with him an immediate sense of mystery, the carnal risk of violence, a transgressive encroaching of intimacy. Up close, Ishmael noted square patterned tattoos covering his entire body. However, "For all of his tattooings, he was a clean, comely looking cannibal."

Queequeg and Ishmael became instant bedfellows. Both on land and sea. And throughout the story Melville compares their intimacy to that of a loving couple, as witnessed in chapter 4, the morning after Ishmael and Queequeg meet at the Spouter Inn, when Ishmael wakes to find "Queequeg's arm thrown over me in the most loving and affectionate matter. You almost thought I had been his wife."

Manly strength, adventure, and fraternity were common themes in many of the comic books, westerns, and Tolkienesque fantasies I had read before arriving in Ms. Briscoe's class. In these stories, however, masculinity was nearly always depicted with a kind of roguish bravado, a real or postured certainty. Men were tough, fearless beings who expressed very little, if any, hesitation regarding their destinies. Rare moments of intimacy emerged only in the forms of jocular playfulness and temporary grief, a momentary sadness over fallen companions whose loss served primarily as grounds for revenge, the manly justification (i.e., heroic impulse) needed to push the plot forward. In any case, these men were void of mystery, lacking the exoticism and sensuality I read in *Moby-Dick*.

No question about it, I was obsessed with Queequeg. I couldn't help imagining him as a dark, heavily inked muscle punk. Yet gentle. A pagan saint. Exactly the kind of guy I wouldn't have minded cuddling me like his wife.

Of course, during this time my hormones were running wild. Puberty. But unlike my pimply faced, voice-cracking peers, there were no cheerleader fantasies exploding inside of me. No hidden hopes of groping beneath the skirt of some girl who resembled Marcia Brady. Instead, I was having erotic daydreams about Queequeg. And, incidentally, it was also around this time that I began to write. Stories mostly. Rugged adventures among men. Good friends—*extremely* good, in fact—who often found themselves in situations like Ishmael and Queequeg, where rooms were scarce, where all the beds at the hunting lodge were already taken, or where late at night their riding posses wound up one tent short on the range.

Needless to say, as a high school freshman growing up in Albuquerque, in New Mexico, in the late '70s, I had never even heard the word "homoerotic." Nor did it occur to me that Queequeg and Ishmael might be gay, or at least have homosexual tendencies. It hadn't even occurred to me yet that I might be gay—not for a lack of sexual attraction to other boys, or, for example, an undeniable crush on Coach Staggpole (yes, *Staggpole!*), my hairy, six-foot-four gym instructor, but for lack of a definition about what my attractions meant. Ms. Briscoe, however, clearly knew. One day after class, as I lingered beside her desk, asking endless questions about shipmates and manly adventures and men sharing beds at sea, she explained to me that Melville himself had spent long portions of his life on shipping boats, and that many of the things he wrote came from his own experiences, others from events he'd witnessed firsthand. "Besides that," she added, "there are lots men, especially today, who share the same bed just because they want to. Either for sex or love. Some by choice, but most because that's just who they are." Her tone was deliberately matter of fact, contrary to the laughter that erupted from her, years later, during the summer after my first year in college, when I confessed to her, anxiously, before telling anyone else, that I thought I was gay. "Ha!" she said, joyously—she'd known it from Queequeg on. "So when did *you* finally figure it out?"

—⌁

"There won't be a funeral," Julie said, her voice steadier now than the last time we spoke, anchored against doubt, as if she had been practicing the words for hours: There, Won't, Be, A, Funeral.

It was late in the afternoon in Berlin, the courtyard beyond my window ceding the autumn sunlight to long-toothed shadows and the first purple hints of night. Three days had passed since I had promised to call Julie back. Though I had tried many times, the moment I lifted the phone my hands began to shake, forcing me to set it back down. Moreover, I felt tired. Practically all of the time. I was actually lying on the couch, asleep again, when Julie called, waking me up. Embarrassed, I struggled to appear alert.

"She probably had it in her will," she was saying. If anything, Julie's voice sounded thicker today, slightly hoarse, but calmer too. Without reproach. "She didn't want a big ceremony," she added. "Well—*really*—no ceremony at all."

Having cut the conversation short three days before, I forced myself to keep it going now, at least as long as Julie wanted to talk. "So what's John planning, then?" I asked. "He must be doing something."

Julie cleared her throat. "I'm not sure," she said. "I'll have to ask Curt."

―❦―

Joyce was fifty-six when she died. I had known her for twenty-eight of those years, half of her life, and well over half of mine. During the weeks following her death, I often thought back on the summer before the accident, when she and I were having lunch at the Flying Star café and she confided in me how concerned she had been by the tone in my recent e-mails from Berlin. Concerned by the feeling of isolation she gathered from them. Concerned by the fact that I only mentioned one close friend and that I hadn't dated anyone seriously since I'd moved from France. She wondered aloud if trying to navigate yet another language and culture was taking a toll on me, making it difficult for me to write.

In spite of my growing doubts about living in Germany, I did my best to convince Joyce that I had, unintentionally, overdramatized my situation there. My German was improving, I insisted, though in truth I'd barely progressed beyond ordering beer and schnitzel off the menu at More, a popular restaurant in Schönenberg, and directing cabbies toward my apartment in Mitte—*Ich möchte bitte in die Jagerstasse fahren*—usually on Saturday nights, whenever it was too late to catch the U-bahn home.

A look of mock consternation crossed Joyce's brow. "As long as you're finding time to write," she said.

"Of course," I replied. "*Really*. Everything is fine."

I couldn't tell whether or not she believed me, but, regardless, she seemed to accept my need to stick close to the moment at hand. I had only been in Albuquerque for few days by then, visiting my parents, and yet the dry heat and arid skies, the smoky piquant scent of roasted green chilies were already making light of whatever life I might have been struggling against elsewhere. An uneven smile opened across Joyce's face, erasing her frown as she pointed toward the shiny convertible Thunderbird parked outside. The car was a gift to herself, from herself and John, and she quickly suggested we go for a drive.

Joyce steered us by several of the newer buildings in town, mostly on Central Avenue (Route 66), near the university area and downtown, as well as a few of the sites where John, an architect, was working with builders on upcoming projects. We talked about people we both knew, about local politics, architecture, and books (I'd finally read *The Line of Beauty* by Alan Hollinghurst, and she was in the middle of *March* by Geraldine Brooks), before, as the afternoon wore thin, she took me to the ACLU offices, showed me her volunteer's desk, and introduced me to one of the lead attorneys there, a dark-haired and handsomely broad-shouldered man, about the same age as me, who also happened to be gay and single.

That was the last time I saw Joyce alive. For months after the accident I was haunted by the image of her sitting behind the wheel of her aqua-blue convertible, smiling at me, a light blue baseball cap protecting her pale, freckled skin, dark sunglasses covering her eyes. Most importantly, I couldn't forget her insistence that I write, nor could I forget my lie. Joyce had read every word I'd ever published, and every time I thought of her, beyond the wit, intelligence and charisma, beyond her generosity and unconditional support, I thought of *Moby-Dick* and Queequeg, of my first short stories, those ridiculous adventures among men that she and Queequeg inspired. Stories only she had read. And I was confronted by my continuing desire to prove her right: to prove that I was, in fact, a writer. Only now, I wondered, just as she had, if my real-life adventures had become a hindrance to my writing.

―◌

Eventually, a reunion for Joyce at the Hispanic Cultural Center in Albuquerque replaced the funeral. Family and friends were invited to stop by anytime between three in the afternoon and seven at night, on a Friday three weeks after her death. I imagined this to be exactly the kind of casual setting that she would have liked. And yet the very informality of a reunion as opposed to a funeral made it difficult for me to summon the effort I knew it would take to return home so suddenly. This event, unlike a traditional funeral, left me unsure of what to expect; I didn't have a strong sense of who would be at the center, or when, and I questioned whether or not by going I'd truly get the chance to mourn and celebrate Joyce's life with mutual friends. Besides, by the time the final details made their way to me, it was far too late to arrange an affordable flight. I felt disappointed—isolated—denied the possibility of sharing my grief. Even so, more importantly, I felt relieved. Selfishly. Now I had an excuse to grieve exactly as I wanted. Self-indulgently. Cowardly. From a safe distance that allowed my constant crying (the desperate unseemliness of it!) to remain invisible to those who might have needed me to behave differently. People like John, for instance, who rightly deserved my strength and support.

Instead, that Friday, I flew to Paris, as planned, where I behaved miserably, refusing to see friends with whom I had set up coffees, lunches, and dinners weeks in advance—no L'Etoile Manquante or *confie de canard*—telling everyone I was too sick to leave the apartment. The following Wednesday, I begrudgingly caught the metro down to the Ile de la Cité, the Préfecture de Police, where I begged a French immigration official for documents I no longer believed I would need. And, on Thursday, landing back in Berlin, I immediately called Felix, calling off our weekly espresso at Café Einstein. At the time, no particular reason for canceling came to mind, but deep inside I must have known it was the first step toward leaving Berlin.

Teenage Riot

Notes on Some Books That Guided Me through a Profoundly Hormonal Time

Alistair McCartney

Prologue

I turned thirteen at the end of 1984. By then I'd already figured out two things: that I was gay and that I wanted to be a writer. Growing up in a Catholic household in Perth, Western Australia, I kept both things to myself for a few more years. But as I figured things out by myself, secretly, slowly, I read. Compulsively, fervently, promiscuously, like only a teenager can. No one reads with the libidinal intensity of a teenager.

So let me give thanks, just like Marcus Aurelius at the start of his *Meditations*, to some writers who came before me, who formed me as both a gay guy and a writer. Let me take you on a nonchronological tour of some books that sustained me.

Tennessee Williams

Williams's plays were probably the first homosexual literature I ever read. I read them because I could read them without anyone suspecting a damn thing. I had a book of plays with *The Milk Train Doesn't Stop Here Anymore*, *A Streetcar Named Desire*, and *Sweet Bird of Youth*. It had a picture of Brando on the front, sweltering and sulking in that T-shirt.

I read the plays so long ago I don't quite recall the experience, but I know I got off on the atmosphere, the neuroses, the languor. I'd read the stage directions and everything. I think Williams taught me to read between the lines—boozy older female equals boozy aging homosexual, warped melodrama equals homosexual epistemology. He taught me the incredible power of the dissolute, of the covert.

Yukio Mishima

My mom bought me *Confessions of a Mask* for Xmas one year. At my request. The book had a white cover, with a picture of a handsome shirtless Japanese guy on the front. I think it was Mishima himself. I haven't read that book since, and to be perfectly honest, I remember absolutely nothing of what was inside. (Sorry, but this problem, the problem of memory, will arise throughout this essay.)

Though I do remember that around the same time I read it we were studying Japanese history at the Catholic boys' school I attended in Fremantle, and we all had to do presentations. I chose Mishima's public suicide by seppuku, aided by some guy he was romantically obsessed with, who, if I remember correctly, failed in helping out his beloved. Some other guy had to finish the job and do the beheading. Of course I didn't mention the homo aspect of this in my presentation. I just talked about how "honorable" a death it was in Samurai tradition and the politics behind it.

But secretly at night I fantasized about finding someone who loved me so much (maybe David P——, who sat in front of me, or Angel B——, in the seat next to me) that he'd help me commit ritual disembowelment for some vague political agenda. It was like something was born in me when Mishima's stomach was sliced open and his intestines spilled out. Thank you, Mishima, for teaching me how to talk about something without talking about it and instilling in me a lifelong devotion to the art of morbid, violent eroticism.

Jean Genet

I had this great secondhand copy of *Our Lady of the Flowers*. I forget where I bought it. It had a really tacky cover, some cheesy but still erotic shot of a semi-naked guy on the front. Born in 1971, coming of age in the 1980s, I was still lucky enough to get a taste of that era when great literature could be found in dime-store paperbacks. That era where high art and homosexual pornography weren't mutually exclusive. When queer writers were seen as having the ability to see into the human soul. Before the gay writer became affixed to a community, turned into a commodity.

Our Lady blew my mind, Genet's attention to the weird magic of childhood, his wandering, digressive prose style, his blurring of fiction and nonfiction. And of course his lineup of guys, Alberto and Maurice Pilorge and Weidmann and Darling, every one of whom was impossibly male and impossibly good looking, "as are all the males in this book," Genet wrote, "powerful and lithe, and unaware of their grace" (Bantam, 1964, p. 160).

In this time long before the Internet, before I felt brave enough to buy a porno mag and when I still relied on the underwear ads in the daily newspaper, this book was my nightly companion, just as writing served Genet in prison. I'd read it and jerk off, then turn off the light and slip the book into that special place of honor, between the wall and the side of my bed.

Edmund White

Of all these guys, Edmund's the only one who's still alive. The only one I ever got to speak to. He's my Facebook friend, for chrissakes.

Of course, I never would have imagined this would happen, that afternoon after school when I finally got up the courage to get *A Boy's Own Story* out of the Fremantle library. I'd been eyeing it forever, its cover with the dark-haired boy in the purple tank top, but getting it out would mean something; it would implicate me. I was still writing heterosexual fantasies in my diary, yet to finally inscribe on paper, like a legal statement, *I am gay.*

Hiding the book in my school bag and smuggling it home, I devoured it in my bedroom. Even though the book was set in a decidedly pre-Stonewall America, amid the sexual repression of the '40s and '50s, its world still resonated with me, reminded me of my Catholic boy world. A world divided into sissies and real boys; real boys were the ones you wanted, obviously. That first chapter with the speedboat and Kevin and his glowing white jockey shorts still occupies me today. From Edmund I learned how to reflect truthfully on the past, how to illuminate it. Oh, and the power of the word "corn holing."

Allen Ginsberg

Like every teenager, I went through my Beat Period. Somehow reading about them, their polymorphous couplings, was as important, if not more important, than reading works by them. But still, their work meant a lot to me. I bought my copy of *Howl* from this great bookstore in Fremantle, found it in the poetry section up the rickety stairs. That little black-and-white book, small enough to fit in the palm of my hand. I went straight back home and sat up all night, reading it from front to back in one sitting, not just *Howl* but the other poems too. I read it exactly like Allen would want his teenage boys to read it, like a monk, ecstatically. (Why has reading become so damn polite as an adult?) From you, Allen, I learned about looking *into* the world to see it, setting it on fire. I learned about the necessary relationship between writing and ecstasy.

William Burroughs

Reading Ginsberg was easy compared to Burroughs. I got the Paladin paperback (1986) of *Naked Lunch* from this amazing basement bookstore in downtown Perth, Black Plague, run by this cool junkie Clint, who selected each book in his store according to his taste (I really should thank him too, since he played a major role in my aesthetic education.)

The Paladin edition had this great painting on the front, of a blue-gray face screaming, Manhattan in the background. Boy, was I in for something when I read that book. I think it was the first real "experimental" book I read. A couple of pages of story and then suddenly, the book breaks down, dissolves and keeps dissolving for a couple hundred pages. But in adolescence there was no such thing as difficulty, and I read every word. Even the introduction with the transcripts of the obscenity trials and Burroughs's essay on addiction. How jubilant I felt when I got to the end with that image of a city under endless construction and those strangely moving fragments of words, "No good . . . no bueno . . . hustling myself. . . ." "No glot . . . C'lom Fliday" (p. 235).

And of course could a book have been more erotic, all those locker rooms and moldy jockstraps, all those ejaculations and ass-fuckings and hangings, all those boys: Carl and Joselito and especially Mark and Johnny served me well, nightly.

Herman Melville

I'm pretty sure I read *Moby-Dick* because of Burroughs; that was a book he admired. I read it dutifully. Every word of the damn glossary. Though not dutifully enough to finish it. I confess I found it kind of boring at the time. I couldn't see beyond all the blubber; it wasn't nearly as riveting as when I revisited it recently.

But there were sentences I lingered on and returned to again and again: "Upon waking next morning, about daylight, I found Queequeg's arm thrown over me in the most loving manner and affectionate manner. You had almost thought I had been his wife. . . . I could tell that Queeqeug was hugging me. My sensations were strange. Let me try to explain them" (Penguin, 1988, p. 28).

Just as I lingered on the inscription to Nathaniel Hawthorne.

From you, dear Herman, I learned the art of a big crazy book, the dual role of digression and obsession.

Oscar Wilde

While we're on the subject of sentences, what could be a more homosexual sentence than the opening to *A Picture of Dorian Gray*: "The studio was filled with the rich odor of roses, and when the light summer wind stirred amidst the trees of the garden, there came through the open door the heavy scent of the lilac, or the most delicate perfume of the pink flowering thorn" (Penguin, 1961, p. 7).

Reading that book, with its black cover, the distorted face of Dorian drawn in gold, was like an initiation into the sacred cult of the homosexual. Just like that open door in the first sentence, the book opened up a world for me. I read it during one summer holiday. It seems most of these books were read then, to ease the boredom.

It wasn't quite as racy as I hoped, and sometimes the arguments about aestheticism bugged me, but what book could be better for a boy still deep in the so-called closet? Unlike a bunch of these other books, I didn't have to hide it from my parents.

"I have grown to love secrecy," Basil says (p. 16), but even the book's coding couldn't contain itself, kept spilling over into breathless avowals. I remember getting slightly feverish as I read Basil's description of why he adored Dorian: "The merely visible presence of the lad—for he seems to me little more than a lad, though he is really over twenty—his merely visible presence—ah! I wonder can you realize all that means?" (p. 16). Everyone should thank this guy. Without Wilde, there probably wouldn't even be such a thing as a homosexual writer, maybe even a homosexual as we configure it today.

Jean-Paul Sartre

Ok, not a gay writer. Surely Sartre was too remarkably ugly to be homosexual, a bug-eyed ugliness that would only carry power in a heterosexual economy. And *Nausea* is not a gay book by any means. Though I do vaguely remember that the character of the autodidact is some kind of pervert?

But I have to include this book. I got *Nausea* during my existential phase—I can't remember if that was before or after my Beat phase. I also bought it at Black Plague bookstore, the Penguin paperback, with a painting of Dali's *Persistence of Memory* on the cover. Like a number of these books I read it one weekend, not doing anything else, just pausing to eat or jerk off or listen to a record, the Smiths probably. Sartre introduced me to the idea of a sensibility. I read *Nausea* wearing my black polo-neck sweater, smoking the Gauloises I'd gotten downtown, which literally made me nauseous. Not a homo book but a profoundly homosexual moment.

Sylvia Plath and J. D. Salinger

Apologies to the authors in advance for not getting entries of their own. They deserve it; *The Bell Jar* and *The Catcher in the Rye* happen to be two of my favorite novels ever.

I'm only lumping them together because I read them back to back one summer vacation. I must have been twelve or thirteen; one of my older sisters, Julianne, was reading them, and she handed them down to me. I was very aware that I was reading something *mature*, especially with Plath. That's deadly important to a kid.

Like Sartre, neither of these books is particularly gay. Though I do recall some "pretty sexy stuff," as Holden would say, in *The Bell Jar*, and there's that interesting moment when a guy hits on Holden in *Catcher*.

Both authors taught me that to write, I didn't have to sound like a member of the Bloomsbury Group. I could write in everyday language. My own voice, whatever that was. And they both offered decidedly queer perspectives on the world. I've never read a truer expression of adolescent discomfort with the world, maybe human discomfort, than *Catcher*. Plath opened me up to that decidedly gay identification with the highly strung female persona, from the very first sentence: "It was a queer sultry summer, the summer they electrocuted The Rosenbergs, and I didn't know what I was doing in New York" (Faber and Faber, 1966, p. 1).

That summer I embarked on my own form of mania. I noticed the hairs on my legs were sprouting, and disturbed by their appearance, I sat on our back steps reading these books, cutting off the hairs with my mom's sewing scissors.

Epilogue

I had a bunch of these books next to me as I wrote this. Not my old copies—they're somewhere in Australia, lost or in boxes or on the shelf in my old bedroom in Willagee, where these rituals were conducted—but the ones Tim and I have in our house in Venice. Leafing through them, it reminded me of the intensity of that time. These books were like strange fathers to me, their twisted child, teaching me stuff about writing and sex that my own dad would never teach me. Although I've since lost interest in some of these books, at times even rejected the authors like a son rejects his dad, they all still pulsed with a certain urgency.

It got me thinking. Do teenage gay boys still read literature to learn about identity? Or does it all come from TV and the web? Does the Internet leave any room for the imagination? Maybe I'm just old fashioned, but it got me a little worried. And reminded me of the real importance of books as a conduit to identity. The importance of passing books and a sensibility on or down in the guise of a writer, a teacher, a lover, a friend.

My Radical Dads

David Groff

Yeah, Walt Whitman. Yeah, W. H. Auden. Yeah, Frank O'Hara. Yeah: great granddaddy, granddaddy, daddy, along with a bunch of other sperm donors gay and straight. But as a queer poet, I think my true daddy is Bette Midler.

I confess that my knowledge of the Midler oeuvre is highly incomplete, and that her voice can make my skin crawl—though not as much as Barbra's. My diva gene is, sadly, recessive. But Bette encompasses for me two of the three personas of the queer sensibility, assuming that there is such a thing as queer sensibility. (As critic Jeff Weinstein once said, "There is no such thing as a gay sensibility, and yes, it has an enormous impact on the arts.") In our culture as in our lives, there is the Bette of Sophie Tucker jokes—bawdy, ironic, take no prisoners, subversive, transgressive. There is also the Bette who is CC Bloom in the movie *Beaches*, all embodied passion, syrup, and need—the woman who bleats about the wind beneath her wings. Now, blend the DNA of Sophie and CC with that of the curator of the Western culture museum—say, Cavafy but without all that sexy nostalgia—who winces delicately at mentions of bodily functions like sex, but whose bowtie spins when he beholds great art. Now you have the triune god of gayness—and gay poetry, or so I always thought.

As a poet I have long wrestled with my mad mothers Sophie Tucker and CC Bloom, as well as that crystalline, impeccable if infertile dad-curator. The great gay poets loom and lower, too. I have been bombasted by Whitman, gotten my face ground into the grit by James Merrill's Weejun, coughed as Auden puffed his dismissive cigarette my way, felt the spittle of gropey Allen Ginsberg, been dissed at the gallery opening by the passionately droll Frank O'Hara, found myself teased and tongue-tied by Ashbery at dinner, and judged myself unworthy to lick Thom Gunn's boots. My daddies all demand different, contradictory duties. If my heart belongs to daddy, which one?

Even though I had done the MFA thing, I came of age not in the poetry scene but in the New York book-publishing world. Except for remote figures like Whitman and Auden, I wasn't reading that many gay poets—or rather, I wasn't educated to read them as particularly gay. In grad school, one straight professor avowed that Whitman died a virgin—that his men were metaphors of yearning, his carnality thwarted, theoretical. Only later, as I loitered looking for sex on the same downtown New York streets that Whitman wandered, did I realize that here was a man who had done a *lot* of hands-on research. Like me, he even kept lists of his tricks. As for any paternal fairy dust wafting onto me from encountering real live gay poets in New York, I might as well have been in Iowa. I never met Ginsberg, Ashbery was a face on West 22nd Street, and Merrill was the elfin and impossibly erudite reader of poems at the 92nd Street Y. James Schuyler might as well have lived in Marrakech rather than in the Chelsea Hotel that I glimpsed from my bedroom window. With the exception of straight male teachers like Stanley Plumly, Stephen Berg, and Larry Levis, I was finding most of my exemplars gay and straight on the page—Auden, Wallace Stevens, Louis Simpson, Elizabeth Bishop, and maybe a little chatty Frank O'Hara. An exception came from my single meeting with glamorous, gay New York poet Douglas Crase—the love child of Ashbery and Merrill and literary godson of Richard Howard—whose expansive, urbane, essayistic poems in his book *The Revisionist* opened me up to the possibilities of rhetoric, history, and place. But mostly I composed my early New York poems with a degree of queer cluelessness, writing what I wanted to write about: family, sex, mortality, urban urgency—and, increasingly, AIDS, which increasingly shadowed me and my brotherhood.

As AIDS pervaded my life, I found myself needing to see how much I could include in my poems of the lives and losses of my brave and diminishing friends. To do them justice, I had to admit into my poems some of the passion, paradox, politicized fury, tragedy, and grievous black comedy that I was witnessing and experienced. As an editor at Crown Publishers, I published two anthologies that showed a path to that kind of poetry. The first was *Out of This World*, poems from the St. Mark's Poetry Project journal *The World*, a book edited by Anne Waldman, which included a lot of queer and otherwise aesthetically and politically radical poetry by writers like Eileen Myles; the book was an often-discomfiting shock to me, what with my essentially Presbyterian poetic education. Also at Crown I published the first *Poets for Life* anthology, edited by Michael Klein, a collection of poets gay and straight responding to AIDS. I had a complex reaction to their work. Some of them employed a meditative attitude that struck me as a staggeringly if understandably inadequate response to a pandemic; these poems made AIDS feel somehow generic, just another opportunity to bemoan the bummer of fate. Yet many of the poems—especially the ones written by gay men—were breathtakingly moving, immediate, and effective, often drawn from closely observed truths of AIDS in the life—as in the poems of Mark Doty, a frontline witness to the trauma of AIDS.

Another AIDS poet, also in *Poets for Life*, pushed past the tropes of the elegy—Paul Monette, whose two AIDS novels I would publish, and whose incredibly fierce book *Love Alone: Eighteen Elegies for Rog* shocked and startled me. The cascading, unpunctuated paragraphs of these poems about his lover Roger Horwitz—an end over end, breathless, gasping rhythm—evoked in their very breathlessness the headlong emotions not just of sadness but that element of grief that is the hardest to evoke: anger. Imagine—anger in a poem! Who knew a poet could be angry? I realized I had somehow assumed that the default pose of a late twentieth-century poet was domesticated melancholy. I was especially impressed by the brutal Sophie Tucker sass in Monette's poem "Buckley," a highly butchy and bitchy retort to the suggestion made by the eloquent American fascist William F. Buckley that the government tattoo the asses of HIV-positive gay men, so that their serostatus would be readily identifiable to their sex partners.

Buckley

favors castration or failing that a small
tattoo on the upper thigh in the thick-haired
swirl by the balls hot and rank in a Bike
no shower hockeysweat Buckley's upper
lip fairly puckers at the thought or else
a scarlet letter F I guess but cubist
Buckley's in no rush he's breaking bread with
Lady Couldn't-You-Di and sailing to
Byzantium for the weekend moonless nights
he lies on deck and Dictaphones the tale
of Bucko Bill countercounterspy and Company
Ubermensch Turnbull and Assered to the tits
stoically libidinous if pressed
at tennis a prince and *vingt-et-un* how far
from the terminal wing the suites are ask
the doe-eyed cons in Sing Sing Buckley keeps
in cigs and Nestlés pleading the dago guv
for Clemenceau the traitor every peace
is dirty pink triangles have a nice
retro feel & for quarantine there's islands
off Cape Ann so bare and stony no Brahmin'd
be caught dead in its lee shore a Statue of
Bondage blindfold torch snuffed a whole theme park
of hate monorail geek-dunk Inquisition
daily 10 and 3 heigh-ho mouse-eared dwarfs
in Future Perfect a mushroom cloud like spun
sugar oh Buckley the thing is I agree
about Soviet wheat the Shah the Joint Chiefs
can have all the toilet seats they like but
somehow your pantaloons are in a froth
to cheerlead the dying of my pink people
covered with a condom head to toe St. Paul
of the boneyard guillotining dicks bug-eyed
which reminds me who does the makeup on
Firing Line Frank E. Campbell how did you

get to be such a lady without surgery
I want my F for fag of course on the left
bicep twined with a Navy anchor deck
of Luckies curled in my tee sleeve just the look
to sport through a minefield beating a path
to smithereens arm in arm friend & friend
bivouacked 2 by 2 odd men out so
far out they can almost see over the wall
no more drilling Latin to meatbrain boys
not 50 before they're 30 not skittish
and not going back in Bill no matter how
many cardinals sit on your face oh rest
easy the spit on your grave will pool and mirror
the birdless sky and your children's children
kneel in the waste dump scum of you a popish
rot greening their knees and their Marcos earrings
and spring will maggot the clipped Connecticut
yard of your secret heart ink and bleed me
name and number and I will dance on you

Monette's deceptively controlled elegies and screeds made many of us squirm, but for me he was making a huge poetic leap forward. He re-engineered a form to fit the extremity of his times. His subjects—his male lover and an impossibly enormous epidemic—were radical in themselves, even as his themes were timeless.

Monette, Doty, and other poets like Melvin Dixon, Thom Gunn, and Tory Dent were willing to address HIV not just as a personal and social calamity but also as an implicit but rich and awful metaphor for the challenges we all confront around the body, love, death, and justice. Like the most potent metaphors, AIDS is also real. I wish more poets, gay and straight, would take on AIDS as the kind of resonant subject that many of the most groundbreaking poets embrace—the way Adrienne Rich did with the vagaries of language, or as Whitman did with metaphor of the nation, the body, and the self. When the writer Richard McCann spoke of perceiving Whitman's poems of the Civil War, in *Drum-Taps*, as poems congruent to the war against HIV, I heard the voice of the erotic, tender nurse, honoring the vital men he saw dying even as he grieved for his nation and his vision of comradeship; his lament was contemporary.

All these poets—along with other writers who wrote from the power of the human voice in the world, like O'Hara and Schuyler—prodded me toward trying for greater poetic authenticity. The act of confronting HIV, and the call to come out of the closet, require you to be square-in-the-face honest. When you write and then rewrite—and even when you think you are being truthful—you have to learn and then relearn what is authentic to you and what is bullshit. The bullshit can be pretty seductive for a while—the poetic gestures, word games, and conceits that arise dazzlingly from the rational left brain, and that can result in notional, often sterile poems. And just being out of the closet doesn't mean you are writing authentically; some of our best con men are openly gay. But as I labored for three hundred years on the poems that became my book *Theory of Devolution*, I felt I couldn't *not* try to tell the truth of what I saw happening. Otherwise my writing would be untrue, boring, and bad.

For me, being truthful meant getting even queerer, ideally in tone (whatever a queer tone means) but in content, too. I felt I had no choice but to write about dead boyfriends, orgasms so fierce they were little deaths, and the hurricane of HIV that swept away some of us like Fire Island beach houses even as it left others of us inexplicably standing. To ignore AIDS, or to transmogrify it into a rich and strange amulet of loss, just wasn't justice. I would risk being as treacly as CC Bloom, as coarse as Sophie Tucker, and as austere and bowtied as that museum curator, but I had to strive for a balance that felt forthright, resonant, perverse, and subversive.

These days, I'm once again struggling for a balance of art and authenticity as I write and rewrite poems for a new collection, to be called "Clay." Clay is the name of my boyfriend. He has been HIV positive since 1984.

After the example of all these bold poets, what good poet withholds? I've never understood how a poet born in the twentieth century could declare he wasn't a homosexual poet but a poet who happens to be homosexual. That's like declaring on Manhunt you're straight-acting and straight-appearing and no fats or fems please—and we know just how good *those* types are in bed. To me, being gay is like being male, or

David Groff

female, or American, or white, or black, or privileged, or poor—it is, whether you like it or not, an integral, defining element of our identity that we ignore at our peril. Being truly out summons each of us to work to surmount the queer fears that life breeds into our bones—the fear of exposure, of vulnerability; of dropping some bead of untoward or inartful emotion; of disempowerment and estrangement; of the reactions of parents and straight friends who understand only so much; of the snide dismissal by critics or tenure committees.

Being an openly, truly queer poet does *not* mean we have to write about hot sex, longtime lovers, leather, Castro Street, or Proposition 8, though it would be nice if more of us did that. No one has to write queer. Yet our summons to authenticity does demand that we each examine and explore—over a lifetime, fearlessly—what it means to us as poets to be homosexual. If we deny the vitality and significance of our homosexuality, if we shrug it off, if we are out of the closet but (to use the word employed by legal scholar Kenji Yoshino) *cover* for ourselves— discounting or disrespecting our gayness, ostentatiously normalizing it, ignoring it like a beautiful birthmark—then our poetry is fucked, and not in a good way. Our ashes will end up as good as heteroed.

How many of us are truly, regularly out in our writing? We may be out to friends and colleagues, and committed to fighting for our rights, but what barriers do we consciously or unconsciously erect to wall off our queer possibilities? Sometimes I worry we regularly de-gay our work before we even write anything, the way we can de-gay our homes before our parents arrive, stripping the nude postcards off the refrigerator, sticking the photos of our smiling bare-assed friends in the bedside drawer along with the lube and the photo of the dead trick with the visible lesions. How many of us twenty-first-century writers are as open to the animation of homosexual vitality as Whitman was in 1855, cruising New York streets some forty years before the term "homosexual" was even coined? For all their apostrophes and extravagances, Walt's poems remain as glisteningly radical as the day they rolled wet off his press. They are unmatched in their forthright rendering of desire and their uncompromising elevation of men-loving-men as a central metaphor of human adhesiveness and the American story. And how many of us are as queer and unapologetic as that poet who righteously sashayed through McCarthyite America, talking love and art and Lana Turner?

Being truly, openly queer involves not just an obligation to authenticity. It is, I believe, part of a summons to new creative opportunities. Our queerness points out our special path to a renewal and fresh inclusiveness for our literature.

It took me a long time to realize that my gay daddies, for all their different aesthetics, were offering me a single directive. After *Theory of Devolution* came out, I went through a painful and destabilizing period of self-questioning. Having written poems in some isolation, I was now wriggling into the community of poets gay and straight—a community characterized by cacophony. As I perceived my poems in a larger literary context, which is a poisonous pastime if undertaken for more than sixty minutes a year, I felt as if my various daddies had become an admissions committee, all grilling me for inclusion in schools that demanded contradictory advanced placement tests. Should I struggle to ape the elegant, offhand eloquence of James Merrill? Might I abandon linearity and try to be a 99-cent store Ashbery? Should I follow my apostle Paul and wave my raw nerve? Should I sharpen my eye like Doty, and find my own square inch of redemptive beauty? Could I be funky and quotidian, a Schuyler without a diagnosis? In January 2005, while I was on a writing retreat on the frosty Delaware seashore, I reached a crisis. Walking the blisteringly cold beach, I heard all these Jeremiahs—and their crossbred sons, my talented big brothers and contemporaries—screaming and urging and declaiming manifestoes in my head. It was a clusterfuck, and I was getting *chafed*.

Then I realized I didn't have to choose. I could talk back to my daddies. I could pluck the cigars from each of their mouths and take a puff, then put the cigar back. With a certain willful fuck-you-ness, I can blend my own genetic cocktail, savoring each daddy less for his aesthetic than his authenticity. You don't have to kill your daddies to become a man, nor do you have to mirror them. As I work through my lineage, I find myself sparked by a notion that underlies the hope of social and political progress and of the hardworking paterfamilias—that deep down, every good daddy wants his boy to grow up to be a better, more successful man than he is.

Our gay forebears offer us two related traits: their bravery, and the shock of their content. They tell me being a queer writer is a real opportunity because, if we want, we can boldly go where no writer, even

Whitman, went before. In the new century, we have fresh chances to advance their legacy. As the late, great gay-daddy poet Reginald Shepherd posited, we are entering the era of what he called the "post avant garde." Poets of many aesthetic attitudes are converging, shrugging off some of the anxious rigidities that have recently delineated poetic identity and fenced out those whose poetries differed from theirs. Moreover, in our new era, even as we can engage in radical ventures in form—ventures that may be largely exhausted—and can experiment with the fracture of literary language and intentions, we can also pursue what I call *radical content*.

Radical content calls for writers to vitalize their work by writing about subjects and themes that have been excluded from our roster of options because we think they are unliterary, shameful, political or public, commonplace, squirmy, or the realm of experts. These subjects and themes are ones we have so far lacked the balls and the language to pursue. Using all the forms, words, passion, and art at our disposal, we can infuse into our writing the stuff that preoccupies us in life and too seldom shows up in on the page: astrophysics, Project Runway, Darfur, ecology, lovemaking, medicine, Barack Obama, AIDS, Bette Midler. As gay men, we can of course write about all that stuff. Yet we have a special summons to queer matters. We can write about our relationships and our marriages—subjects oddly not often broached directly or deeply in much of our work—and about growing old and not dying young, about our bodies, about how we crab our way through the world and swim in the mainstream, about Bette and even Barbra. We can wave our wedding rings or slap a few faces; instead of buttoning up our shirt collars to please the priests of the Temple of Letters, we can show them a little chest hair. We can invite those priests to come up and see us sometime—up at our place, the home complete with the naked photos and those cerise throw pillows. Such radical literary action would do our daddies proud. It would be wind beneath our wings.

The Mentor I Never Met

Janet Frame

Aaron Hamburger

I learned about Janet Frame's death in the *New York Times* during my morning subway ride to work. Since her passing in 2004, her reputation has spread somewhat, though she's still relatively unknown outside her beloved New Zealand. I might never have discovered her if not for Jane Campion's film based on Frame's autobiography, *An Angel at My Table*, a movie I saw by chance in the summer of 1991.

Frame grew up as one of five children in a close-knit, poverty-stricken family in rural New Zealand. A passionate reader and budding poet, she became painfully morose when two of her sisters drowned in separate accidents, one ten years after the other. After being mistakenly diagnosed as schizophrenic, she endured eight years of electroshock therapy in asylums and was slated to undergo a lobotomy when a book of stories she'd published won a literary prize. Frame was discharged shortly thereafter and traveled to Europe, where she felt as out of place in the trendy literary world as she had in mainstream society. Eventually she returned home to devote her life to her art.

The afternoon I saw *An Angel at My Table*, I was a confused eighteen-year-old loner studying art in Paris with a class of Americans. Earlier that day, I'd sat for several hours in a park struggling to get my stubborn pencil to make the shapes I saw in life appear on my sketch-book. I'd always had trouble making friends and had hoped to find at least one kindred spirit in a community of artists. Instead, I felt lost and timid around the other students, who were more interested in getting drunk or hitting on cute French people in clubs than producing art. While my roommate went out at night, I huddled in my dorm room with a drawing, or more often scribbling in my journal about how lonely I was. Even if I'd wanted to join the crowd, I was too afraid of asking to be included. It didn't help matters that I was slowly realizing I was gay.

However, after leaving the movie theater showing *An Angel at My Table* that warm afternoon, I felt strong, even proud of my alienation. I decided that the reason I hadn't befriended any of the other students was simply that I was a much deeper person than they were. I wanted to express my thoughts rather than paint pretty pictures of parks. I wanted to be a writer, and writers didn't need anyone, only their books and typewriters.

Back in the States, I bought and promptly devoured Frame's *Autobiography*, a thick volume originally published as three separate books (only one of which is actually titled *An Angel at My Table*). At first I fell under Janet Frame's spell because I identified with her personally, but as I learned more about the business of writing, I began to appreciate the mastery of her craft.

What impresses me most about Frame is the bracing clarity with which she sees the world, physically, psychologically, and philosophically. Fearlessly sacrificing her own vanity, she describes herself in vivid, revealing detail: her fuzzy hair, her decaying teeth, and "the continuing war of some jewelery [*sic*] with my body. . . . Bracelets always broke, necklaces were too small, brooches came apart, earrings unclasped or were too tight." She writes memorably about how poverty affects her physical appearance, and by extension her social status. Here she describes her increasingly tight school uniform, which her family can't afford to replace:

> [The uniform] pressed on all parts of my body; it was torn and patched and patched again. . . . Also, I knew that my homemade sanitary towels

showed their bulk, and the blood leaked through, and when I stood up in class, I'd glance furtively at the desk seat to see whether it was bloody, and when I stood in morning assembly, I placed my hymn book in one hand and shielded either my back or front, whichever was bulkier with my other hand. . . . I could never understand why no one "formed twos" with me in assembly or physical education, when the command was given. . . . My shame was extreme; I concluded that I stank.

Frame's admirably calm and frank precision neatly avoids ostentatious self-pity and lends her shabby uniform and bloody towels a quiet dignity.

Frame is equally perceptive in describing her environment, which she infuses with her own feelings of hurt and awkwardness. While describing the farm ritual of bull castration, she evokes her longing for a childhood nirvana suddenly and ruthlessly destroyed by her sister Myrtle's death:

> I was unable to understand the mutilation performed on the bull calves when they were a few months old and we, who had been feeding them, had grown fond of them. The operation was usually done at night, in secrecy, by a strange man who hurried away, leaving the bull calf hot-nosed and bleeding between its legs. There was an element of ugliness brutality, unhappiness, in the deed and in the casual way my parents answer my questions. . . . I knew that if Myrtle had been alive, she would have told me honestly with her mixture of fact and rumour, "They've cut its things off so it won't be a wild bull."

Frame doesn't see careless barbarism as unique to humans, however; she sees the same potential for brutality in nature. Her painstakingly beautiful descriptions of her beloved New Zealand landscape with its "moonscape of burned bare hills" are tinged with unease:

> From my first sight of the river I felt it to be a part of my life (how greedily I was claiming the features of the land as "part of my life") . . . through all its stages of fury, and reputedly now and then, peace, to its outfall in the sea, with its natural burden of water and motion and its display of color, snow-green, blue, mud-brown, and borrowing rainbows from light; and its added burden rising from its power, of the dead—withered or uprooted vegetation, the bodies and bones of cattle, sheep and deer, and from time to time, of people who drowned.

There's no need for Frame to explain which "people who drowned" she means here.

Yet the *Autobiography* transcends gloomy solipsism, not only thanks to its beauty and unexpected flashes of humor but also because its story represents the larger problem of the role of the artist in her society. While recounting her personal misfortunes, Frame suggests that people who see life's horrific complexity clearly and honestly become outcasts because of their gifts. Perhaps this is one reason her work is often reduced to the "exploration of madness" genre, as it was in her *Times* obituary. Frame herself resisted this kind of pigeonholing, and in the *Autobiography* she refers dismissively to ill-informed reviewers who critique her work based on "a few biographical notes (not provided by me) that referred to 'insanity.'"

These critics miss that the "insanity" Frame describes within the asylum walls is only a symptom of the general insanity of dehumanization that we who live outside those walls struggle with every day:

> I was impressed and saddened by their—our—capacity to learn and adhere to and often relish the spoken and unspoken rules of institutional life, by the pride in the daily routine, shown by patients who had been in hospital for many years. There was a personal geographical, even linguistic exclusiveness in their community of the insane, who yet had no legal or personal external identity . . . only a nickname, no past, no future, only an imprisoned Now, an eternal Is-Land without its accompanying horizons, foot or handhold, and even without its ever-changing sky.

The asylum becomes a microcosm of our own world: hostile toward the needs and identity of the individual, increasingly obsessed only with the present, and all too prone to slide into the madness of war.

Frame's portrait of life in the mental hospital (described in lengthier detail in her novel *Faces in the Water*) is devoid of graphic theatricality, but is nonetheless horrifying. She makes us feel as if we are witnessing the capricious injustices of a totalitarian regime, for example, when a doctor holds up a quote from Virginia Woolf in one of Frame's letters as a proof of schizophrenia. And when Frame is saved from her lobotomy, she condemns the arbitrariness of her transformation from loony to star patient with understated indignation:

Instead of being treated by leucotomy, I was treated as a person of some worth, a human being, in spite of the misgivings and unwillingness of some members of the staff, who like certain relatives when a child is given attention warn the mother that the child is being spoiled, spoke pessimistically and perhaps enviously of my being made a fuss of. My friend Nola, who unfortunately had not won a prize, whose name did not appear in the newspaper, had her leucotomy and was returned to the hospital.

After leaving the asylum, Frame travels to Europe, hoping to "broaden her experience." In England she falls in with a circle of bohemians, whose pretensions she sends up with a wink and a nod:

> I realized that my new friends were not used to connecting writing with publication. "You mean you've published a *book*?"
>
> "A book of stories, and I've a novel being published soon. Only in New Zealand," I added hastily, trying to diminish their shock and restore plain curiosity to their faces . . .
>
> Someone said, "She's published a book!" She called to the others in the kitchen as if summoning them to deal with an emergency. "Quick. She's published a book!"

Rather than lapse into broad satire, Frame points her lens back to herself in a surprising reversal. She's more awed by these ne'er-do-well dreamers than they are of her:

> My friends impressed me; they were gifted, intelligent, learned, more than I could ever hope to be. . . . I lay marveling at the poetic dreams and the apparent confidence of those who seemed to become poets and painters simply by the spell of utterance; "I'm a poet, I'm a painter."

Later, while satirizing the latest literary craze, she implicates herself once again:

> Following the publication and popularity of Colin Wilson's *The Outsider*, there was some prestige in being "outside," quite unlike my experience in New Zealand when the prestige lay in being "inside." . . .
> I visited sleazy clubs, becoming a member for the evening to gain admission. I met prostitutes, male and female and listened to their

stories, gaping impolitely as I cherished my growing "experience of life" and quoting to myself on many occasions, "I sit in one of the dives on Fifty-Second Street . . ." The direction I had set myself, however, was too clear for me to be waylaid for long. Wasn't it time I applied myself to my writing?

As Frame's reputation grows, she revises part of her next book to please the critics, her agent, and her publisher. The result is a piece of work that pleases no one and everyone. In the process, she learns a valuable lesson about the writing life:

> A writer must stand on the rock of her self and her judgment or be swept away by the tide or sink in the quaking earth: there must be an inviolate place where the choices and decisions, however imperfect, are the writer's own . . . as individual and solitary as birth or death. What was the use of my having survived as a person if I could not maintain my own judgment?

Words are what I lived that hell of poverty, death, and torture for, she tells us. Words are literally what saved her from "being swept away by the tide or sinking in the quaking earth" in that New Zealand asylum. What sense does it make to betray words now for a review or a pat on the back from a publisher?

The price for Frame's valiant independence, however, is loneliness. When she decides to leave England to come back home to New Zealand, she has no one to say goodbye to, and has to ask a librarian to do her the favor of "seeing her off."

For years wherever I moved, Janet Frame's *Autobiography* sat on my desk. Occasionally I'd pick it up and stare at the picture on the cover of her autobiography, her wide grinning face framed by turbulent swirls of hair, eyes narrowed with laughter as she cradled the typewriter nudging her breasts.

The book followed me as I studied English at the University of Michigan where I fell in love for the first time with a handsome young Spanish major, to San Francisco where I had my heart broken, to Prague where I patched myself up again, then to New York where I went to grad school and began work on a story collection titled *The View from Stalin's Head*, which eventually became my first published book. And though I no longer use writing as an excuse for feeling lonely, I still try to follow Frame's example in my work. I search for telling details instead of indulging in flashy metaphorical loops. I strive for sentences that suggest emotion with the right balance of words rather than bludgeon readers with self-conscious bursts. I look for ways to connect my obsessions to larger universal dilemmas. And I try to resist the latest stylistic trends by aiming to produce the kind of fiction I want to read.

Shortly after *Stalin's Head* was published, I was browsing through a used bookstore when I came across a slim blue volume titled *The Lagoon*, a British paperback edition of Frame's debut story collection that had saved her life. (When it was released, Frame had been so worn out by electroshock therapy that her publishers chose the title.) Half-afraid I'd be disappointed, I bought it.

I quickly fell in love with *The Lagoon*, which, after having read the *Autobiography*, was a compelling lesson in how a writer weaves details of her life into fiction. In these twenty-four stories, Frame distills the sad details of her childhood into dense Jungian fairy tales that resonate with allusions to songs and folklore. Here, for example, is the opening to one of the stories, titled "The Secret," about when the thinly fictionalized Janet learns of her thinly fictionalized sister's fatal heart condition:

> My eldest sister was called Myrtle. She had dimples on her knees and curly golden hair and she could pinch me very hard when she was wild with me. She was all filled with a longing to be grown up. Once she went for a holiday down south where snowberries and penny oranges grow on the hills, and people keep bees, and have orchards where the grass is wet and silver with frost in the morning, and the fallen apples go squelch, squelch underfoot. Down south Myrtle fell in love with Vincent.

The paragraph is a marvel of poetic compression, tremulous with the emotion Frame packs into her carefully arranged words, like the subtly alliterative power of "when she was wild with me," and the thrillingly apt choice of "wild." Also, there's lyrical effect of "fallen apples go squelch, squelch underfoot," almost like a song, and the lovely "snowberries and penny oranges." I have only a faint idea of what snowberries or penny oranges are, but I sense them. I see them. I want to know.

Aaron Hamburger

I feel the same away about Janet Frame as I do about "snowberries and penny oranges." Though I never met her, as I studied her obituary in the *New York Times*, the facts of her life were so familiar I felt as if I'd lost a beloved mentor. My only regret is that I failed to express my admiration for her work while she was alive. All I can do now is to share that admiration with others, to keep reading her, and to keep writing.

The Case
of the Undone Novel

Richard McCann

Sometimes, but not often, he would work on his novel, my now
long-dead father. Those evenings, he set up a wooden step stool
in the living room of our small suburban ranch house and then placed
his battered Underwood atop it, so he could watch his favorite TV
shows as he typed—*Gunsmoke* and *Perry Mason*. I knew his novel was
about his childhood growing up in a mining town in central Pennsylvania, between Johnstown and Altoona, and even though I never read
it, at least not back then, when he was still alive, I knew from his having
described it to my brother and me that he had included within it real
things from his own life: how his family had been so poor when he was
a child, for instance, that they'd sometimes had to eat for dinner only
what they called "coffee soup," made from breaking up stale bread
crusts into the black coffee leftover from breakfast. How he'd seen his
first plane when it flew over a thicket where he was picking blackberries
with his father, a railroad engineer who always called him "honey-
bunch." How when he was ten a pot of boiling laundry water had tipped
over from his mother's woodstove and burned him so badly he was
scarred all down his left side, from his rib cage to his ankle. Afterward,
he was kept in bed for over a year, so long he'd had to learn how to walk
again, he said.

As for the rest of his literary life: he admired the poems of Walt Whitman, or so I learned long after his death, when I came across the love letters he'd written to my mother in the months following their first meeting, cribbing long passages from "Song of Myself" and "I Sing the Body Electric" and mixing into them his own descriptions of my mother's breasts and genitals. I know he loved Erle Stanley Gardner and occasionally boasted of having read over fifty of Gardner's Perry Mason novels, including *The Case of the Perjured Parrot*, *The Case of the Duplicate Daughter*, *The Case of the Lucky Legs*, *The Case of the Terrified Typist*, and *The Case of the Counterfeit Eye*.

I know that his novel was important to him, because whenever he inserted a new page into the typewriter, feeding the paper into the platen and turning the knob, that page was always accompanied by four sheets of carbon paper sandwiched between four sheets of delicate onionskin, so that he always made a total of five copies on which he then penciled his meticulous revisions. I know that in the late 1940s, a few years before I was born, he wrote a letter to my maternal grandmother, asking her for a loan sufficient to a year's pay, so he could leave the job he hated—in those years, until he reenlisted in the army, where he eventually achieved the rank of lieutenant colonel, he was a repo man for Commercial Credit. He felt he needed to work instead, he told my grandmother, on completing what he described in his letter as a "great American novel." My grandmother declined his request by return mail, writing that she would be glad to send as her gift instead a brand-new 1948 Dumont television—a "12-inch Teleset in a Meadowbrook console cabinet"— that cost $525, a sum equivalent to $4,919.25 today. It was on this television that he later watched *Gunsmoke* and *Perry Mason*.

The Case of the Dubious Dumont, he might have said.

Or perhaps he might have simply said "thank you," or perhaps even nothing at all. He loved watching TV as he sat in his red La-Z-Boy recliner, with me and my brother and our dog Mickey lying on the floor in a semicircle around him.

In any case, I do know that in the dozen or so years between writing to my grandmother for a loan and his sudden death at the age of fifty from fulminant liver failure, he wrote a total of thirty single-spaced pages.

I know this because I have one of the carbon copies of his manuscript right here on my desk beside me now. Across the top of the first page, he has typed in caps the words "A NOVEL," and below that, in a more modest rendering of both upper- and lowercase, he has typed "by Richard McCann."

Yes, I was the son who was named for him. I was the one who became a writer.

I was eleven when he died.

After that, I'm not sure what I felt toward him, if in fact I ever knew before.

The summer before his death, at our family fishing camp in Pennsylvania, I could see his disappointment at my squeamishness each time I asked him to bait my hook with the night crawlers I hated to touch. By then, he'd already begun telling me not to play so much with girls. Once, when he overheard me gossiping with a classmate on the telephone, he told me, "You don't need to be a Chatty Cathy."

I know I missed him after his death. Sometimes, for instance, I'd find myself suddenly standing in silence before the opened door of the hall closet, staring at his army uniform, which my mother kept stored there, enshrouded in a plastic dry cleaner's bag. But even though I could have never said it then, I also know that I sometimes felt relieved to be no longer subject to what I took to be his scrutiny. Over time, perhaps in guilt, as a response to my relief, or perhaps because I had somehow imagined without even knowing it that he had betrayed me by having died, I began to recall him only in fragments, as an accumulation of his tastes and habits. I remembered that he liked ketchup sandwiches. I remembered how he looked standing in the middle of Pine Creek in his rubber waders, casting his line for brown trout. I remembered that, the opposite of my mother, he preferred Ford over Chevrolet.

Each Sunday for almost five years after my father's death, until my mother remarried, my mother, brother, and I drove to Arlington National Cemetery, where my father was buried on a hill just below the Tomb of the Unknown Soldier, to kneel before his headstone and recite a half-dozen Hail Mary's and the Lord's Prayer. Afterward, we drove to the Hot Shoppes restaurant, where I always ordered the fruit cocktail for my appetizer, because I felt it to be a sophisticated choice, the kind I imagined myself making in the years to come, after I moved away and my life became my own.

I'm not sure how it happened, then, that I was the one to come into possession of my father's novel. I remember that I had it with me in my freshman dorm at college, in that rundown double room I shared with Mike Cregan, a sophomore who was somehow five years older than I and who talked about almost nothing but the German carnival side-show he claimed to have visited the previous summer, at which he'd paid an extra five marks to see a blonde Fräulein getting fucked by a donkey. Mike once told me that he had two wishes: to marry a nice girl he could take home to Connecticut, and to revisit that carnival side-show, although I don't know if he meant to realize them in that order.

In retrospect, I suspect that I simply asked my mother for my father's novel. By my freshman year, I'd received in response to an aptitude test that I had sent in to the Famous Writers School what I believed to be an encouraging personal letter, given that it seemed to have been hand-signed by Bennett Cerf himself. By then, I'd started to tell people that I was a writer, even though I had written almost nothing except for a few haiku leftover from high school. It was then, I think, that I came upon the idea of completing my father's novel.

I'm not sure why or how I conceived of doing this. I do remember, however, announcing the plan to my mother, who granted me her approval and reminded me, as she often felt the need to do, that my father had really loved me. I remember that my plan seemed to me almost a *practical* decision, as if I'd figured out that if I were going to be a writer, I'd be smart to join the family business, where I'd already had a head start, although, in retrospect, it's clear that writing was never my family business and that my motives were murkier and more complex than I then knew. What was I doing? Was I attempting to negotiate between the actual grief that I must have felt after my father's death and the guilty conscience I had for having sometimes wished, when he was alive, that I could escape his baffled and critical gaze, as if I'd somehow contributed to his dying by not having been the sort of son he surely wanted? I knew he would not have appreciated the poster that I'd hung over my dorm room bed, a larger-than-life photo of Bette Davis in *All About Eve*. I knew he would have continued to worry about the kind of boy I seemed unable to stop myself from becoming, a boy whose anxious laughter was too sudden and too shrill, a boy who could not keep his hands still while he was talking. Was I planning to complete his novel as some kind of atonement? Was I hoping that by entering his words, I might somehow come to know him?

How could I have understood myself then? I was seventeen. Only six years had passed between my father's sudden death and my going off to college—a drop in the bucket, as they say, at least from my perspective now. I am sixty-one years old. I have now lived more than a decade longer than my father did.

Whatever my motives, here's what happened, at least as I now recall it: one night that fall semester, I sat at my battered dorm room desk, reading the novel's opening pages, a notepad and a pencil at the ready beneath my gooseneck study lamp, should I have wished to start writing. Mike sat opposite, on the edge of his bed, clipping his toenails.

There was a protagonist, Johnnie Kirwin, a good but mischievous boy, an eighth-grader, whom my father had clearly based on himself. There was a setting, Bishop, Pennsylvania, an almost exact facsimile of Patton, Pennsylvania, population 2,023, the coal-mining town where my father had grown up, its shingled houses covered with coal soot, its empty lots piled with cast-off slag and smoldering boney. There was a scene of local miners parading on John Mitchell Day, honoring the president of the United Mine Workers of America who had been orphaned at six and then sent down into the mines to work. There was a town tramp, Vera, who loitered, smoking a Fatima cigarette, almost nightly beneath the lighted marquee of the Majestic Theater. I took note when I got to the Majestic. Once, while visiting family in Patton, my father had taken my brother and me to the Majestic Theater to see Elvis in *Blue Hawaii*.

But pretty soon I felt bored, thumbing through pages. It was the same boredom that I'd felt as a child when my brother and I were sent to Patton for two weeks each summer to stay with our uncle Pete and aunt Martha. Each day, after they left for work, we wandered their old house, trying to figure what to make of it, with its coal cellar, its steep back staircase that led only to a closet, and its dark, curtained rooms with their heavy window shades pulled down and their walls lined with blue-hued Maxfield Parrish prints and old family photos and framed religious mottos—WHAT IS HOME WITHOUT A MOTHER, TO THY CROSS I CLING, LOOK UNTO ME AND BE YET SAVED. . . . At night, after supper, our Uncle Pete drove us to get ice creams at different Howard Johnson's along the Pennsylvania Turnpike, some more than fifty miles away.

Bored by the novel, I thought that maybe I needed to take a break from reading it. I put the pages back into the folder in which my father had kept them. I leaned back in my chair and smoked a few Viceroys. Then I looked through a jar of loose change until I found enough coins to go downstairs and buy a Coke and a Clark Bar. After I ate the Clark Bar, I went outside and sat on the stoop to drink the Coke.

By the time I went back upstairs, Mike had gone to bed and turned the lights out. He liked always to be the first in line at the cafeteria for breakfast. I don't remember what I did after that. Possibly, I made my way across the room through the dark to put my father's novel in a drawer and straighten up my desk. Possibly, I just went straight to bed.

But I do recall that I did not look at my father's novel again, not that night, not that year—and not for more than forty years. I think I gave it back to my mother. Later, I think, she gave it back to me. And then it became one of those things, a memento mori, that periodically rises from a cardboard box that one is either packing or unpacking for a move.

And then I came across his unfinished novel a year or two ago, while I was packing up my own papers—literary manuscripts, photographs, ephemera—to ship to the university library that now houses them. At the last minute, I packed the original of my father's novel among the works that I'd written. What else to do with it? I thought. I have no children.

After the special collections librarian assigned to the task had processed and catalogued everything—13.2 linear feet, in 16 boxes—the director of libraries invited me to speak at the opening of what was now termed the Richard McCann Archive—my father's name as well as mine, I kept thinking, because by then there was no one left alive, except for my oldest brother, who remembered that that name had once belonged to my father before it ever belonged also to me.

For the day of the opening, the library arranged an exhibit of items from my papers in glass tabletop display cases around the lobby. In one, there were multiple drafts of the first story I'd ever published, along with a few family keepsakes that I'd described in stories, like my mother's silver brush and comb set and my great-grandmother's black mantilla. In another, on the far side of the lobby, there was a stack of yellowing pages bound together with a black banker's clip.

I went over to examine it. There it was: *A Novel*, by Richard McCann.

A woman was standing beside me, also peering into the case.

"Did you write that?" she asked. When I looked at her, I saw she was wearing the kind of matronly dress my mother used to call a "DAR Bemberg sheer"—something stern yet flowery. She was holding a cocktail napkin into which she'd folded some cheese and crackers, part of the library's celebratory repast.

"No," I said. "My father did."

She looked back down into the display case.

I didn't know what else to say, though for a moment I wanted to tell her how my father had sometimes sat in the living room after dinner, pecking out an occasional paragraph on his Underwood while watching *Gunsmoke* and *Perry Mason*.

"Oh, I see," said the woman. "Your father was a writer, too."

Yes, I thought to say. Yes, my father was a writer, too.

But was that really true? After all, hadn't he really been just a hobbyist—no different from a Sunday painter, say, or a man seated at an upright piano, pounding out "Chopsticks"? That's how I'd come to describe him to myself over the years. Occasionally, I'd find myself telling some friend or other about my father's unpublished novel—his "great American novel," as he'd once described it—and the friend would invariably ask, "So, tell me—is it any good?"

"No," I'd say, "it isn't good." I'd go on to explain that it was sentimental, that he hadn't reached too far into his own material and hadn't imagined his characters—his mother and father, for instance—as distinctive or possessing complexity. Sometimes, I'd add that I could have shown him how to fix it—if he'd lived, that is.

Why did I feel the need to speak of him like this—to disparage what he loved and to repudiate whatever bond we had between us, no matter how great or small? Was I attempting to settle some old score, to triumph over his anxious disapproval of what he regarded as my girlishness? Was this my way of punishing him for his having died?

The woman walked away from the display case without an answer from me. When I closed my eyes, standing there, I could still picture my father in our old living room, seated before the typewriter, in his faded fishing shorts, white T-shirt, and cotton slippers. He always changed out of his army uniform the second he got home from work. He said he felt more like himself that way.

He is rolling a piece of blank white paper into the platen, backed with the four sheets of carbon paper between four sheets of onionskin. Once he has the paper straight along the page guide, he looks up for a bit at the Dumont in the corner—maybe it's *Wagon Train* this time, or maybe *Have Gun Will Travel*. When the commercial comes on, he looks back down at the typewriter keys and pecks out a word, which he then regards: Is that the right one? Is there one that's better? He is resuscitating what he recalls of the coalmining town where he grew up. I know that place. Sometimes he took my brother and me along with him on his car trips to visit relatives who'd stayed behind. Once, he drove us past a few sites of his childhood, which my brother and I regarded in silence: a culvert by the tracks, where he played after school with other boys; the McCrory's 5 & 10¢ Store, from which he was occasionally allowed to buy some necessity, like galoshes; the railroad yard where he first went to work at thirteen, sweeping out the locomotives.

Who is this man I now recall sitting at night in his small suburban living room, the picture window at his back, periodically pausing to light a Pall Mall or sip from his beer glass before returning to his work, setting down on paper what he needs most to remember from what will prove to be his not-long life? He types. He erases. He draws on his cigarette. He types. This man was my father. He was Pop.

I opened my eyes and, for a moment, when I looked back down into the display case, I felt a sharp and even almost extravagant pride for my father and his unfinished novel, as if somehow I'd just published it.

Yes, he was a writer, whether he succeeded or not.

At least that's how I felt that day, standing in the library.

It's not what I felt back when I was a freshman in college, when I decided to put my father's novel aside and return it to my mother.

As soon as I abandoned my father's novel, I hatched a new scheme for becoming a writer: I would write stories for *True Confessions* and *Real Story*, since I'd heard that confessions magazines were always looking for new talent and that they paid two cents a word. All of my stories were always told from the point of a view of a woman, of course, and they all followed the familiar formula: first sin, then suffer, then repent. I wrote "I Hitchhiked through Hell" and "I Can't Forgive My Sister." I wrote "My Husband Is a Bigamist" and "I Can't Walk down the Aisle to the Altar." I sent each one out to a magazine as soon as I completed it. None was ever published.

Fugitives

James Allen Hall

My first semester of college in a sun-drenched town, half an hour from Daytona Beach: I spent all the time I could in the dusty sunless expanse of the library. Maybe I was martyring myself, but for the first time in my life, I felt like I had access to information that could save my life. It was dark and cold and I was utterly alone, so why was I terrified and sweaty-handed as I pulled a book called *A History of Homosexuality* from its sleepmates on the shelf? I took the book quickly, keeping its spine against my body so no one would know what I had touched, what had touched me. I walked my fugitive self down the grim stairs, down to the grimy basement. My prison was my freedom.

A year later, I came out to my poetry professor. She photocopied the entirety of Mark Doty's *My Alexandria* and gave it to me, after making me promise to buy the book at some point. I walked quickly back to my room, lowered the shades, and read. I'm not ashamed (though perhaps I should be) to tell you I read it first for the sex. That's the kind of college boy I was: under the sheets, lights off, thinking poetry would get me off.

And here's how Mark Doty describes sex in "Days of 1981," one man servicing the speaker

                    on the bleachers
        in an empty suburban park, and I reached
        for anything to hold onto, my head thrown back

        to blueblack sky rinsed at the rim
        with blazing city lights, then down to him:
        relentless, dazzling, anyone.

The eros of the occasion transfixes the speaker into loving the "blueblack sky" and the "blazing city lights," graduating sex to literal sensuality. Here's a description of penetrative intercourse—of hot sweaty hairy daddy-on-daddy action—from the poem "Lilacs in NYC":

        You enter me and we are strangers
                to ourselves but not
        to each other, I enter you

        (strange verb but what else
                to call it—to penetrate
        to fuck to be inside of

        none of the accounts of the body
                were ever really useful were they
        tell the truth none of them),

        I enter you (strange verb,
                as if we were each an enclosure
        a shelter, imagine actually

        considering yourself a *temple*)
                and violet the crush of shadows
        that warm wrist that deep-hollowed

        collar socket those salt-lustered
                lilacy shoulder blades
        in all odd shadings of green and dusk . . .

        blooming in the field
                of our shatter. You enter me
        and it's Macy's,

James Allen Hall

some available version of infinity;
     I enter you and I'm the grass,
covered with your shock

of petals out of which you rise
     Mr. April Mr. Splendor

I can't think of another poet who would interpret the asshole as the unfolding delights of clothes and home décor and well-lit good cheer of a department store.

I'd never met an "openly gay" poet on the page before. I didn't know what to expect from that moniker. I guess I thought what set me apart from my friends was desire, and that gay poets would write about their erotic existence. As if straight poets don't. And, if they don't, maybe they fucking *should*.

Of course there's sex in *My Alexandria*, as elsewhere in Doty's work, but it's described so beautifully. It titillated my vocabulary. After I read the book again, I am in love with Doty's fierce elegance, his precise descriptions, the control he wields in braiding together disparate narrative and lyric threads. Mark Doty changed the scope of poetry for me. His poems gave me permission to write my queer life: to see as beautiful what I thought would destroy me. Or, as he writes, refusing to be the drama queen I sometimes twirl into — "Enough, / it wasn't that way at all."

One thing I love about poetry, perhaps more than any other of its qualities: when you revisit a poem, years after its initial pleasures, something new waits to rise up out of its waters, shimmering at you with a look that says, "I've been here all along, waiting for you to ravish me."

What drew me first to Mark Doty's work was that it was unabashedly out, but without calling attention to itself. It was the mid-'90s, America was awash in identity politics — the way it has been swimming in some version of that ocean since, perhaps, the Puritans marked the Atlantic with their voyage. These poems, however, spoke from the inside of a community, broadcasting from the front lines of outcast and taboo desire, from where people were falling sick and dying. Not just people: a man's beloved.

How foolish I was to think desire animates only our longing for orgasm — and reading Doty's poems, I found a longing for the world, a wish to rinse it beautiful, to make from the devastations something wrought and gritty and glimmering. There's a wholeness to Mark Doty's vision as a poet that I became steadily enamored with over the years. His poem "Fog," for instance, marries three narratives of gardening, occult divination, and the speaker's husband testing HIV positive. There's a sweeping democracy in his poetics: the world we're bound to is bound to us as well, and a poem can reveal connection between disparate experiences—reveal that they are, in fact, the threads of the same cathartic tapestry.

It was something I was trying to do in my own poems at the time: to build a place for the "real toads" (to quote Marianne Moore), to make feeling *real*. I fell enslaved to the ways Doty used narrative to build to a lyric moment, the way he'd rudder and steer the poem with statement. He has a singular way of deploying description so that, in one moment, it grounds the poem and, in another, lifts the poem too.

I'm the kind of person who's always felt drawn to the galvanizing and searing statement, the "Daddy, daddy, you bastard, I'm through" of Plath. There's some of that force in Mark Doty's work, but it isn't the characteristic drive throughout the poems. Where Plath prefers a blunt-force trauma kind of statement, Doty seems to prefer inquiry. Doty seems always to look, to hold something in his hand, cock his head, and ask, "What fragment of heaven made you?" There is no sacrifice of power in the querying—instead, Doty finds the liminal space of the question to be one fraught with power, a space where possibility charges its nuclear reactors. Take, for instance, the relatively early poem "Tiara" from his first book, *Bethlehem in Broad Daylight*. The poem begins by telling us that a friend, Peter, "died in a paper tiara." The narrative of the poem progresses, and Peter's friends gather at the wake, where someone makes an offensive and hurtful comment that Peter "asked for it"—"it" being his death, probably due to complications from AIDS. The speaker of the poem is chagrined, at the least, and iron-jawed angry at the most. The poem's end has Peter in a kind of heaven, which the speaker imagines "poised over the realms of desire,"

> huge fragments

> of the music we die into
> in the body's paradise.

Another poet would end the poem here, on "paradise," and it would be a fine ending. But Doty teaches us to push to something more unexpected, and what he comes up with is so thrilling, I have to quote the entire end, which is just one interrogative:

> And given
>
> the world's perfectly turned shoulders,
> the deep hollows blued by longing,
> given the irreplaceable silk
>
> of horses rippling in orchards,
> fruit thundering and chiming down,
> given the ordinary marvels of form
>
> and gravity, what could he do,
> what could any of us ever do
> but ask for it?

There's a rhetorical question that resounds mightily in the music Doty makes—the thundering and chiming fruit, the hollows that echo with horses' hooves through the orchards. The description lends its lyric, exacting intensity to the force of the question that ends the poem better because it forces us to breathless begging for the end. It enacts the very structures of desire.

Another poem's end I'm fond of quoting is more gentle and yet no less forceful in its asserting wisdom. I return over and over to "Visitation," a Provincetown poem that describes a whale swimming into, then out of, the harbor. The speaker uses this event to meditate on grief—his first reaction is that the whale will get stuck, that it will die a beached thing:

> That, in those days, was how
> I'd come to see the world:
> dark upon dark, any sense
>
> of spirit an embattled flame
> sparked against wind-driven rain
> till pain snuffed it out. I thought,

> *This is what experience gives us,*
> and I moved carefully through my life
> while I waited . . . Enough,
>
> it wasn't that way at all.

The speaker changes course in his own "salt-flooded folds / of the brain." The poem teeters on the borders of elegy and praise, and what follows is the speaker's gorgeous description of the whale and the harbor, until

> even I
> couldn't help but look
>
> at the way this immense figure
> graces the dark medium,
> and shines so.

The poem ends with the speaker shaking his head and addressing himself, as well as his audience:

> What did you think, that joy
> was some slight thing?

"Salt-flooded . . . brain," the speaker notes, leaping from the whale—the exploring and endangered other—to the self, going interior in a way that would make Emily Dickinson proud and jealous.

Mark Doty finds power in powerlessness, in the abdication of normative perceptions of authority. He's a fugitive, pressed to the margins, the invisible space where queer men have always been pushed—and where they have always made vibrant, Technicolor lives. In "Visitation," for instance, the whale's endangerment speaks to the persona's, and how it changes the speaker. Every poem is a journey for Mark Doty, it seems. The place we start—the burning building in "The House of Beauty" or the garden in "Fog," or the light post on which someone has placed the sign "Homo Will Not Inherit"—is never the same place we end up: "gorgeous," the speaker says at the end of "Homo Will Not Inherit"—"and on fire. I have my kingdom." There's a fierce expression of voice, but it sings from a place of inquiry and finds in it not a quandary but a resolve. Doty dwells in possibility. Description, tone, metaphor—the craftsman's tools—allow him to lift veil after veil, seductively, yes, but also in order to wed the known to the unknown. He names the world so that it might slip his grasp, so that it might grow even larger with wonder, so that it might once more become a world I want to live in.

In August 2001, I moved to Houston to study creative writing. The University of Houston was the only program to which I applied, because I was ignorant, and because I wanted to study with Mark Doty. A year later, I sat in two of his workshops—Nonfiction and Poetic Forms. Mark is perhaps one of the most adept teachers I know; he reads widely and voraciously. He was as good a reader for me, a Doty devotee, as he was for students who were more linguistically experimental. And he was generous and positive in his critiques—I'd even go so far as to call him tender without sacrificing honesty.

My poems as a student in 2002 were in pretty bad shape. I was writing heavily coded, uncontextualized image-narratives. I was trying desperately not to write what about a subject matter that was haunting me. They were the kind of poems that would elicit silence in workshop— they stunk up the joint that badly. My personal essays for the nonfiction class, though, elicited a different response. It was in Mark's class that I was introduced to the lyric nonfiction form, which braids elements of image and metaphor with the telling of true stories. And it seemed to come natural to me, maybe because I am blessed with a colorful family and a mistrust of—or lack of memory for—chronology.

After the nonfiction class one day, one of those blazing and humid days Houston is known for, Mark and I walked back toward the main building. He was encouraging me to write a memoir, and he asked me suddenly, "James, do you really want to write poetry?"

I don't remember if we actually stopped in our tracks right then— but that's what my brain remembers feeling. My heart sank into my stomach, my kneecaps. My poetry hero thought my poems were shit. And he was right.

"Yes," I said, and then, "I want to write about my mother, but the world doesn't need another bad mother poem."

"James," Mark said, and now we had stopped, "if you want to write about your mom, then write about your mom." I don't think he was exasperated, but his voice rushed a bit: *then write.* I don't know if straight white male writers ever experience that moment of being granted permission to voice. And I never thought I'd be that kind of writer either, honestly. I was the kind of queer who'd been an activist, who'd marched outside of ultra-homophobic mega-churches, who once seduced a self-identified ex-gay telephone operator at Exodus International into having phone sex. My drag name is Betty Crocksucker: I'm not a hold-back kind of guy. But somehow the idea that a gay man writing about his mother was formulaic-with-a-capital-Freud had taken residence in me. Mark was kind to say what he said. I'm sure he thought it was an ordinary statement, nothing that broke open the heavens for him. But his encouragement, and even the slightest hint of exasperation in his voice, did just that. The world may need many more "mother poems." But it certainly didn't need the drivel I was writing before I allowed myself to voice what was urgent inside me.

Forget that you know me—my certain sins, my two-times-ever drag persona, my great and desperate need to write. Picture me in an airport. I haven't slept very well. It is twelve hours after a friend called to tell me he was HIV positive. I love him more than anyone in the world.

I am reading Mark Doty, forcing myself to read especially the poems about Wally. Seated next to me, a soldier in travel fatigues asks me for a pen, a blank look in his eyes, as if I am part of the puzzle he is trying to complete in the book folded in his lap. We sit across from a jumbo-screen TV: Libyan revolutionaries driven in retreat by pro-Gadhafi forces, nuclear reactors spewing radiation miles across Japan, New York's governor meeting with members of a gay-rights group. I am trying to stop the feeling that I've been injured in a private war. I'm not allowed to broadcast the details of that war, for fear I'll betray my friend. When the story about the governor finishes, the soldier mutters to himself, "I hate homos."

I think of my friend, alone and scared for months, and carrying much too heavy a burden, how he said he'd considered killing himself. And how this man next to me has casually expressed a sentiment not so different—they both ended with another gay man demoralized or dead. I think of a world without my friend, who saved my life once. I feel vulnerable, violently expatriated, in the wake of the soldier's half-breathed confession. What could I say?

I am not looking at him when I say, "I do not want you ever to die," and from my periphery he looks stunned and shifts uncomfortably in his seat, and I point to the book I am reading. "It's the last line of this incredible poem," I tell him, and he nods because he understands the word poem but not how it can be incredible, and says he reads *Goodnight Moon* to his son before bedtime. Then my flight is called, and when he offers it back, I tell him to keep the pen. I want his hand where mine had been. I think of him going off to Afghanistan, some remnant of homo oil blessing his trigger finger.

On the plane, I am searching for my seat, people looking toward me but not at me. I think again about the poem, the ending to "Turtle, Swan." The speaker has entered a dark movie theater; his eyes haven't adjusted. He's looking for his beloved, but finding only pairs—not the solitary man he needs to sit next to in the dark. Here's the end:

> I don't know
> where these things we meet and know briefly,
>
> as well as we can or they will let us,
> go. I only know that I don't want you
> —you with your white and muscular wings
> that rise and ripple beneath or above me,
> your magnificent neck, eyes the deep mottled autumnal colors
> of polished tortoise—I do not want you ever to die.

I don't know where that soldier's gone now: only that he had to say goodbye to his wife and son, replacing his "father" identity for "fighter." And he has no idea that what he said to me that day in Syracuse sounded like fighting words: I will hurt what you love the most. Sometimes I feel the threat in the world so much, I want to run. When I look to Mark Doty's poems, though, I am returned to myself more whole, more human. I have a more capacious heart. These poems salvage my courage. I am ready to say, *Enough, it wasn't that way at all.*

Some Notes on Influences or Why I Am Not Objective

Michael Klein

Confessionals, or I Am the Opposite of Edward Albee

I recently did an interview with Edward Albee, who insisted that writing about oneself is boring because one can't be objective about oneself. You write *through* yourself, he said. Because he never courted subjectivity, he called himself a writer before he called himself a playwright, because he couldn't find any kind of writing that he was good at until it came to playwriting. All of that *any kind* of writing must have been too objective.

Then, he wrote *The Zoo Story* and thought, well, that wasn't too bad.

I am the opposite of Edward Albee.

I have always wanted to write *through* myself in order to write *about* myself. I am shamelessly subjective, but not single-mindedly autobiographical. I want to be a *personal* writer.

Harold Bloom said in an interview: "I teach, think, read and write personally. What else could I be? What are we all here for? Objectivity is a farce. It's a myth. It's shallow. Deep subjectivity is not easy—it's very difficult—it's what you try to educate people into."

So, when it comes to influences, I am also very subjective and attach myself to my influences. I responded to the *subjectivity* of music, before I responded to books.

I *listened* to confessions.

I thought all confessions came wrapped in music, the way Laura Nyro's "Eli and the 13th Confession" came wrapped in a hyacinth-scented lyric sheet. Along with "Eli . . . ," Tom Waits, Leonard Cohen, and Joni Mitchell were also in the air. And there were other kinds of the American harmony and dissonance in music that had no words, and it all felt confessional: Aaron Copeland and Charles Ives and the German staircase-like atonality of Paul Hindemith.

I practiced and played on an out-of-key piano my mother stuck in a corner of the living room and tried writing—like every teenager who writes—songs about being alienated in a world of giants, and all wrapped around metaphors about being gay and all influenced by everything I was listening to. I let everything in. I couldn't sift influences. Then, I read some books and matched the music to the reading and then the meaning of the reading and the living in the reading to the writing.

Bodies of Influence

Inside the music that you actually sit down and listen to is the idea that something ephemeral has a logic, and that idea interests me as a writer. Saying what happens, telling a story of some kind (although narrative has never been as important to me as syntax and cadence): *story as the shape of something*—this is what I looked for at the beginning.

I wanted *influence* to wash over me.

I wanted to be *a body of influences.*

And, I wanted a *style* to show me what to talk about.

Wanting style is probably a modern idea for an artist. But anything worth doing is worth overdoing. Is demanding style a homosexual tendency?

If there is a homosexual aesthetic, it hits the air as style.

Every *difference* finds a style so that it can be seen.

Books had style.

Books had covers.

I Judged Your Book by Its Cover

Remember the cover of Richard Brautigan's book *Trout Fishing in America*? If you don't know it, it's a photograph of the author with some chick (they were chicks, then) posing in a park in front of a monument. The original print run didn't even have the title on the cover of the book (you had to look at the spine to know what book you were holding in your hands). And while it may sound strange for a writer to say this, that photograph, that book (the words in the book, the *Brautigan*) was one of the things that made me want to be a writer.

Brautigan seemed to let the whole world come into him, then turned it into something we could read. He made writing seem utterly organic and natural, and so, of course, it was strange, too.

Brautigan had a *style*.

And before I even got to what was inside the books, I was enamored with the book covers and who actually designed them at around the same time I was enamored with film music and the people who made that: fascinated by how art could also be *presented*: the way you got in. The *ticket* into the theater of the mind.

I once lived with a man who always took the cover off the book he was reading. While I was fortunate to be living with someone who actually read books, I was surprised that he stripped their clothes off. Without covers, books all look the same.

Then, years later, after the man who took the covers off, I walked into a party in a loft that a writer was subletting for the summer to work on his book, and all the books were turned around in the bookcases so that all you saw were the slightly open white mouths books have when you face their spines to the wall.

"I don't want to be influenced," he said.

"Why not?" I said.

I always want to be influenced.

I want to sort out my life through all of its influences.

What I Take Out

I went to the library and took books out every week. In the beginning, it was all poetry. Poetry was short. I could read a lot of books of poems, which meant that I could read a lot of books. I wanted to read a lot of books because I wanted to know how to make one. Poetry made me smarter about language and gave me a way of looking through the world into something that almost resembled it.

Michael Klein

I read the books alphabetically by the poet's last name: Antin, Bly, Corso, Cummings, Duncan, Ginsberg, Jones—that sort of thing. Except for Whitman and Wordsworth, most of the poets I liked lived at the beginning of the alphabet, and most of them were men. But that isn't true now. Now, I like a lot of poets who live at the end of the alphabet: Olds, Rankine, Rich, Ruefle.

And I read plays. Plays were short, too. I read Beckett, Kopit, and Williams.

In plays and poetry I was attracted to the brevity as well as to the sadness and despair. I didn't read to get happy. I didn't read to be entertained. I watched movies to be entertained. I danced to get happy. I read to understand how people who couldn't or shouldn't survive, survived.

I Choose

After D. H. Lawrence, my high school English teacher assigned E. M. Forster and said, in a stunning reversal of pedagogical habit, that we could read any book Forster had written, which meant that I (for there was no "we" in this instance, no rest of the class, just me in my seat in a sea of *Passage to India* readers) could read *Maurice*. I chose *Maurice* because I knew it was about queers and because it was a book published after his death. I chose *Maurice* because it was a confession—even though it wasn't *or was it?*—E. M. Forster's confessional, because now/then he was dead. And I was reading something he didn't want people to read until he was dead.

What struck me most about the book was how the relationship between Maurice-of-the-manor and Scudder-of-the-boathouse was a microcosm of the relationship a free society has with a closed one—what each of these gay men represented. Here is where I read that homosexuals lived in two worlds, while most of the world lived in one world.

And Scudder wasn't only *open* about his sexuality. He was open about his life and to the world beyond and including his sexuality. He was a happy homosexual, which also meant that not being a homosexual would have made him unhappy. Being with another man actually made him *happy*. The sex with Maurice made him *happy*. There weren't a lot of happy queers in literature when I was reading books in high school.

There was an unhappy queer only a room away—teaching another English class. Mr. Harnett walked into the ocean into his death on Fire Island one weekend while I was reading *Maurice*.

"He was queer," the school said.

Posthumous Lit

I was drawn to posthumous lit—the morose (mature?) shadow over anything literary in my childhood's psyche.

My mother worked at Farrar Straus as a copyeditor and used to bring home rolls—they were rubber-banded rolls then—nothing bound—of galleys of the books about to be published. And every week, she also bought home the current issue of *Publishers Weekly*, which—as it still does—had those enticing "Forecast" pages: books that were coming up.

I still get excited about books coming up, but, in the fall of the Republic, there aren't as many books to get excited about as there used to be books to get excited about.

One day in that part of my youth, I was excited by a poet named Sylvia Plath, who had a book called *Ariel* coming out, which *Publishers Weekly* referred to as "poems written in the last days of a woman's life"—or something very close to that (it was the idea of something that *lived* (a book) beyond your own living that caught me).

It feels like the first real book of poetry I ever read—that is, that completely absorbed me, because knowing that the woman who had written those poems had taken her own life meant—and this was the first time I actually *felt* this idea—that writing had very high stakes (even if I didn't understand what some of the poems were about). I wanted to write poems with as much fire in them as those poems of Sylvia Plath's, but only if it meant that I could live.

Then, after the first poem, I wrote another poem.

I Will Tell This Story
the Way I Choose

Shaun Levin

It's a puzzle to me, considering where I come from, how I got to be where I am now, here in London, living as a writer, getting books published, knowing all sorts of poets and authors, some in real life, some through letters, some—admit it!—through Facebook, all of us recognizable to each other, even if just through pictures. Sometimes I think: What takes a shy, bullied (but willful) white boy from a small port town on the tip of Africa and flings him across the continent, to the Levant, then later across Europe, thwacked like some dodgem car along the up and down sides of a triangle, propelled by the caprice of history and a momentum gained by centuries of pogroms and wickedness, to land up writing on a damp island among the offspring and survivors of the twisted and vicious English?

And then to make a career out of writing about the homosexuals, to be a queer Jew immigrant small-town writer-in-exile sustained, on the whole, by a community of dead writers, none of whom, as far as I know—and I know—cared about England or its Literature.

What am I doing here?

Rewind.

I was brought up in a part of the world remote enough for the Europeans to feel they were free to raid its land and debase its people.

To a large extent these practices continue in some form or another in South Africa, although today the country is still remote enough for the Europeans to feel untroubled about neglecting it. My people came to Africa at the end of the nineteenth century, penniless, ignorant of the land they'd been enticed into. We'd escaped from Lithuania, victims of an age-old hatred that is, in most parts of the world, still fresh and vibrant today. Sometimes the only way to deal with injustice is to get out.

My strongest memory of growing up in the harbor town of Port Elizabeth is a desire to leave. Perhaps that is a common desire among queer people—among all writers!—especially those of us who have grown up in the small towns of the world. By the time I was fifteen, my family was packing its bags and getting ready to leave for the Promised Land, a place in which we arrived not exactly penniless (no white person leaves South Africa penniless) but definitely ignorant. We moved to a town in Israel called Ashkelon, a town even smaller than the one I was born in. This was my chance to reinvent myself, to hide inside a new language.

The countries that have made me are wicked places. Immoral and damaged. But maybe the world is like that. And writing—art in general—is the antidote.

I don't remember how I discovered Jack Kerouac. It might have been through the couple I babysat for while I was still in high school, just before I went into the army. I think they had a copy of Ginsberg's *Howl* on the bookshelf in their bedroom, maybe even on the same shelf as *Sensual Massage for Couples*, which I leafed through and masturbated to while their newborn baby slept.

My first copy of Kerouac's *On the Road* is the 1957 Signet edition; it's here on my shelf in London. I bought it from Steimatsky's bookshop on Dizengoff Street in Tel Aviv. Even back then the book looked used, yellowed; it was the only copy in the shop—as if it had been sitting there since the 1950s, the bright yellow sun on its cover scorched into the orange background. The card of the cover is crumbling, flimsy, bits of it falling off like plaster from a ceiling. Inside I've written "1981"—I was eighteen. A year later I'd go into the army, more or less the same age Jack was when they expelled him from the Navy for constitutional psychosis.

For a long time I thought it was *this* book that had changed me, but really it was the biography, the Ann Charters book about Jack Kerouac, the one she wrote in Sweden during her exile from America. I read it upstairs in that house in Ashkelon that summer before the summer I went into the army, in a room furnace-hot (this was before they installed air-conditioning), but it was my refuge and my cave . . . I built a fire on the threshold. I slept on a pile of mattresses to keep the *tokolosh* away.

I remember the chunkiness of the biography. The solemn painting of Kerouac on its cover, him in a light blue shirt with a green vest underneath, his black hair shining with Brylcreem. In her introduction—although I could be misremembering this—Ann Charters writes that she left the United States in protest against the war in Vietnam, and I like to think that my leaving Israel in the mid-1990s was in the same tradition. Exile as protest. Baldwin in Paris, Hemingway, too, and Joyce. Leaving in order to understand where we're from, who we are; to save ourselves.

I keep being instructed by the dead.

I keep wanting to hit the road.

One scene from the Kerouac biography informed the writer I became. The scene takes place in City Lights bookstore in San Francisco, Allen Ginsberg reading from "Howl" or "Kaddish," I can't remember which, and Jack moving among the audience with his cap in hand, collecting money to go out and buy wine for everyone. That image made me. The image of a writer who does for others, who makes things happen, who likes it when everyone is having fun. That has been a driving force for me. Although I am a loner and my work is primarily autobiographical—and even when it's fictional, it looks autobiographical—I see myself as a socially committed writer. I enjoy making projects happen. That's why I set up *Chroma*, the queer literary and arts journal, and why I recently set up Treehouse Press.

At the heart of it, too, is a desire to be part of a gang of living writers all in the same room drinking wine and reciting poetry!

The summer after the summer I discovered Kerouac, I went into the army. For the month or so of my basic training I carried with me, sometimes in my pocket, my copy of *On the Road*. Israel was fighting a war in Lebanon, and although I was not a combatant, I was sent to the front. I can't remember what I read during those years, and maybe when one starts to have sex in earnest, reading falls by the wayside. Sex and war are a lot to deal with, and I have spent most of my writing life trying to make sense of both. War is just beginning to surface in my work. Sex has been there for a while.

Who taught me to write about sex? And by sex I mean desire. I mean the things we do with our bodies when we are naked in the company of another body. I mean the way we watch each other and touch. Where do we find the words and the ways to write about this? The impetus and the permission. Where do we find our writing ancestors? They find us. Our teachers? They find us. When the student is ready, the master, etc. The *High Risk Anthology of Forbidden Writings* came to me from somewhere, and with it came John Preston. By the time I encountered Preston's work I was out of the army and writing short stories in Hebrew, taking my first steps as a journalist in the Israeli press. I'd even given myself a Hebrew name. My transformation, into a thing I was not, was complete. I thought I could get away from me, away from the bullied small-town girl/boy *moffie*.

But in the *High Risk* anthology Dennis Cooper said I didn't have to, that I could say what I wanted to say, and still not be as outrageous as him! Essex Hemphill said: Say it. David Wojnarowicz said that nothing was too filthy, no thought illicit. But most of all it was John Preston's voice I heard. He told me that all I had to do was fuck and write about it. If I wrote frankly and openly about fucking—the abandoned doing of it and the intellectual understanding of it—I'd be fine. I could make a career out of that!

I read *Mr Benson* and *I Once Had a Master* and any other stories and essays by Preston I could find. I wanted to live like him (this was long before I became a slut and a daddy), to have my days filled with desire, to have a master, a brutal and caring lover like Pedro. And I wanted to write like him. But in order to do that, I'd have to go back to English. To write with depth and precision about lust and the flesh, we must revert to our native tongues. The decision to stop writing in Hebrew and to return to the language I was born in was like diving into cool water. I was like a fish flung back. I was dolphinesque. The first story I wrote, and I wrote it almost in one breath—about a cross-dresser buying new stilettos, then being fist-fucked by his boyfriend—was accepted immediately, and then I did it again, and again. I got a story into *Honcho*, then into *Inches*. The editors of those two porn magazines gave me the confidence to keep writing.

I never wrote porn. I never wrote to titillate, to excite.

I was almost thirty at the time, doing my degree at Tel Aviv University, taking a class in African American literature. That could have been the first time I encountered Zora Neale Hurston, but I have a feeling it was before then; perhaps she was mentioned in the Intro to American Lit class the year before. And perhaps — I think Italo Calvino said this — whenever we read a classic it is as if we have always known it. *Their Eyes Were Watching God* was an epiphany, and with it came its author. Zora was the I-don't-give-a-fuck woman, the I-go-where-I-want woman dancing, tongue-in-cheek, to the band's narcotic harmonies. I was not going to be the white guy sitting there drumming the table with my fingertips while everyone else worked themselves up into a frenzy. I would not behave myself. English literature could not teach me this, Shakespeare could not teach me this, not Dickens, not Thackeray, not even Martin fucking Amis. I would be like Zora. I would tell my story in the way I choose, juggle with this language our ancestors had barely heard of, pull it like taffy, make it sweet and brittle.

The first time I really thought about ways of doing it (writing), the first time I realized that you could *choose* how to tell a story, that a writing voice was both refinable and innate (deep inside, there to discover), was when I came across *Their Eyes Were Watching God*. Taking Hurston's lead, I became a kind of anthropologist, a participant observer in my own queer world. I would write about my own people, revel in variations of my self and its fictionalizations, extract stories from the cryptic places I have access to, the cruising grounds, bathhouses, the bedrooms, and clubs — in Tel Aviv, and eventually in Paris, London, Bangkok, Sydney, New York — those arenas of queer desire, the culture I was born into, initiated into by my peers and curiosity. I would keep writing my own "Eatonville Anthology."

I was brought up by Xhosa women. I came into this world in Africa. There is that to think about when I think about Zora. And when I think about W. E. B. Du Bois and the double consciousness of black folk in a white West that "looks on in amused contempt and pity." And Paule Marshall and Toni Morrison and Jean Toomer and Richard Wright and Langston Hughes, those writers who spoke for a community but were and are completely individual, who gave me the tools to explore my otherness, gave me the language to write about what it meant to be me: a Jew in Africa, an immigrant in the Middle East, a gay man in this world, this "two-ness" that I carry inside myself, that if it wasn't for the dogged strength writing gives me, might tear me asunder.

Zora wrote until poverty and obscurity killed her, Kerouac until self-doubt and alcoholism defeated him. Preston was killed by AIDS. They were writers who, despite racism and homophobia and alcoholism and AIDS-phobia and self-loathing, said what they wanted to say in the way they wanted to say it. Their personal stories were the stories of a time in history, of their generations, their gang. The Harlem Renaissance, the Beats, Gay Liberation, the onset of the AIDS epidemic. They told their own stories first—what it meant to be colored them—and then they told the story of their folk, and through that created a picture of a community, and of themselves in that community.

Our writing ancestors tell us about ways of dying, the options available to us. By that I mean a trajectory, a path, as if the images with which we steppingstone our lives can foretell our end, our deaths, the ways in which we'll be remembered, or forgotten. But how can we know in the midst of all this violence, all this "contempt and pity," how and if we'll survive? So we cling to the images of others to find our own direction, the image of a robust Canadian American with a beret full of coins, a restless blackwoman with a notebook and fire, and a cute young queerboy on a train going to meet his master.

Not just writers make us the writers we are. I owe the writer I am to others, too. To my father, who washed my mouth out with soap for standing on our front lawn and swearing randomly at passersby.

"Next time it'll be a jar of mustard," he said.

My father, a restless fisherman, frustrated poet and philosopher, lover of Jung and dream analysis, who gorged on books and psychology in the months of his dying. Twenty years before that, in the late 1970s when we left South Africa, he'd write letters home on thin blue aerogramme paper, his handwriting lean and upright (like himself), sharing the details of our new life. He left us with journals full of dread and rage, fuming and exorcising on the page the way his spiritual healer had told him to do. "Write out the anger," the guy had said to my dad, "then burn the pages." But my father never did.

Shaun Levin

I have a high school teacher to thank for allowing this immigrant boy to write stories when I should have been writing essays for composition class. An ex-boyfriend who criticized my first attempts at stories, said such disparaging things that it took me years of dogged writing to stop hearing his nasty voice. And Isaac Rosenberg, mad mystical poet, who died long before I was born, almost a hundred years ago in the trenches near Arras, killed on April Fool's Day just months before the end of the First World War. I was a boy when I heard them talking about his poem on the BBC's World Service, which I listened to in bed at night on my bar mitzvah–present radio. Here was a Jew who wrote poetry and was talked about on the wireless. I would aim for that.

And Agnes Makasi, maid and mother, who taught me that stories are told through the body, that we must lay ourselves bare if we want to be heard, if we want our stories to mean anything. Who spoke to me in a language I could not understand, a language that relied on every part of the tongue, the whole of the mouth. Who showed me—we were in the kitchen one afternoon—a picture of a friend she'd grown up with in the township of New Brighton. "She's in London," Agnes said, which seemed then like the epitome and epicenter of freedom, a place to escape to, a sanctuary from the horrors of Apartheid, and by extension—horror, in general. Bullies, homophobia, the homogeneity of the small town, war, political injustice. As if none of that could harm you in London. And perhaps that's why I'm here, now, writing.

Thom Gunn

A Memoir of Reading

Randall Mann

for Craig Arnold

At seventeen years old, in Orlando, Florida, I found, in my Language Arts textbook, my first Thom Gunn poem, "On the Move." (And lucky me, because I had something of a Keats hangover, which is to say that I was writing unromantic Romantic lyrics with titles like "Conversations with the Wind.") Though I didn't have the words for it then, I was stirred by, maybe, the sturdiness of Gunn's diction and line, the "uncertain violence" of birds in the first stanza of the poem. (A gust of swallows "spurts across the field" like eco-porn.) And then, in the second stanza, comes Trouble:

> On motorcycles, up the road, they come:
> Small, black, as flies hanging in heat, the Boys,
> Until the distance throws them forth, their hum
> Bulges to thunder held by calf and thigh.
> In goggles, donned impersonality,
> In gleaming jackets trophied with the dust,
> They strap in doubt—by hiding it, robust—
> And almost hear a meaning in their noise.

Um, hello! This is Brando meets back room; the gleaming bikers, out of control, ooze control. I admire the conflation of the birds and the bikers—of nature and not-sure—their "movement in a valueless world," and my suburban, not-quite-out, not-quite-poet, have-*got*-to-get-out-of-Orlando younger self might have been drawn toward this poem's formal rebellion; its seductive, cautionary "part-solution" of the final line: "One is always nearer by not keeping still." What I do know is that it was exactly the right poem at the right time.

Eventually I left Florida and made my way out to San Francisco, and that's where I really started reading Gunn, all of it, and in all the wrong order, first *The Man with Night Sweats*' startling, stunned ache of elegy, and then *The Passages of Joy*, then back, all the way back to *Fighting Terms*, then *Boss Cupid*, and so on. I love *The Passages of Joy* best, though, its everyday chronicle of the curious, formal, free poetry that is San Francisco, of the love and the fog and the drug-fucked nights. My copy, which I found on generally pre-gentrified, hooker-happy Polk Street, has this Don Bachardy drawing of Gunn on the back, bulgy jeans and studded belt and leather band and tats and wife beater, and I thought, yeah, this is good; this is what I need. This is not tweed.

The book starts with "Elegy," a scrupulously enjambed piece about friends who "keep leaving me"; it's tempting to read this through the lens of AIDS, though it's nothing to do with that, written before the scourge; still, I'll admit that it's hard not to imagine Gunn as a kind of seer when the penultimate stanza goes like this:

> There will be no turn of the river
> where we are all reunited
> in a wonderful party
> the picnic spread
> all the lost found
> as in hide and seek

What I like best about *The Passages of Joy* is that it's a darkly humane rendering of how gay men relate, and fail to relate, to each other in San Francisco, the "open city," as he says in the poem "Night Taxi," "uncluttered as a map." (As an aside, August Kleinzahler, in his lovely essay on Gunn in *Cutty, One Rock*, wrote, "To travel with Thom was to participate in an erotic mapping of San Francisco out of the bus window." For me, this is what it's like reading Gunn.) *The Passages of Joy* is lubricated yet queerly compassionate: in one poem, after a night out, the speaker ends his run in the sheets alone: "I calm down, / undress and slip / in between them and think / of household gods." Even his drug dealer, in the poem "Crystal," is made vulnerable and civilized, he who "looks nobler every year": "Inside the crowded night he feels complete."

Or, one of my favorite Gunn poems, "San Francisco Streets." This is a clear-eyed, trimeter/dimeter allegory of a certain kind of social climb in San Francisco's gay Castro district, variations of which I have seen — okay, participated in — in this gay ghetto in which I live. The boy discussed in "San Francisco Streets," fresh from "Peach County," who by degrees "rose / Like country cream — / Hustler to towel boy, / Bath house and steam," has become a jewelry clerk, and "at last attained / To middle class. / (No one on Castro Street / Peddles his ass.)" Indeed. And yet, despite the boy's prettiness and shopgirl status, when "Good looks and great physiques / Pass in procession," the speaker thinks he catches something, a "half-veiled uncertainty," in the boy's expression. Gunn, in his assiduous, cool, tender construction, lets that seemingly offhand detail, "half-veiled uncertainty," betray the queer currency of the piece, which is beauty and youth, not truth; which is the quick rise of the unlined, and then the incremental, pitiless decline. The poem ends with advice that takes on the air of menace, the last two lines of which I have thought, sometimes, I ought to have tattooed on my forearm:

> Better remember what
> Makes you secure.
> Fuzz is still on the peach,
> Peach on the stem.
> Your looks looked after you.
> Look after them.

Before I met Thom, I had two sightings of him in the city. The first was in this shady little pseudo-leather bar in the Castro (everything's a bit pseudo in the Castro) called the Detour: he had on a leather jacket, and he was leaning against the chain-link fence (don't ask) that was rigged up in the middle of the bar. The second was on the corner of Carl and Cole Streets in the Cole Valley: it was noonish on a Sunday, and he was dragged up in leather, head to toe, waiting on the N-Judah streetcar, off, maybe, to a Sunday bar crawl south of Market Street. When I think of Thom, more often I think not of the brief time I knew him but of these two images, the spidery lean of the handsome would-be trick in a bar, the unrepentant leather-in-broad-daylight wait. The possibility.

I'm writing this in 2009; Thom would have turned eighty this year. He was a great talker, self-possessed yet humble, a genius with the grant to stamp it, rakish in the most winning ways. Oh, yeah, and he could write like hell, in particular about the complications and machinations of queer longing—in, say, the poem "Sweet Things," one of my faves in *The Passages of Joy*, where two men run into each other on the street, and the names are half remembered, but not the lust. The speaker says: "When he shakes my hand I feel / a dry finger playfully bending inward / and touching my palm in secret." And that finger bending inward, the palm touched in secret, the restraint and promise and things unsaid and stark control, say as much about Gunn's aesthetics as about this proxy speaker. But then, there is no artificial line between the quotidian and the literary in Gunn, and his refusal to pedantically separate the two is one of the reasons why "Sweet Things," why Gunn's work, not only rewards my attention but also moves me. And so, let me end with the end of the poem:

> We know our charm.
> We know delay makes pleasure great.
> In our eyes, on our tongues,
> we savour the approaching delight
> of things we know yet are fresh always.
> Sweet things. Sweet things.

Queering an Italian American
Poetic Legacy

Peter Covino

I intend to highlight a trajectory of a personal queer and marginalized poetic practice that looks at language as predominantly and perpetually unstable, reconstituted, and at times even sculpted into meaning. I've been drawn quite literally by the provocative title of this volume (*Who's Yer Daddy*) in thinking about the development of a queer poetic aesthetic and how my own poetic "daddies" influenced me. Of course, as someone who has written a lot about incest and paternal sexual abuse, this fatherly sphere of influence remains incredibly overwrought, but I hope in this brief essay to do justice to the complexities of writing poetry as a psychoanalytic process that is equally engaged and thwarted by the creative and intellectual, and by primary drives, the sexual among them. I will briefly consider a few queer and/or marginalized poets who have influenced me most and continue to influence me—queer here is not used merely to signify and encompass gay identity but it refers also to concepts of otherness, and outward or bold acknowledgment of difference. My goals involve recognition of the poem's performative or queer effects shaped, simultaneously, by willed and uncontainable psychic processes. For me, this queer trajectory intersects and spills over into a growing understanding and growing complication of poetic identity and the evolving fields of American and specifically Italian

American poetry—and how I perceive myself in conversation with these fields.

When I conceptualize a reconstituted language, here, I'm mostly gripped by the overwhelming cultural impact of Paul Celan, who famously incorporated at least four distinct cultures and language systems in his poems—Romanian, German, French, and Russian. I would like to fantasize that my journey has been as rich and varied, but it hasn't—not yet at least. I'm mostly influenced by the Italian dialect of Sturnese (close to the Neapolitan dialect, which is heavily inflected by Spanish), and then English and Italian in that order, the order in which I learned these languages. The "word-caves, courtyards, chambers and drop or [trap]doors" that Pierre Joris and Jerome Rothenberg (*Poems for the Millennium*, 154) highlight in Celan's word choices is a frequent mantra when I teach and when I edit my own work. I ask myself questions like: Where did this particular sound, or word, come from? What language? What resonances does this word have with others that are or are not on the page? How has the word/sound/idiom translated/migrated (or immigrated) into English? How can I emphasize the other physical spaces, associations, and connotations of words and phrases without making the poems seem obvious, mannered, or too studied. Yet, I get impatient when poems are too hermetic or so word slick that the meaning has to be pored over and guessed for no apparent or hard-earned reward. Celan seems to me to have a perfect ability to withhold and to engage: the knotty word textures, the compound nouns and adjectives, the striking and frequent neologisms, the relative short length of the poems, even as many accumulate into series, suggests some sort of psychic mastery and confidence that appeals. Of course, poetic daddies—like our own poems—often call us back for more thorough reckoning, to figure out what it is about these poets that have so affected us and continue to haunt, or provide solace and continued, available joy. I don't claim to know all of Celan's work or all of Whitman's or Cavafy's or O'Hara's (other key influences) with any sense of authority, but every time I read them I discover and rediscover poems I love. I'm not a big fan of publishing too much without considering the larger poetic landscape; more committed reading of existing poetry and the privileging of the reading experience would help lots of poets, perhaps, realize that the work is not as original and interesting as we may always think.

Sense and Silence and
an Aversion to Conformity

As Celan and many others no doubt value, silences in poetry are at once problematic yet liberating. Poetry allows me/us to listen more methodically—to physically and sculpturally struggle with the words I am conjuring and/or trying to form/recall—in less restricted ways. The poem becomes a site of discovery in this type of multilingual handiwork: the visual schematic that emerges is the evidence of a mental effort to translate sounds and experiences, which often shift as they move from one language and/or dialect into another and then into English. Not surprisingly, since the struggle to articulate becomes so palpable and immediately interactive at a level of mental activity, many poets wonder if we're making sense. Fortunately, I cherish one of Charles Bernstein's dictums (which I may be misattributing) from my days as his student at City College: "Making sense in poetry can be overrated." This injunction no doubt refers to any poetic process that in any way constrains the production of poetry more than it is already constrained, by conventional rules of linguistics, grammar, and syntax, and so forth. Oftentimes the self-conscious disavowal of grammatical rules is specifically what Bernstein's poems are about; his influential theorizing on language poetry and experimental poetics speaks to me most when it involves a deeply intuitive yet surprising process that fights against "cultural self-regulation and self-censorship" (Bernstein, *A Poetics*, 1). Bernstein further claims:

> Poetry is an aversion of conformity in the pursuit of new forms . . . of putting things together or stripping them apart . . . ways of accounting for what weighs upon any one of us, or that poetry tosses up into an imaginary air like so many swans flying out of a magician's depthless black hat so that suddenly, we breathe more deeply. (1)

I can trace the first time poetic language affected me at profound and deeply conscious and unconscious level to the mid-1980s when I was a studying abroad in Rome, in a contemporary Italian poetry class taught by Giorgio Bassani—the Jewish Italian poet-writer who is famous for his novel *The Garden of the Finzi Contini* (1962); the movie of the same name by Vittorio De Sica won the Academy Award in 1971. Bassani was passionate about poetry and published several poetry collections before he had wider success as a short story writer and then novelist; the relative lack of recognition for his poetry strikes me as especially regrettable. Like Celan, Bassani was heavily influenced by his work and learning in several different languages and varying linguistic systems; Bassani, who spoke English with a thick accent, was trained in classical languages but also was an accomplished translator of Emily Dickinson's poetry, in addition to translating widely from the French. Before *The Garden of the Finzi Contini*, Bassani wrote an amazingly lyrical and elegiac novel called *Gli occhiali d'oro* (1958), translated most commonly in English as *The Gold-Rimmed Spectacles*. I recently learned that a little-known film based on the novel appeared in 1987, starring Rupert Everett and Stefania Sandrelli, around the time I studied with Bassani, almost thirty years after he wrote the novel, which may account for his renewed fascination with the work during those years. The short but riveting novel, a mere 140 pages about a respected middle-aged doctor, Athos Fadigati, was the first queer-themed book I ever read in Italian. The doctor's name is a transliteration of the Greek and Italian meaning roughly "the exhausted one from the holy mountain," and this sort of clever word play is ubiquitous.

Bassani suggestively chronicles Dr. Fadigati's intimacy and illicit affair with a much younger, wayward male boxer/student, who eventually humiliates and betrays their relationship by publicly punching the doctor in the face in a crowded beach resort hotel. The events and consequent scandal quickly lead to the doctor's loss of prestige, livelihood, and eventual suicide by drowning in the river Po—what has always seemed to me to be a tortured homage of sorts to Virginia Woolf, as well as a bizarre presage of Celan's suicide. You can imagine the complex intellectual awakening and conflicted coming-out story the book propelled, as hushed secretive words, carefully parsed, resonated for the first time as I delved on: "Ebbene, ho sentito dire che è . . . che era 'cosi' 'di quelli' . . . a parlare di argomenti indecorsi, e dell'inversione sessuale in ispecie, c'era chi ricorreva sogghignando a qualche parole del dialetto che anche da noi e' sempre tanto piu cativo in confronto alla lingue dei ceti superiori (Bassani, *Il romanzo di Ferrara*, 174) ("Oh well, I've heard it said that 'he's an . . .' that he was 'like that' 'one of those' . . . to speak of those indecorous issues, sexual inversion especially, there were those who resorted, sneering, to some dialect word that even by our standards was always much more derogatory with regard to the language of the upper class" [translation mine]). In addition to the stuttered speech and the obvious difficulty of acknowledging a same-sex relationship, *sogghingnando*—which means "sneering" or "snarling"—is particularly sound heavy, onomatopoeic, and disturbing to hear in this context.

Bassani was fiercely defensive of his daring choice to explore the interrelationships between queer identity and the plight of Italian Jews in the late 1930s shortly after the promulgation of the racial laws that would lead to the deportation of some twenty thousand Jews and the extermination of eight thousand, roughly 15 percent of the Italian Jewish population (Luconi, "Recent Trends," 4, 13). Bassani is never moralizing or reductive in his extended examination of homosexuality; street names, names of piazzas, bars, and restaurants of Bassani's native city of Ferrara are plainly detailed, which give the novel a heightened air of authenticity, acceptance, and realism, in spite perhaps of his well-documented feelings of perpetual exile and his conflicts about writing in what had become the language of his oppressors.

In Bassani's seminar I also studied the radically queer and leftist work of poet-filmmaker Pier Paolo Pasolini for the first time, and Bassani spoke out publicly about Pasolini's murder (in 1975) by a gang of gay pick-ups, allegedly hired by the right-leaning government of the time. Pasolini was also Dario Bellezza's mentor and the mentor of Bellezza's best friend, the more acclaimed poet Amelia Rosselli, whose *Variazioni belliche* (*War Variations*, 1964) was translated by Paul Vangelisti in 2004. Bellezza, who died of AIDS-related complications in 1996 and would be buried near Amelia Rosselli in the non-Catholic cemetery in Rome, is largely ignored outside of Italy, and he's been a major influence on my work; I'm currently translating a significant variety of his poems—with the goal of completing a selected volume in English.

How multicultural poets process language and how multiculturalism and queerness still seem underappreciated in their interrelationships continues to interest me, and I am especially focused on the transition of Latin into Italian and how so many words and sounds made it into English and why others did not. For example, the words *consternare* and *conflittuale*—"consterned" and "conflictual"—have always seemed like perfectly useful words to me, though they are not standard in English

and evidently awkward. Poetic language can often reclaim and recon-
textualize awkwardness; and part of my contemporary project in poetry
is to ensure that a queer language be preserved while also recovering a
language that may have been queered out of the history during that
transition into more standardized English.

Toward an Integrated and Inclusive Sociopolitical Vision

While I value the tireless creative impulses of experimental poets and
their strong intellectual desire to challenge as many rules for poetry as
possible, I equally value the need to communicate more immediately in
poems that have personal and/or political goals that inspire direct, visceral
responses. Tory Dent is one of those poets whose wild associative leaps
and powerful subject matter takes my breath away and then lets me
breathe more deeply, both because her work is relentless and overwhelming and because it is necessary and vital all at once. The headlong
rhythms, skillful repetitions, line breaks and careful pacing, and the
brave subject matter all reward renewed reading and listening. Two
notable and instructive poems especially worth revisiting include "The
Murder of Beauty/The Beauty of Murder" and "Spared," both from her
debut collection, *What Silence Equals* (1993), as they illustrate that
simultaneous daring and complex intensity that I value.

I do not believe we can separate the social and political realities of
our lives from the poetry we produce, nor should we. Further, poetry
has the power through its concision of detail and lyricism to remain
more memorable, perhaps, in an age where close reading and listening
continue to evolve because of the challenges of new media. Why not
allow more unruly elements and content to enter our poems? The type
of poetry I value most tends to be deeply emotional and psychologically
engaged. In an era of increasing poetic hybridity, I'm not necessarily
interested in arguing about the relative value of any one particular
school of poetry versus another, whether we're discussing experimental
poetry, post-confessionalism, the next generation New York school,
elliptical poetry, etc. I just want the best work to move and grow and
to keep moving and keep expanding confining parameters; but I also
want people to read more poetry and try to grapple with some of the

profoundly troubling sociopolitical issues poetry raises. Writing poetry for me becomes a basic and functional way of trying to discover as many fundamental truths about myself and the world around me as I can. In this way, I feel terrifically provoked and challenged by Jack Spicer's assertion that "talking as a poet is heartbreakingly difficult if you want to talk honestly" (Gizzi, *The House That Jack Built*). As a poet, I always strive to talk honestly: at some point in every poem I write I feel a need to strip aside artifice and relax the craft and ask myself, Is there something essential here that's worthwhile or good? Can this work matter? While I value humor in poetry, I'm not consistently interested in the merely clever or sharply ironic. As a former professional social worker and as a gay immigrant man of Italian descent, I feel passionately aware of my otherness and comically aware of the dangers of becoming a poster child for a Benetton-like advertisement. I often prefer poems that err on the side of sentiment instead of those that are filled with biting irony in the service of no redeeming emotional or social issue. I much prefer those poems that are extreme and psychologically probing and uncontained, even if sometimes they fail—as long as they do so desperately, with some sense of urgency, playfulness, or rigor (or all of the above)—while keeping stridency in check, as much as possible.

Postscript

Queer Italia: Same-Sex Desire in Italian Literature and Film (2004) has been formative for me in thinking about these issues of literature and identity theoretically; but, above all, the close reading and writing of poetry can yield amazing and pleasurable insights. For many of the poets I've cited, ethnic and cultural identity and the need to express oneself fully and with regard to one's sexuality have continued to be a vital challenge. There seems, sadly, also to be some sort of implicit intersection between expressive queer identity and increased homophobia and bullying, which can lead to suicide and/or suicidal ideation. And I'm struck by the work that volumes such as this one can do in helping us specifically to think about how literature and poetry can continue to shape and save lives. I am excited about rediscovering other gay poets and some of my friends' and peers' work, too. When I first started writing, Mark Doty's and Michael Klein's poetry were hugely important to me—and still are; Doty has become relatively canonical already, and it is impossible to say how many gay poets he's supported and influenced—David Groff among them and others included in this collection. For a short while, I would socialize with Michael Klein in New York City, and I found him enormously exciting, hysterically funny, and penetrating, sort of the bad boy Phillip Seymour Hoffman of poetry, and I think about his work and influence regularly. Of course Michael has gone on to have lots of success as a nonfiction writer, but I suspect folks will begin to appreciate and encourage his poetry again too. I am likewise influenced by the generosity of the conversation and panels this volume has and will engender: Mark Bibbins has been a friend for a long time, my first queer poet friend; Brian Teare's first book won the Brittingham Prize, and I was a finalist that year so of course when it came out I devoured it. Jim Elledge's wide-ranging and tireless poetic and scholarly work has been a huge influence to many of us; and he helped introduce my work to a larger audience when he published my chapbook for the Frank O'Hara Prize. That contest presented a generation of new gay poets, such as Ron Mohring and Aaron Smith, among others—not to mention the added attention the prize gave to the judges—terrific idiosyncratic gay and lesbian writers like Tim Liu, Reginald Shepherd, and Maureen Seaton, to mention just a few. I think stating the obvious can be important and empowering, and that's a poetic sensibility for me as well.

We write these essays and attend conferences and literary events in the spirit of fostering community: sometimes communities develop as a result of conscious effort, but just as often we develop productive connections and "entanglements" through flirting or other conscious and unconscious means. These realities and tensions affect people's work and perceptions. Yet we just as readily dismiss these realities or actively thwart them in search of something purer, which in effect can be likewise as abstract. In this age of unchecked global media, the gay poetry world can seem even more frenetic and feel like a minefield we have to negotiate, especially if you think too hard about what others say or perceive. Many of us write because we have to, because we get better at it, even if we can't negotiate the politics of our various writing communities well enough; we persevere because after a while there's nothing else we can do better.

Works Cited

Bassani, Giorgio. *Il romanzo di Ferrara*. Milan: Arnoldo Mondadori Editore, 1980.

Bernstein, Charles. *A Poetics*. Cambridge, Mass.: Harvard University Press, 1992.

Celan, Paul. *Poems of Paul Celan*. Edited by Michael Hamburger. New York: Persea, 2002.

Cestaro, Gary P., ed. *Queer Italia: Same-Sex Desire in Italian Literature and Film*. New York: Palgrave Macmillan, 2004.

Dent, Tory. *What Silence Equals*. New York: Persea, 1993.

Gizzi, Peter. *The House That Jack Built: The Collected Lectures of Jack Spicer*. Middletown, Conn.: Wesleyan University Press, 1999.

Joris, Pierre, and Jerome Rothenberg. *Poems for the Millennium: The University of California Book of Modern and Postmodern Poetry*. Volume 2, *From Postwar to Millennium*. Berkeley: University of California Press, 1998.

Luconi, Stefano. "Recent Trends in the Study of Italian Antisemitism under the Fascist Regime." *Patterns of Prejudice* 38, no. 1 (March 2004): 1–17.

Rosselli, Amelia. *War Variations*. Translated by Paul Vangelisti. Los Angeles: Green Integer, 2004.

Vanity Fairey Interviews Writer Noël Alumit

Noël Alumit

G od fucking dammit," yells Noël Alumit, waving around a letter from his doctor. "I have to go on cholesterol medication." He crumples up the letter and throws it across the room. "I lost fifteen pounds and gave up sugar so I wouldn't have to go on medication. After all that work, I still have to go on it." He stands quietly for several seconds, then sighs. "I don't know how those HIV-positive guys do it. Taking all sorts of meds. And here I am quibbling about taking something for my cholesterol."

He occupies a small apartment, filled with books and art. He lives in Silverlake, a trendy part of Los Angeles. "It wasn't always trendy," he says. "I grew up around here. I stayed here because it was affordable then—with lots of artists and gay people and people of color. Then the gay people died. Then the brown people were bought out. Then the artists were replaced by people who managed the artists . . . I'm getting worked up—"

He abruptly stops talking. He pulls out a cushion and sits quietly on the floor. He meditates for nearly twenty minutes. I sit there and look around. Buddhist icons spread here and there. I notice a red protection cord around his neck. He looks up and says, "I was raised Catholic, but Buddhism seems to fit me better."

Noël Alumit seems to be at a crossroads. Last year, he won the James Duggins Prize, an award reserved for writers in "mid-career." He's forty-three years old and pondering the future. He invites me to sit on the floor with him. I sit down and we talk books, writing, and plans.

_ᴄ⌒

Vanity Fairey: Who was the first author to make an impression on you?

Noël Alumit: I'd have to say Shel Silverstein. His children's book *The Giving Tree* made my heart cry. It was a story about a boy's relationship with this tree. The Tree loved the boy dearly. As the boy grew, he kept wanting and needing things. The Tree did its best to provide for him, even when the boy grew to be an old man. The Tree was still there for him. I was only a little kid, but I remember that story truly moving me. I still think about it. That's how you know when a book is good. It makes a lasting impression.

VF: Did you read lots of books as a child?

NA: Yeah, I guess more than most kids. I read a lot of books in comic book form—graphic novels they're now called. I read *Dracula*, *Frankenstein*, *The Invisible Man*—books little boys like to read.

VF: Who was the first gay writer to influence you?

NA: It was Arnie Kantrowitz. He wrote *Under the Rainbow*, a memoir about the gay rights struggle. I read it at the Echo Park branch of the LA Public Library. It was the first time I'd read of the gay experience.

VF: Did you like it?

NA: I did. That was probably the first time I was really introduced to the gay aesthetic. When I picked up *Under the Rainbow*, I didn't know what it would be about, but I knew it was going to be queer friendly. Just from the title, I knew it was a play on Judy Garland's "Over the Rainbow." Even then, I knew Judy Garland was somehow a gay icon.

I was a little uncomfortable with it, too. Arnie Kantrowitz talked about how he liked to knit, and I was just a kid then. I thought that was a faggoty thing to do. Men don't knit, but I was a self-hating teenage boy. What did I know?

VF: What was your next gay book?

NA: Well, I'd always been a fan of Montgomery Clift. I picked up whatever I could read about him. Patricia Bosworth and Robert LaGuardia wrote biographies about him. I considered them gay books because it had gay content. They were portraits of a closeted life.

Bosworth wrote a very respectable book on Clift. LaGuardia wrote something a little more steamy, a little more sexy. I knew LaGuardia was a gay writer. I could pick up on it. He spent more time talking about Clift's romantic dalliances. I do have to say that LaGuardia, who has passed away, had an influence on my own career.

VF: How so?

NA: LaGuardia's book *Monty* was the first bestseller for a fledgling agent named Albert Zuckerman. *Monty* became the first bestseller for Zuckerman.

VF: Why was that important to you?

NA: Al Zuckerman ended up becoming my agent and selling my first novel, *Letters to Montgomery Clift.*

VF: What a coincidence.

NA: Well, it sort of reinforced how a book can have a lasting effect way beyond an author's lifetime. LaGuardia had no idea how his book or life would shape another person's life, his career. I have to say that finding an agent is always a difficult experience. The actual agent may not read your manuscript at first. It might be an intern who does the first read, then recommends your book to the agent. One of the problems I had with *Letters to Montgomery Clift* was that most people didn't know who Montgomery Clift was. Fortunately, people who worked under Al Zuckerman knew. They better.

VF: Did you read anything else as a teenager?

NA: I really got into S. E. Hinton. I enjoyed her coming-of-age novels of teenage boys. I loved William Wharton. His books *Birdy* and *Dad* really meant a lot to me. I also discovered Charles Bukowski. His short story collection *Hot Water Music* was shocking to me. Up until that time, I hadn't read anything like that. I've always liked troubled characters, but these people were truly broken. It felt like I was reading about a vicious rape. However, I could see my world in his world. He wrote about places I knew about. I lived in those down-and-out areas. It was meaningful to me, because those stories were the closest to my surroundings. I didn't live that kind of life, but I saw the people in my neighborhood that he was talking about. I'm glad I discovered him. I hadn't read anything by him since, but that short story collection gave me permission to write about truly ugly things. There were other books that dealt with desperate, broken people, but those stories made their lives poetic. Bukowski didn't do that. Some people simply have brutal lives till the end— there is no poetry there.

A writer who did have a lot of poetry and who also influenced me was Harold Brodkey. His first book, *First Love and Other Stories*, is one of my favorites. He was very different from Bukowski. His broken people went to Ivy League schools and had a different kind of intellect than Bukowski's characters. I appreciated that.

Even though it wasn't said out right, I could sense that Brodkey was attracted to men purely by the descriptions of the guys in the stories. It was clear that Brodkey was fascinated with guys. Later it was revealed that Brodkey was bisexual, and he eventually died of AIDS.

VF: I know AIDS work has played prominently in your life.

NA: Yes, it has. In the '90s, there was a lot of work being done in the gay community to heal the pain of AIDS and how it affected us. A poet named Joel Tan gave me a flyer to a writing class at the Gay and Lesbian Center in Los Angeles. I'll always be grateful to Joel for that. That was my first foray into the literary world. A lot of writing about AIDS happened in that class. There were men in that class who started writing but eventually died. I think of James and Brian, who were lovers, and they took that class. They're no longer with us. In a way, I write because they can't anymore. We were starting our careers; mine continued.

Frankly, it still hurts to think of all the artists and potential artists we lost to AIDS. I think that one of the reasons our country is in turmoil is because there wasn't art being created to help us grow or learn. We really did kill a little of our country's soul.

VF: During that time, when all of that grief was going on, how did you deal with it on a literary level?

NA: I don't think I knew it at the time, but I turned to another part of my identity to deal with it. There were moments when gay writing was so painful that I needed to turn away for a while. I began paying attention to Asian American writers, and how they were exploring American life. I was working for East West Players in the early '90s. East West Players is the country's oldest Asian American Theater Company. They were reeling from the casting of white actors in "Yellow Face" in the musical *Miss Saigon*.

There was an important sense of community there. I became influenced by playwrights Philip Kan Gotanda and David Henry Hwang. There was a big sense of multiculturalism in the 1990s, something I thoroughly enjoyed. The Asian American Writers Workshop was active in Los Angeles, headed by two lesbians. I felt a sense of purpose as an Asian American to write stories so we can be heard.

I also read Amy Tan's *Joy Luck Club*, a book that I loved. I enjoyed the female perspective in the book, and actually identified with some of their struggles. However, Asian guys I knew at the time didn't take too well to the *Joy Luck Club*. They thought there was a lot of bashing of Asian men.

I can see that point of view. Part of women's fiction sometimes is to write about overcoming the oppressiveness of men. In this case, Asian men. Then came discussion among my Asian male peers about how we fit into this world. The Asian men I knew were resentful of how Asian women in fiction seemed to always go for the white guy. It didn't help that famous writers like Amy Tan or Maxine Hong Kingston chose to marry white guys. The sense of building up the Asian male image became part of my psyche. For the most part, I make the Asian men in my fiction physically attractive. In my first novel, I make Filipino Bob and Japanese Logan good-looking fellows. In my second novel, I made the three key Asian men in that story handsome or beautiful.

VF: Will all your male characters be gorgeous?

NA: [*Laughing*] Not necessarily. At this time in my writing life, the men that I've created have been guys I'd personally want to date.

VF: So far your characters have been Asian or Asian American. Do you see yourself writing about other people?

NA: Do you mean white people?

VF: Other people.

NA: Yes. I already started. I've got some short stories that I'd been thinking about. I'd been thinking of honoring my acting roots. You know I started off as an actor. I got my BFA in theater. I'm thinking of writing about actors, all sorts of actors. Yes, even white actors.

VF: Do you think you can pull it off, writing about non-Asians?

NA: Of course. I read white authors writing in the voice of people of color all the time. I read straight authors writing about gay people. I can write about anything I want.

⁓

He looks at his watch, signaling to me that the interview is over. I get up to leave. He remains on the floor. He says, "My mind is still agitated. I need to meditate a little more."

With that, I quietly exit his apartment.

The Four of Them

Thomas Glave

regarding so much of what they have meant and still mean to me:
the world, and more

Gordimer

But then once upon a time, in that beleaguered and ancient corner of the world, the brave white woman who loved language and stories and true things (and who in that place where blacks were so loathed never forgot the truth that she was white) decided not to leave. Decided not to leave the country where the blacks were loathed and indeed treated like dirt, or in fact far worse than dirt, and the whites mostly smiled upon it all, despite (or more often because of) truncheons cracked against black heads in the townships by white police officers, and tear gas sprayed by them without care throughout places like Soweto, places like Boipatong, places like Sharpeville and Ulmazi and Imizamo Yethu. The brave white woman who loved words didn't have to stay there in the (especially for blacks) beleaguered country—the place increasingly deplored by the entire world—and write about all of it: the blacks beaten and tortured in prisons, on the streets, and in their own homes; the blacks and conscientious whites arrested and jailed without hope of a fair trial; the famous black man who spent more than twenty-five years in prison, beaten and tortured, but who lived to become president, beloved throughout the progressive world; the lies of the government about the secret police; and more, and more, and so much more. She didn't have to stay there in the maelstrom. And maelstrom it was, for couldn't they have done to her what someone had done to one of the brave white men? To Albie Sachs? Bombed her car or home as was done to him in the neighboring country, in Mozambique? Or had her placed under house arrest, as had been done to so many others? Passport confiscated, citizen's rights and privileges rescinded, telephone tapped?

She never forgot, of course—and never let others forget—that whatever *could* have happened to her (but didn't) *would* have happened in a far worse way to black people, and did.

She didn't have to stay there and write, steadfastly, about *us*: about black people; about black people who, as her characters, were, like her white characters, complicated; sometimes quixotic. Real. In doing so she did something monumental—monumental, yes—that very few white writers anywhere have ever done.

She was, in truth, one of the very few white people who showed me that white people really could be more than just white; they could, from time to time, when they did their best, actually be *human beings*.

And so if a brave white woman could risk her blood and limbs in that place so terrible because of what it did to both blacks (in every way) *and* whites (mostly spiritually, sometimes physically) and all in between, could I, who also loved language, do something brave as well?

Could it be possible to write the unwriteable? Write something about, for example, a man burned alive in Jamaica *in our time* because he loved—because he desired—other men? Could one write about men loving each other but also (literally) torturing each other? Write about (*but summon from inside*, some voices whispered) the torment of intimate emotional cruelty or the torment of (while manacled in some secret room) feeling lighted cigarettes stuck to one's testicles?

Could one write about the men-loving white men who hated blacks? About the black men who hated white men or—far worse—sometimes themselves?

And write about the black women who deeply loved black men and each other, and our children, but spat at men like me the acid-bile of the word *faggot*?

She did not leave. Nor flinch. Like some of the other brave ones of all colors, *she* stayed.

And so here is my faith—what has become my faith, a voice inside me whispered long ago. My faith partly because of her and those very few like her. Faith, here, where, against what might once have ended with a rope around my neck or a bullet in my brain, I will stay.

Lorde

But in fact this is not a poem
                        Audre
                            it is not a
                                  poem nor an
encomium nor anything like that anything
                                  hagiographic   no not at all because I
                               know I know now more than ever after
                          that book about you after
                    Warrior Poet especially after it that
            you are not a
      goddess
as I foolishly (callowly) had once believed you to be
        not hagiography this is not but simply a
letter to you Audre: one that requires
                      white spaces on the page or not many white spaces because
well there is so much to say isn't there and not enough
          time not enough space to add up all the words of
               gratitude Audre for all of your   strength your
                                power   and
        (Caribbean girl   *Eastern* Caribbean girl)
for all the years Audre of your saying and
               articulating and
                    enunciating the
unsayable   *the* unsayable   the
              unspeakable   about
          us about you about
because this is who we are the crucial words let them be known and
       let us all and each be seen Audre heard and
         the sum of all the parts making the whole making the

---

person making the

me

articulate it: black   and

Caribbean and man-loving and

all of it the sum of the parts making the whole and

before reading you before that declarative language Audre not knowing quite

that it was possible to be

black and

homo and

Caribbean and

Jamaican

and *immigrant* and

writing about it

naming it

across these geographies of

nation and self and

Kingston   the Bronx   Clarendon   Trafalgar Park   Aenon Town   West Village

Norbrook   Emancipation Park   Mona   Treasure Beach   Hope Pastures   Harlem

and so thank you Audre for the language and the

manifold ways to say it and *know* it and   *feel* it, Audre   and

but no   NO   this is not a poem, Audre

nor a damned encomium

it is merely a

(but how well you know it)

deep

oh let it be *deep*

calling

calling of your name

Audre

Audre woman

womanpoetvoice

voice and power   *language that helped—that helped us—*

Yes   :

Baldwin

Dear Sir, Dear Father—

You came to me in a dream quite recently—indeed, many years after

Thomas Glave

I first found you entirely on my own in a bookshop somewhere. In that time, long before the intimate dream, I found you . . . but how to say? Not quite mine, I think, though you always were. Found you elusive, sometimes elliptical: qualities that daunted and entranced, and which perhaps you inherited from Mr. James, whom you loved, or from the magisterial church, which never left your deepest blood. You were just beyond my reach in those younger days, Father, and possessed of a knowledge too terrifying (one of your favorite words) for me to occupy. That knowledge had been bitterly won by all of those who had come before us, and by you; it began with love and anger, and exploded with rage, and ended with love and anger. Yours was a rage that, for the longest time, I could not fathom (or refused to fathom), though I myself possessed it; it was a storm that I could not (would not) countenance, though its bloodfury crackled just beneath my skin, and especially beneath the skin of my more-often-than-not smiling face: the sometime protection of the clown, or the coward, or the much-beaten child, or the pre-suicide, or the lunatic-psychotic, or the dreamer . . . or the man already dead. It was the fury of *To be black and conscious in America is to be in a constant state of rage*, you said, and *Father, teach me, I prayed, but please not so harshly, not with such rage* . . . but the bloodfury, yours and mine and all of ours, was, in the cauldron of america unavoidable. (Coming from Jamaica, our island hearts did not, I know now, wish to learn that bloodlesson so soon.) And perhaps in denial of your anger— for it did scald, and scald again, with but a glancing look upon the page of your conjured worlds—I thought for some time, chose to believe, that *my Father—this one, the black American one—speaks from a profoundly different religious tradition than mine, and that is why he is so very angry: yea, for his is the African American sermonizing voice: that thundering and poetic richness that runs through his very American blood and which he would not have been able to escape had he turned his flesh inside out and exposed it to one hundred suns, then turned it back on itself again. And black Americans are*, I thought, *unlike Jamaicans, always so very very angry* . . . the uninformed ruminations of an unexposed child. A child listening to *that voice*, I thought, *unmistakable, unerring in its reach, heard by one in barbershops and on street corners, in front of storefront churches and chicken-and-ribs joints alike, from Harlem to Memphis to Cleveland to K.C. to D.C. (especially Southeast) to American Beach to Decatur to Charlotte—and, God knows, onward to Chicago (try the south*

*side first), Gary, Detroit, and straight on back down to N.O. You know it,
you feel it. But it was not mine. It was not—is not—the reserved, preserved
formal poetry of my true-true people's Anglican church, heard in one hundred
and more Jamaican country towns. It was the language of my black
American cousins and my black American Father, and Father, we still
scorned you all and yours then, did we not? We in the archipelago thought
ourselves better than you all in the U.S. of A., did we not? And as if all that
were not enough, Father, remember this: that no one—no one at all in
school, when I began formally to study you—ever, ever said anything about
you loving, needing, wanting other men.*

How could I have known then just how very much I had always
needed you? How much I would discover how in fact I had always
needed, so urgently, to love you?

You came to me recently in a dream. But all the things you told me
in the dream you had told me before, years ago; I remembered. Still, I
needed you at the time of this recent dream as I had needed you long
ago but had not known it; I needed you to tell me again all that you
had told me in dreams years before, so that as I listened—by God, as I
listened—I could feel *your* hand once again on my forehead, Father, and
your voice once again at the back of my throat: your voice telling me
once again, *Go on, go on, child. Do it. Just do it. Yes, child, just go on.
Don't wait for the fire. For the flames will come as sure as Gabriel; as will
the rage. Do not wait. Do not stop. Just move. Move,* you said.

The only thing for which I have not forgiven you—and for which I
may never forgive you—is that you died.

Yes, you died. But you did not leave me

Fatherless,

Father,

nor without brothers.

Morrison

And so it was, Lady, that Someone offered you language; offered it to
you brilliantly, in a golden glove outfitted with silk and festooned not
with glittering rubies (which, for your purposes and by your measure,
might have been gaudy) but with pearls: quiet, understated, simple.
Themselves. And from the sea. Pearls, the sea, very old voices, much

memory, a listening, an attending, and thenceforth arrived Sula. And later Sethe. Paul D. Jadine, and Cholly. And Joe Trace, and Stamp Paid, and Guitar and Milkman and Ruth, and more, and still more. One could never imagine a time when there would not be more from you, but that time will, we know, come. We know it as a dreaded fact, as one understands — *knows* — that one day one's most beloved will have to die — as will all of us. Yet the bounty of what has been imagined and offered on the page abides and endures. (Endures, yes: for when Ms. Welty died — someone whose visions you admired, as I have — in my case, the correct word would indeed be *loved* — I thought, Well. Well, now. The truth is that the world ought to end just now, I thought. It should end as it ought to have ended when, in 1992, Ms. Lorde left this place. As it ought to have in 1987, when Mr. Baldwin left. But the world did not, astonishingly, crumble when they departed, as it did not, amazingly, when Ms. Welty moved on. Miraculously, it all will, all of it, somehow be all right. We have their words. The pages and the voices speaking out of them. Something — *something* — survived, and survives.)

And so it was, Lady, that something in your windings and byways on those pages reached out to that small boy in that place — that often not very nice place — quite far from where you were, and told him, unquestionably, utterly confidently (and quietly, *softly*), that he too — he! — could do something along the lines of what you had done. Could at least do something that began with (but did not end only with) imagining. Through all of his lonesome hours, through each of his alone hours (lonesome and alone, yes: for few around him wished to spend much time with a faggot then; few much use, except to hurl stones or actual refuse at his head, for a faggot then), he wondered about them, those people: Pecola, Sula, Sethe, Paul D., the ghost-daughter herself with her depthless black eyes and unlined hands, and all the others. *Where had they all come from*, he wondered, *and how had the Lady imagined them?* — questions that pondering them, reading them, would not answer entirely, but would in fact deepen — lengthen — in time. The depth and length could often be fearsome . . . — *But if she could do it*, he thought, that little brown boychild girl-eyed faggot, *then* may*be*, may*be*, he dared to think (but what a laugh! What a dreamer! — so others in his world, had they known of his yearnings, would have snorted in his direction, even spat at him, over his ridiculous head) — *just maybe*,

I could do it too. Someday. Somehow, he dared to think. Little ridiculous, pathetic stupid faggot. Sitting there thinking. Dreaming. And reading. *But keep it all to yourself,* he thought, *far from harmful hands and contemptuous eyes.*

And so, Lady, he read you for years. Read you with devotion. With utter devoutness in the pursuit that was, for him, virtually prayer. (But also escape. God help him—help *me*, Jesus Lord, to escape.) And watched you. Watched you carefully. Scrutinized you with a gaze as unstoppable as it was resolute. *The steel within.* He possessed it. The steel that one must possess when loathed.

He scrutinized the proud carriage of your shoulders and head, Lady—that gray head, increasingly gray and then dreadlocked across the years—that said that you, like those before you (and about whom more often than not you had written), had—*have*—dignity. Grace. Possibility. *We* have dignity, irrespective of what the nations at large tell us, what the many scowls and curled lips at large tell us: we of this color and other colors. *We* are possible. We who originally came from (no, were *wrenched* from, as one would rip out, with a clenched fist, the intestines of a still-living person), that place so long ago and far away across the waters.

And so it is possible—in fact hugely necessary—to recount our stories. To remember them. To not have them languish among the many, the innumerable *disremembered and unaccounted for.* Do you remember? Lady's language in the wake of a grieving ghost: *This is not a story to pass on. So rememory it,* he thought, using the word conjured out of the mouth of that needful ghost, and *re-member* . . . no matter how painful. No matter how many wish not to remember, and will not, and cannot. Remember if only because of *all* the pathetic little shit-faggots still lying broken-boned in darkened corners, sucking (if they still are alive) flame-blackened thumbs. Remember if only because of all the necks broken by hemp knotted and hung from trees, and the "fire-cooked blood" that *she* wrote about. Remember the dead and dying children on scorched fields, the people screaming in black underground places with their hands cut off and their genitals singed, and the fact that so many of us everywhere still are not—cannot yet be, will not be for some time yet—safe. Remember because *I*, he thought. *Because I am,* he who became me thought. *Because I am one. One with all of them.* All of them who are—who will always be—we.

Jumpstart

Tim Miller

I think a lot about where I come from as a gay man. In fact, thousands of times I have performed a piece about the crucial moment of queer conception, that essential moment when that dyke egg and faggot sperm made moi! (Buttplugs, Sappho, and Vaslav Nijinski are naturally also involved!) Leaving that delicious dream ballet aside, in fact, my cock and tongue connect me directly to the queer Ur-daddy of my personal cosmology. I am woven in with my own canonical poetic queer paternity, the epic transformative vista of Ginsberg (born the same year as my real dad!) and electrical-bodied Whitman. Plug me in and turn me on! More specifically, I am directly hooked up to these queer daddies not only in the mysterious paths of poesy—I love that word, but if you are not careful "poesy" comes out sounding like "pussy" and got me in trouble once at a university in North Carolina—but I am also hooked up in actual hook ups! I am in six direct degrees of sex separation from Walt Whitman, the queer ancestor who all on his own can make me think *Amerika* is worth saving. Allen Ginsberg famously charted his direct sex link, his tongue-y inheritance, with Whitman, and I daisy chain on. Allen Ginsberg had sex, of course, with Neil Cassidy, who fucked with Gavin Arthur (nephew of President Chester A. Arthur), who slept with famous queer socialist Edward Carpenter, who canoodled with Whitman. Fortunately, Edward Carpenter kissed and told; he shared with his intimates what he and WW did in the sack! Their sex seemed to be pretty much in sync with these lines from Father of the Nation Walt . . .

> I mind how once we lay, such a transparent summer morning;
> How you settled your head athwart my hips, and gently turn'd
>   over upon me,
> And parted the shirt from my bosom-bone, and plunged your tongue
>   to my bare-stript heart,
> And reach'd till you felt my beard, and reach'd till you held my feet.

Since around twenty years ago I had sex with my beloved friend David Roman—dear love of comrades and all—whose first sexual experience was with Allen Ginsberg in Madison, Wisconsin, when he was eighteen, thus I get to share in that sex family tree. I am connected, jumper cable linked in actual wet tongue to tongue. I claim my History of Tongues, of queer sub lingual exchange, of the family tree of breath. This is the real history of arts and letters: Who kissed who? Who fucked who? Who fucked over who?

I have to admit, I made every effort to get to one less degree of separation from Whitman as a young queerlet. When I was a teenager in NYC, I tried for months to get Ginsberg to bone me. I followed him all over the East Village my first months in NYC, held his Tibetan bells for him on St. Marks Place readings at the macrobiotic café, would stand outside his apartment just a couple of blocks from mine. But Ginsberg liked his boys to present as straight, so I was not a blip on his radar. Nonetheless, like I said in my aforementioned history of tongues, I had sex with David Roman, who had sex with Allen Ginsberg, who had sex with Neil Cassidy, who had sex with Gavin Arthur, who had sex with Edward Carpenter, who had sex with Walt Whitman: Daddy of our American Tongue.

So where's my prize? I want a dinette set, or a gift bag of Aveda products, or at least a twenty-five-dollar Barnes & Noble Gift Card that I will end up never using. I want to share the wealth too, of course. All the people I ever had sex with—and there are a lot of you, certainly enough to fill a ninety-nine-seat Equity Waiver theater—that whole army of my lovers are thus within *seven* degrees from Walt Whitman. You may reasonably ask, "*What difference does it make?*" After all, haven't all of us, women and men, Monica and Bill included, had sex with Walt Whitman one way or another? Perhaps the skin-to-skin sex family, the mysterious transfer of tongue to tongue via loving touch, may not matter all that much anyhow. That intimacy, that spark, can happen in so many other ways: a classroom seminar, a sweaty performance somewhere in Wisconsin, or among the high school speech contest kids doing my work in competitions all over. My words, my tongue really, guiding theirs over new paths and bilabial plosives! Those gorgeous two-lipped, bilabial "Bs" and "Ps" joyfully spitting and farting their way into consciousness. My favorite sound is that popping speech we wetly produce on our lips and tongues. This is our real genealogy, our actual connection to our ancestors. This is the gorgeous, unprovable, but certain truth that inspiration, aspiration, heart, and hope mysteriously pass from one tongue to another.

While I am acknowledging the forefathers—and foremothers too, but that is another essay—I need to also face the more vexing concomitant question, "Whose Daddy Am I?" Gulp. Well, let me slip out of my threadbare, yet still flattering, Peter Pan costume and own my Inner Daddy. I think about this identity a lot as I travel and perform all over the country working in universities with young artists aged eighteen to twenty-five, queer and otherwise. I love that I get recurrent, annual stops at places like Southern Methodist University in Texas or University of North Carolina School of the Arts, so I get an ongoing relationship to so many students at lots of schools. (This is why I have eighty Facebook friends among the undergraduate cohort at Virginia's James Madison University of all places!) Clearly, in the transformative heat of a sweaty theater or rehearsal studio, I am trying to challenge these young artists to dig deep toward the narratives and poetics *they* need to perform. In this endeavor I am definitely talking on the hat of guide, pedagogue, creative *Pater Familius Queerus*.

But I am also very interested in how this happens without any direct, embodied connection. There is a small battalion of high school kids who perform my work in speech contests all over the United States. Now speech contests, though without the fantasized glamour of the *Glee* show choir phenomenon, actually have many times more students running all over their states oral interpreting up a storm than doing covers of '70s power rock. I did speech contest for a couple of years in high school, most memorably with my Dramatic Interpretation of Anthony Burgess's dystopic novel *A Clockwork Orange* extolling *Ultra-Violence* and the *Old In-Out-In-Out*, as Alex would say. It was clearly my way of engaging a queer antibourgeois posture as a fourteen-year-old and shocking the judges of speech contests all over Orange County. I imagine that the young folk who are choosing to do monologs from my shows published in my various books are doing it for very much the same reason. If you snoop around YouTube you can find these mostly queer young men performing my work for speech contests. One of these young performers has more hits on YouTube than I do performing the exact same piece of mine, *My Queer Body*. But then, he is an adorable seventeen-year-old Texas hottie performing my piece—the one I mentioned at the beginning of this essay about being a gay sperm—in the privacy of his bedroom, with his rumpled bedclothes visible in the background.

I have gotten to know a number of these young men. Kile Akerman, who as a senior in high school won the 2008 state of Illinois speech championship performing a monolog from my show *Glory Box* about marriage equality, said of the experience:

> When I read your play going into my senior year of high school I was immediately enamored. Your story resonated with my own story of collecting my queer identity. Obviously, as with any story, mine differs substantially, but there is an undeniable overarching message of love and acceptance which I think most of us can attest to entertaining as well. Not having any "good gay role models" your performance *Glory Box* showed me that there were people like me who were able to share their words and their struggles. I became distraught that in the current state of the world, I too might have a bottle of Colt 45 malt liquor thrown at me from a passing truck like you did. That I might be denied the ability to share my life with the person I love. This sort of realization makes you want to do something with whatever tools you have. At the time, the tools I had were a knack for performance and a venue with which to perform. Just like that, I set out to do what little I could for the movement by sharing the stories that speak to a larger collective queer understanding.

Jackpot! For me, this is hitting the slots just right in Vegas—three cherries line up, and the treasure pours at your feet from this proof of the mysterious ways we speak to each other: across time, across generations, across the written word, across life and death itself.

Why does this thrill me so much, I wonder? I am so aware having these jumper cables in my hands wanting to exchange juicy sets of electrical creative techniques, activism strategies, and possibilities with young artists thirty years my junior. Is this the fifty-two-year-old getting a big dose of *memento mori* and wanting to pass things on? Probably. Is this how the guy who never had kids—though a lesbian couple is Facebook messaging my partner Alistair and me daily for our sperm!—tries to extend his psychic DNA reach through this kind of creative mentoring? Again, probably.

As much as I value this kind of disembodied daddyness through my books and social networking presence that gets manifested at speech contests in Nebraska and Tennessee, there is something very particular about that real-time exchange in the studio. At Performance Space 122 in New York City, a space I cofounded thirty years ago and ran for three years, I am figuring this out in a new way. And where but PS 122 could I so keenly mark my own life-changes, my own journey from boy to man? I hadn't even reached my full height when I first set foot inside the front door at PS 122 at the age of nineteen. I looked like a little boy then, and now I look like my dad! Well, like a thinner, gay version of my dad. Ah mystery!

I am currently doing an emerging queer performer mentorship project at PS 122 that has been very charged for me. Two of the three, Kamelle Mills and Brigham Mosley, are gay artists I have worked with over the years at SMU, and now I am getting to keep an eye on them as twenty-three-year-olds and nurture their work as we bring it to their first professional performance in NYC. I love the feeling of getting to embolden them to do things in their performances. My goal is not to encourage them to make performances like how I would do it, but to do performances that I *can't* do. Not just because I have three decades on them, but because I am not an African American gay man from Texas like Kamelle, or a young woman paying for college by being an S&M sex worker like Katie O. Somewhere in this is also an insurance policy that bodies, performing bodies especially, carry these paternal sparks across time and generations. Hopefully, these young artists will all outlive me by thirty years, and in the same ways as I carry a bit of Ginsberg or Wilde or Whitman in me, they carry some of my performances, teaching, politics, and joy forward.

There is such an exquisite conversation that goes on between this complex present that we occupy as it swaps notes with the past and the future, with the dead and the not yet born. Those jumper cables are truly electrical and singing as all those tongues and beds and words and performances that preceded us keep pulling us forward to the future.

Caliban

Dave King

Gay-boy friendship, pre-gay: what curious magnetism draws us to each other, even before we've acknowledged the sex? Recalling the little coterie that orbited my friend D in those years, I think of dancing in our dorm rooms. I think of learning the lyrics to *No, No, Nanette* and performing "I Want to Be Happy" impromptu on the staircase, long after lights out. My God, I remember a slew of dull winter evenings when other boys gathered to hear me read aloud from *Auntie Mame* and *The Wind in the Willows*, no one doing the obvious math, no one looking too deeply at his own soul. Then we'd return to the world and be mainstream again, some of us kissing or even fucking a hippie girlfriend, each of us donning the oddly tailored mantle of early-'70s masculinity. For the world then was one of communes and righteous politics, guitar feedback, both types of Deep Throat, Warren Beatty, H. R. Haldeman, and TM. How did a Y-chromosome fit into all that? And how did a Y-chromosome jibe with nostalgia fashions and unisex hair—so very neutering on pubescent boys—or with the supple sexless buzz of the drugs? In a few years we'd be seniors, and when our birthdays rolled past we'd rooster up and register for the draft. Already I'd spent years imagining the war, which I saw as a ghoulishly heightened Boy Scout Jamboree, set in a rainforest and calibrated to expose my failings:

my cowardice and lack of patriotism; also my little girl's throwing arm. The wandering eye I still believed I could keep secret.

Perhaps we all had such worries, we eight or so blithely accepting friends gathered for winter story hour. In the end, though, it was not Vietnam that took out a quarter of our number; a decade later came the virus. And in the valley of the shadow of childhood? No one was yet gay, and friendship was largely a matter of instinct. Each of us hid himself behind screen concealments; all of us trusted the scrims the others put up.

My friend D commanded a room. Outspoken and boisterous, he had a terrific laugh and strong opinions and an air of being fully himself, even at fourteen. And flair—*flair!*—which came down to a personal dress code, an iron will, and a cool walk I attempted to emulate. We looked nothing alike, but we had the same first name, and I was a competent if crude mimic. So is it really any wonder people saw us as one person?

I don't recall how we met. He'd entered our prep school the year before I did, and by the time I arrived he was part of the stew. For a while during my first term, we weren't yet friends, and I wandered the campus draped in the bleak identity I'd packed up and brought from home. Really, it was like some dry husk I stumbled around in, even as I attended classes or dragged my fat butt to the soccer field, even as I tried out for drama and band. Who knows how this husk appeared from the outside, but inside stood a boy who'd grown up shy and indifferently nurtured, who lacked the imagination to do other than succeed in school, who'd already mastered the fine art of being forgettable. Whose blandness and docility must have been convincing, as they went un-questioned, yet who nevertheless roiled with unexpressed . . . unexpressed *what*? Desire, certainly; that was central. And a decent sense of humor, which I was wary of revealing. But also bitterness and contempt and fury, a blunt sense of power and victimhood and need. Also ambition— inchoate and deeply buried—arrogance—buried deeper—and (does it even need stating?) a big chip on the shoulder. People described me as *nice*.

Had D also a secret soul: some measure of grief, those same longings? At fourteen, all I saw was charisma. I saw that walk, which took posses-sion of the world. I saw confidence and insouciance, which bent the universe to his will. His social ease: how he could enter a gathering. How he took on those foreign bodies: teachers, other students. How he'd launch into banter with any stranger at a concert, at a political demonstration or in a shop or on a bus or any of the places we went, me invariably tagging along. And how in conversation he'd tap lightly on a person's jacket to draw them in or emphasize a point. I'd been raised to keep to myself, but D courted intimacy and reaped bonhomie in return. It was a trick as magical as a sleight of hand.

I watched him reorder the planet to his priorities. He was the first person I liked who would carelessly skip class, and he made doing so irresistible. Small rebellion, of course, but I was an immature fourteen. Hour after hour we'd lie on his bed, listening to his records and drawing in pen and ink. Then D might decide he needed a cigarette, and out we'd head to where he wouldn't be caught smoking. The nearby riverbank or the little town, which had a restaurant and a candy store and a couple of junk shops. Picking up a brooch made with iridescent butterfly wings, D would hold it to his chest, then abruptly to mine, then he'd warble a line from a Nina Simone album. Outside the shop, he'd pin the brooch to my jacket, smoothing the corduroy over my tummy, and declare that I could *not* seriously defend *Jesus Christ Superstar* as art. And yes, looking back, I see how my sense of him was never objective, nor even correct. For what I felt then was no reasonably considered judgment, but the ardor of a boy who'd fallen under a spell.

For all I saw to adore in D, I can't say what he saw in me. Perhaps he wanted a sidekick, or maybe it really was the pre-gay gravitational pull. Maybe friendship itself is like crime: merely motive plus opportunity; and perhaps D was the maguffin. In any case, at some point he decided I was funny, for what's vividest in my memories is the project of making him laugh. Before long, he was promoting me as a wit, and it was as though he'd dubbed me a duke or some other nobility, for in my whole short life I'd been called *studious* and *well behaved* and even *gentle*, but no one had detected any interesting traits. Then D dowsed out the wellspring of personality, and the reaction was like a three-year drunk.

Of course, I was *not* a wit, not in any actual sense. I was a bottled-up sophomore who whispered snarky remarks. I could make fun of people's names and dirty up the lyrics to popular songs, and I could do puns and limericks and one or two funny voices. I could make faces when people's backs were turned, and as my shyness diminished, I developed a gift for tart and childish imitation. Of course I could do bitchy.

Is it fair to compare this to coming out? I wouldn't get really laid until after high school, by which point I'd regained a tiny measure of gravitas; but the forsaking of inhibition began with the lovely follow spot of a friend's attention. Before sex or sexual identity, D midwifed a version of me, pressing me to be born as *someone*. And so I was, emerging id-first and desperate—*desperate!*—to amuse.

No doubt a wiser boy would have resisted the challenge, but I hoisted my paltry arsenal and deployed what I had. A performance driven by fumbled uncensoring, for this wasn't maturity or insight; it was the Terrible Twos. In class and out, I gave vent to the contrary, the ornery, the arbitrary, the petulant, the flip, the arch, the high-handed, the irresponsible, the feckless and the critical; and if my aim was a penthouse aerie in Outrageous City, memory suggests that I crashed down more often at an abandoned barn near Obnoxious.

This is not a story of holy wildness (no Weather Underground, no heroin) but rather of bratty prep exhibitionism, in which pranks and petty larceny and juvenile meanness were the sum of the social rebellion. I can't feel much grief for the pranks or the larceny, the exam-time fire drills, liquor runs or filched property. Nor for the portrait of a benefactor held for ransom, nor for the breaking nor the entering. (An incident with a pitchfork is a somewhat different matter.) But I regret the meanness. I don't now see myself as an unkind person, but in courting D's laughter I preyed on weakness, and I couldn't stop. Whoever I could ridicule, I did—not cleverly, as we told each other, but mercilessly and without restraint. For I was so vulnerable to ridicule myself! It must have seemed that to lower my small rapier—even slightly—would mean losing my battle with forgettability.

If this had been prison instead of boarding school, I'd have been his punk; if there'd been sex, his ravenous piggy bottom. But our only jail was a fading New England prurience, so I became Mrs. Danvers to his teen Rebecca, guarding our closeness and our inseparability, winnowing our cohort, constructing a world in which we two were under siege. Beyond the campus lay true and genuine risk, but insulated as I was, I laid siege to the school and the world of adults. Indeed, I was fighting maturity itself, that looming agglomeration of *actual* battles, *actual* achievement, *actual* accountability, *actual* . . . sex.

Dave King

I suppose it cost me an Ivy League education, and I'll pause here to salute the nice admissions officer who offered a glimpse of the conduct report submitted by my guidance counselor. I had to look up the word "vindictive" after leaving his office, but hitchhiking back from New Haven, I was picked up by a certified Beat who got me high and gave me a record album when he dropped me at my exit. And it could be I learned then what undergraduate school might have taught me: you reap what you sow.

To give Prospero his due, D's affection was genuine and his attention generous. If he egged me on, it was youthful appreciation, and that laugh of his could have shivered any wall. But he was not my oppressor, and attention will always be my weakness, though I control my hunger for it now. And in time, we grew up—I, of course, lagging behind. We'd almost finished high school when I sensed I no longer had to perform. When whatever I'd needed to prove I had proven; when I knew D trusted, even before I believed it myself, that there was more in the orchard than quips and barbs; that given the chance, sweeter fruit might be borne. We spent the summer together, then drifted apart.

Some folks do come out seamlessly, balancing *before* with an adjusted out identity. I think D was like this, for he was always—remains—absolutely himself (though again, my opinion's tinged by bedazzlement). But for me, that was not the way. Rooted deeply in caution, I had to take that dry husk to the woodshed and burn it. I had to lay waste to concealment, then scatter the ashes, for there was much to incinerate before I got to desire; the niceness and good behavior went up in the blaze. All the gentleness: *poof!* Then it was all or nothing; at least, it was for me. A battle royal, a jubilee, religious conversion, a Broadway show. A magic carpet ride, an oratorio, a marzipan feast.

Gay-boy friendships, no longer pre-gay. Wouldn't it be lovely if all of us declared together! A whole generation, holding commencement: sheepskins distributed, square hats wafting skyward, photos snapped, and loved ones shaking hands.

Instead, we'd run into each other unexpectedly, we old friends from school. The boy who always was quite a musician, the two who taught children's theater; the dancer, the orchid grower and the singer/waiter and the painter. And the costume designer; what a career *he'd* have had if he'd lived! Here we all were, in New York in its wild days, but for a moment our old selves rose ghostlike around us. Two, three, maybe four years later, on a street in the village, dressed for cruising: a sudden encounter. Or at a restaurant among new companions or at a film.

Or dining by candlelight across from another man. And though there now should have been no question, sometimes those old scrims would totter back up, false and threadbare as a production outdated. The warm surprise of the greetings, the little shocks of familiarity and change. How quickly the war had ended, releasing us into lives we could choose for ourselves! A little gossip upon first spotting each other, the obligatory *you look great*. But longing, as those banalities went down, to move past the fibs of our shared adolescence, to state what—one more remark, a waiter hovering, the friend at the table following quietly along—what now seemed so obvious. Needing also to affirm something vital: I'm the same me, but grown up, maybe kinder. Definitely kinder. More honest now and happier, too! Blushing, *blushing!* And with this, the offer of a seat, a drink. The introduction of the patient friend. This person who, um, loves me—*loves me!* As I am. And with whom I'm in love, too. This is my boyfriend; well, there you go.

My First Poetic Mentor
Was a Welshman Named Leslie

Timothy Liu

Leslie Norris was my first mentor. Fresh off of my mission, I came to BYU with a passion for poetry without actually having read much of it, only Sylvia Plath's posthumous volume *Ariel* and a handful of poems I'd encountered as a high school senior—Lawrence Ferlinghetti's "Constantly Risking Absurdity" and ballads like "Sir Patrick Spence." I'd heard that Professor Norris was the official Poet-in-Residence, a non-Mormon transplanted from Wales, so one morning, I stopped by his office with three poems and asked him what he thought. After thumbing through them, he said, "Actually, these are not very good. But that doesn't matter. I've heard about you, and I believe you are a serious poet. That makes you one in ten thousand! Never forget that. Just remember that you are a poet whether you write good poems or bad poems." I was crushed by his response, rode my bike home in tears. I returned the next day with a new sheaf of poems and asked, "What about these?" After a brief interval that seemed an eternity, he said: "Something has happened to you. These are much better!"

These initial meetings took place in the fall of 1986. In the three short years that followed, I took every course and workshop that Professor Norris taught, from the English romantics to the modernists to workshops of every level, even sitting in on his graduate workshop in my senior year. He was religious about his office hours, his open door the most welcome sight as I wandered the halls of the Jesse Knight Humanities Building. He talked to me about poets from a land I still have never visited, about Vernon Watkins, about Dylan Thomas's famous red and blue notebooks that Thomas kept in his youth and that he mined for the rest of his life. Leslie spoke fondly of his wife, Kitty. I remember the support he gave me when I was struggling to come out of the closet; he told me to get out of Utah, to do my graduate work elsewhere, somewhere I could just be free to love whomever I chose. On at least one occasion, Leslie threw me out of his class, feeling that I was being too cavalier or pompous in my (dis)regard for the work of other poets. I'd show up at his office door prodigally repentant, full of tears and gratitude for his pardon. He kept things real between us.

At a certain point, Leslie said to me, "It's time for you to work with some American poets. I have taught you everything that I know. I have reserved a spot for you in Richard Shelton's workshop at Rattlesnake Mountain in the Tri-Cities. It's about a ten-hour drive from here, so get in your car and go." It was there that I first met William Stafford and Naomi Shihab Nye. I'll never forget hearing Stafford read his poem "St. Matthew and All" or Nye reading her poems "The Yellow Glove" and "What Brings Us Out." There are these moments of initiation into an art form, when the sublime is irrevocably seared into our consciousness. One suddenly feels a certain kind of *possibility*, a sense that one's trajectory in life is about to take a turn. The feeling is incremental at first. You read a poem that stays in the mind. You write a poem that impresses others. But then there's that great leap, Rilke's injunction to "change your life," a command that comes from within, not from without. Leslie was merely the midwife, but back then, I never knew how consequential his thoughtful care would turn out to be.

Several months later, I attended my first Writers at Work Conference, then held in Park City, Utah, and sat at the feet of Marvin Bell, Sandra McPherson, and Robely Wilson Jr., among others. I'll never forget McPherson's inscription in my paperback copy of her book *Patron Happiness*: "With belief in your work." Who knows what these five words meant to her, or how often she might have inscribed them to others. What mattered was that her inscription gave me *permission* to think about my own future as a poet in a new way. Sometimes, vital support and encouragement comes from without, *not* within. It's like we need to know that we can actually *do* this crazy (a)vocation called Poesy. I remember trying to cozy up to Robely Wilson Jr. (then the editor of the *North American Review*), and when I asked "Robely" what publishing advice he had for young aspiring writers, he said, "That's easy: never assume you have a relationship with someone *when you don't*." Ouch. So much for my initial forays into the art of the schmooze. At some point, I enrolled in a workshop taught by Tess Gallagher when she came through Salt Lake. The cult of Tess, Raymond Carver's widow. And the shock of hearing her read a poem like "Cougar Meat." The fetish of having her sign a clothbound copy of *Amplitude: New and Selected Poems*, the red-copper foil embossed on the cover blazing beneath the jacket.

All these pleasures I faithfully reported to Leslie, and upon graduation, he said to me: "I think you should go work with Philip Levine—he has something to teach you." And so I headed off to New Harmony, Indiana, to work with Levine for a couple of weeks before entering grad school at the University of Houston. As it turns out, I didn't win Mr. Levine's approbation, rather his censure of being "a spoiled little yuppie out of California with nothing important to say." Yet in a private conference over a ten-page manuscript, Levine did circle six lines and said to me, "If I had written these six lines, I would've called that a *fucking* day." Working with Levine toughened my skin, my resolve: I would continue down this path *with or without* anyone else's goddamn approval. The thing is this: Leslie Norris made me feel that I *belonged* to the world of contemporary American letters. He'd show me the latest galleys Peter Davison would send him from the *Atlantic Monthly* and say to me: "Tim, send your poems there too. Always send your work to the best magazines—you owe that to your work. Tell Peter that I told you to send him work." Leslie gave me courage to go out into the real world and not content myself with being a big fish in a small provincial pond.

On my shelves is an inscribed copy of Leslie Norris's *Selected Poems* (Poetry Wales Press, 1986). There's a sentence in the opening poem "Autumn Elegy" that haunts me still. Leslie wrote a Keatsian "ode to autumn" every autumn, invited all of us to do the same. Here, he marvels at a landscape, knowing that his peers who've died in the war are no longer able to see it, thus magnifying its beauty and the poet's own sense of duty: "Yet, if I stare / Unmoved at the flaunting, silent // Agony in the country before a resonant / Wind anneals it, I am not diminished, it is not / That I do not see well, do not exult, / But that I remember again what // Young men of my own time died / In the spring of their living and could not turn / To this." During my sojourn at BYU, the AIDS crisis was just in its infancy, a new war whose likes had yet to be seen in this world, and this poem would hold for me a special unintended resonance.

The life Leslie Norris lived made his poems true. He was the kind of mentor who went the extra mile at every possible turn. And I know he did the same for countless other fledgling poets. He taught me that poets do not exist in a vacuum but in constellations across space and time. Through him, I met so many other poets who helped me on my way. And it is through his great example that his spirit now ripples on out throughout his poetic legacy and through all of us who have answered the call.

The World Is Full
of Orphans

Raymond Luczak

I t's taken me years to articulate the defining fact of my childhood: I
was an orphan.

Growing up, I was shuttled between my biological family in Ironwood, Michigan, where there weren't educational facilities for deaf
children like me, and Houghton, Michigan, a university town two
hours away. Over the years, I lived with three different foster families in
Houghton; I stayed with a foster family during the week and with my
biological family in Ironwood on weekends. This went on for nine
years. (I also spent five years in a Catholic school system.)

I longed to fit in with my own hearing family, but in a small kitchen
filled with eight siblings babbling all at once during mealtimes, it was
next to impossible. I wasn't allowed to use sign language, because it was
believed that it would interfere with my speech therapy. If I wanted to
know what was going on, the usual answer was, "I'll tell you later."
Usually, I would see them burst out laughing a few seconds later, forgetting that I was there. Of course, by the time the meal was over, they'd
completely forgotten what was so funny.

I yearned for a world that made sense, and a world where I could
laugh as easily as they could without my straining to lip-read.

I came to understand that if I complained about feeling left out, I'd
be seen as a party pooper. I had to "toughen up." So if I did cry, it wasn't

because I was feeling sorry for myself. It was because I couldn't articulate those feelings that came from not being included as equal to them. I had no words for the loneliness that consumed me worse than paper on fire. I was the boy that no one wanted.

No one wants you if you're too different. In my case, I was both deaf and gay. I knew I was different, but I never questioned why I had to be punished for not hearing like everyone else. Somehow I'd intuited that if I did, I'd be even less popular. I followed the script of being the dutiful boy with clunky body hearing aids that operated out of a harness strapped to my chest, a boy who cleaned his entire plate while alternating between fanciful daydreams and foolish hopes that I'd someday be able to laugh along with everyone. In the world of my daydreams, I was king of all that happened. I became a storyteller without an audience.

___

Books were easy. They didn't require lipreading, or blast me with expressions of frustration if I asked them to repeat themselves, or mock me for not being able to understand dirty slang.

I read voraciously. Words, at first rising out of smoke and fog, began to lend weight to the dreams floating in and out of my head, giving me an unprecedented sense of control. When I read, I didn't have to be the deaf boy on the playground. I could be any character I wanted.

My oldest brother, Mark, gave me Meindert DeJong's novel *Hurry Home, Candy* one Christmas, and it became the very first book of my own. (That it is about a stray dog with no name and no home of his own is eerily prescient, which is probably why I identified with it so strongly.) I read—and reread—that book. I felt as if I had a true friend who wouldn't hesitate to repeat stories until I understood each and every word. If I could count books as my friends, I had to be the most popular boy in school. The problem was, books just weren't cool.

___

The first time I had sex with a man, we were in a library restroom. I was fourteen, and he was of indeterminate age. Even though I'd initiated it, I was still in shock afterward. This was something that wasn't in any

Raymond Luczak

book I'd read, and yet I knew I wanted more. He wasn't afraid of touching me; I wasn't an outcast. That was a new feeling.

I began to hunger for words about these experiences. My dreams became clearer. I didn't know what words could describe my ache for classmates my age and men I'd vaguely known, but my dreams were filled with them. I was in love so often that I was even afraid to say the word "love" to anyone. I was still the boy that my classmates shunted aside.

Being orphaned heightens doubts about one's place in the universe. As long as you don't have someone who loves you just as you are and who doesn't try to change you into something that you're not, you don't have a home of your own. It doesn't matter if you own a house. You're still lost.

Like any orphan, I knew that it would be a matter of time before I was chosen and whisked away to a good home. I waited and waited, with a library book in hand. Each time I read a book, I felt less like an orphan and more like a human being.

—⁓—

Once I arrived at Gallaudet University in Washington, D.C., in the summer of 1984, I soon realized that I didn't have to daydream anymore. I was suddenly among others of my kind, and they all used American Sign Language. I didn't have to strain at lipreading or repeat myself if I'd mispronounced a phrase. What mattered was the clarity of our hands. Those of us with hearing families had experienced the pain of distance that made all of us orphans, and we were finally able to turn to one another for familial solace. We stayed up so many nights, just *signing*. We were truly home.

Lambda Rising, a LGBT bookstore on Connecticut Avenue, NW, was my home away from Gallaudet. Sometimes I couldn't decide which were more enticing: the bearded men who prowled its aisles or the brand-new paperbacks that graced its shelves. Most of the time the men didn't approach me, probably because they'd spotted the hearing aids behind my ears, but strangely enough I didn't feel disappointed by their sudden loss of interest. A brand-new book was a more than adequate consolation prize.

With each purchase at Lambda Rising, and the nearby secondhand bookstore Second Story off Dupont Circle, I began to leave behind the world of mass-market paperbacks for trade paperbacks and Penguin Classics. I had discovered literature, and a whole new world of men whose words would nurture this writer into existence. Works like Christopher Isherwood's *A Single Man*, Oscar Wilde's *The Picture of Dorian Gray*, Edmund White's *A Boy's Own Story* and *States of Desire*, and Quentin Crisp's *The Naked Civil Servant* took me places, emotional and otherwise, that I hadn't known existed. Words weren't mere words anymore. They had *voices*. They were talking to *me*. They were telling me family stories as if I'd always been one of them. They never looked away from me as they carried on at the dinner table! I laughed and cried. And they never cared whether I was deaf or gay as long as I listened. How I loved reading them!

Then I happened to eavesdrop on a book—Charley Shively's *Calamus Lovers: Walt Whitman's Working-Class Comrades*—in Lambda Rising. A chapter described Mr. Whitman bathing naked with a younger Fred Vaughan in the East River off Brooklyn Heights, and even though the fantasy wasn't supported by historical documentation, I was struck by the eroticization of a writer in gay male terms. Of course, I'd read about gay sexual experiences before, but never one of an acclaimed writer in a description that mixed lust, love, and longing in equal measure by someone who'd never met him. It made me want Mr. Whitman, and I hadn't read his *Leaves of Grass*! I'd never thought of writers, even though they talked about sex and its many incarnations in their work, as physically *naked*. Writers weren't just people who buttoned up their shirts, sat on a living room sofa, and talked to me about things after the fact. They were as full of yearning as I was.

Then I read the first edition of *Leaves of Grass*. I wasn't impressed. He seemed so full of babble. Nevertheless, whenever anyone talked about Mr. Whitman and his life, I paid attention. I learned more about him in bits and pieces. If I had read Gary Schmidgall's *Walt Whitman: A Gay Life* back then, I'd have become obsessed with him. (Alas, that book didn't appear until a decade later.)

In the meantime, I came across Allen Ginsberg's poem "Howl." Blown away by his apocalyptic vision of America in the 1950s, I immediately thought of Walt Whitman. I read the second edition of *Leaves of Grass*, which many consider its best version, and I wept at his bucolic and sensuous visions. He wasn't afraid. Experiencing the love of his comrades in the purest form with true abandon had given him the strength and courage to celebrate all that was good—and bad—in life. It was also the first time where I'd seen how one writer could sire another. My English lit classes had of course discussed literary "influences," but I hadn't seen with my own eyes until that moment just how that was supposed to work.

Over the years, I've realized that Walt Whitman was a spectacularly virile man, inspiring one writer after another to celebrate the brotherhood of men in arms with their own kind. Although I don't write like him—nor would I dare to—I still count myself among his many sons. He continues to pat me on the shoulder at times when I feel my writing is going nowhere. He—along with the many writers who crowd my shelves—has given me what my own biological family has utterly failed to give me: the gift of encouragement to stay true to myself.

I write because it continues to be my ticket out of that orphanage.

—⌒—

It is impossible to choose only one influence as my singular inspiration as a gay writer. In this, I'm blessed to have such a loving family reunion each time I browse my bookcases.

I am the son of many fathers who've inspired me with their words and actions, and I hope to honor their legacy with my craftsmanship. I hope to sire others wise enough to know that our ancestors were far greater than I can ever hope to be. I am nothing without them.

Thus, it has recently occurred to me that I'd never really been alone while growing up. Books were my truest family. Whenever a book of mine is published, I release it out into the world, trusting that at least one kind-hearted stranger will adopt it and cherish it as much as I have. People come to my readings, often to tell me how they've enjoyed this or that book of mine. In fact, two hearing poets told me recently that they've reread my collection *Mute* front to back at least three times. This fact touches me deeply more than they'll ever know: it means that I've become family to someone who's chosen to listen. Such are my proudest moments as a father.

The world is full of orphans, and yet how heartening it is to see that, among books, one is never alone!

The Seismology of Love
and Letters

Brian Leung

I felt my first significant earthquake long before I fell in love or knew I would someday become a writer. I was eleven and had grown up in San Diego County, all sage, no sand. The same way I understood that water flows down hill, I also implicitly knew that the ground shook from time to time. I hadn't yet, however, discovered boys, and being in love with one, being loved by one, wasn't a possibility I thought to even imagine. The night of that first earthquake I had fallen asleep in our living room on the tattered green La-Z-Boy that was the last remnant, besides myself, of my mother and father's failed marriage. It was in the darkness of the early morning that I woke. The test pattern for a local station hummed on the television. My mother was working a graveyard shift at Denny's. My sisters were in bed. I did not know why I woke, but in seconds, the earth rumbled to life, the house shuddered and lurched. The shaking did not last long enough for me to be afraid, and when it stopped, I shut the television off and went to bed. Years later, another earthquake would wake me again, a stronger one.

I'm fresh from my MFA, but also thirty-three years old, at a writer's colony in upstate New York. A noted young bad boy of gay literature is baffled. "How can you not have heard of me?! Didn't they make you read gay literature in college?"

"Yes. Some."

"Then obviously nothing worthwhile."

I t's fair to say that growing up I knew more about earthquakes than I did about love and letters. There were, to be sure, standard models in my personal life I might have turned to, my aunt and uncle, for instance, but with no full-time parent in my house and decades before homosexuality was commercial and enjoyed pop culture ubiquity, television was my teacher. I believed I was Fred Rogers's neighbor. I believed he liked me just the way I was, that he liked everyone just the way they were. Sometimes, even beyond his demographic, I'd flip on the television for the comfort of his inclusivity.

One has to venture outside the neighborhood eventually. The shifts going on inside me were tectonic. By puberty, I knew instantly it was men I preferred, exclusively. While my peers, boys and girls, were all "going together," and at least talking about being in love, I was alone. My first sexual crush was Kevin, the county bus driver, who drove the 49 route to the mall, and who I dutifully waited for even though the 48 was a shorter trip. Kevin was in his midtwenties, a long-haired blond with a thin moustache and stringy arms. He was my version of TV's Shaun Cassidy or Leif Garrett. I sat in the front of the bus and watched Kevin's big hands grip the steering wheel. Sometimes I'd fantasize that he'd ask me to mow his lawn and then invite me inside for lemonade. I knew we would be naked together then, but I couldn't imagine what, exactly, we would do. These were the first tremors of my sexuality, uncertain and awkward, and all of them about sex, whatever that was. And by then teachers were encouraging me to write, mainly praised my humor, my attention to heteronormative themes. I'd have saved myself a lot of time if I'd written about Kevin. Maybe if I'd been given James Baldwin's "The Outing."

It's seventh grade and I've written "Hike into Terror," praised and panned by my teacher as entertaining, but a too-dark depiction of family and marriage. "Too many murders."

That the earth moves beneath our feet has always astounded me. When we're out walking, we are floating at the same time on a crust of dirt over a magma sea—a planet pie of sorts. Once, when I was young, I lay on the ground, face up, eyes closed, to see if I could feel the subterranean movement. Nothing. But I knew the ground was moving, that I lived near the edges of where two tectonic plates met. Their intersection creates the San Andreas Fault, causes the relatively frequent earthquakes and the slow drift northward of Southern California. In the year 16 million, San Francisco will be in Los Angeles's back yard.

That I understood from a young age, even at a remedial level, the workings of interior Earth amuses me now, for I could not detect the changes inside myself as I grew beyond puberty. I knew, for instance, that I was sexually attracted to men. I did not know I could do anything about it or even that the feeling wasn't considered normal. What a gesture it might have been, had someone slipped me something by Edmund White or his contemporaries. I was simply floating over my teenage years, unaware that the friction of sexuality and the attendant inactivity was building up. It was lucky, I've speculated, that I was half Chinese, and that my father's traditional Chinese father child rearing, even at long distance, caused me no end of anxiety that I wasn't Chinese enough. I was lucky we were poor, on food stamps for a while, that my mother entered into a third marriage with an alcoholic, annulled it after seven months, and then married again. White heterosexual homogeny was the least of my worries, the furthest thing away from what was my pen's mind happily writing entertaining fiction.

Before major quakes, there are sometimes warning temblors, and I recognize those in the teenage version of myself. A knowing English teacher recommended, off the record, *The Color Purple*. My mother, hearing about the book's controversial status in high school libraries, insisted on reading it as well. When she finished, we talked, and as if she knew exactly what I should hear, she said, "It's not about lesbians. Shug knows Celie deserves to be loved." It was a generous moment that went over my head. That appendage was focused on all young men on whom I had crushes. Not the least of these was Ben, a naturally muscled, slim-bodied guy with a voice that sounded like an untuned guitar.

At a party at Ben's house I found him sitting in his parents' room with a group of other high school guys. Ben was lying on the bed surrounded by these jocks, hicks, and stoners. I jumped up behind him and unconsciously ran my fingers through his soft, thin hair. Though, surprisingly, there was not a single comment from Ben or his friends, their faces became varied combinations of widened eyes and contorted lips. If there could be such a thing as a silent avalanche bearing down upon you, it would feel something like that moment. I looked down and saw what my hands were doing and stopped.

I was aching and did not know it. I thought, at the time, I simply wanted friends. And for a long while in high school, that was true. I saw the popular people and wanted to be among them. Through design and device I achieved that goal but had no idea what to do with myself once I planted my flag on the rather tenuous soil of that new place. The geography, the altitude, was much different than down on the plains where I'd been a geek. But with Ben, and a couple others, I understand now, I wanted to be in love.

I'm forty, established as a writer, enjoying a late lunch in San Francisco with a Baldwin scholar and a notable activist writer, both disgusted with my career. "Listen to her," he says. "You have to talk about what happened," she insists.

I have collaborated with him on some of his Baldwin scholarship, and yet, "I want you to write about us. I want you to write about the truth I am living."

Instead of love, I settled for a first kiss on my high school graduation night. Mark was the editor of the yearbook, *Life*. I was the editor of the school newspaper, the *Horizon*, and the annual literary magazine, *Allusions*. Mark had come out to me as bisexual earlier in the year, thinking, I suppose, I would reveal something about myself. Of course, I merely sat oblivious and still, wondering why he'd chosen to tell *me*. At our graduation party, given by one of the more popular kids and locked down by the parents, I found Mark late in the evening. We ended up in the same tent, surrounded by five other young men. As we lay quietly in our respective sleeping bags, I reached out across what felt like an enormous fissure of space and grabbed his hand. He leaned into me and we kissed for a long time. The world did not rock, nor split beneath me. I simply felt good.

In the morning, I woke before everyone. I looked at Mark, this person I'd kissed the night before. He was indeed male. I said to myself, literally, *oh, I guess I'm gay.* To this day I don't even know how I collected that simple vocabulary. I gathered my things and smiled about my epiphany on the way home. Of course, I was still no closer to conceiving that it was possible for a man to be in love with a man. What I did understand was that it was possible for a man to kiss another man and that was the vein I planned to mine. One might hope such a person, a young writer, might have had the instinct to run to the bookstore or library to read about just what this gay thing was. Alas.

Seen on a seismologist's map, California is varicose with fault lines, the San Andreas a hardened artery that runs through two-thirds of the state. It is a visible landmark, a noticeable scar for most of its span, and many imagine it will be the source of the "big one." But there are dozens of less noticeable faults that the public largely ignores. In Southern California, seismologists warn us, fault lines striate the landscape, run under and through our cities. Not far from where I lived in Los Angeles, an active fault runs through downtown. In Hollywood, a block from the Capitol Records building, a noticeable scarp buckles under the asphalt. We in the southern part of the state are more at risk, we're told, from these hidden faults, than from the San Andreas, the tail of which trails off into the California desert.

In those early years of my sexual activity, there was no model for monogamy, and the call for it, out of community self-preservation, had barely begun. Now, of course, monogamous, same-gender relationships crop up frequently in popular culture, but when I was younger, sex was what gay men were good for and what we were good at, it seemed. It was what *I* was good at. It certainly never occurred to me that I and another man could be in love together, be safe together. Even now this is a difficult concept to explain to my heterosexual friends, that the possibility of falling in love didn't exist in my consciousness. The most understanding of them forget that all of us are products of cultural expectations and few, if any, escape that. A heterosexual assumes falling in love is possible because they've seen an entire human history of it. I should have known about and read Paul Monette.

I did what I thought I was supposed to do, despite the risks. I slept with many men, Travis among them, an ice-skating instructor, legs thick and brown as tree trunks, confident and graceful. He brought me to his bed but would not kiss me on the mouth. On the wall hung pictures of him and a male student in various poses. He took off his clothes and then mine. He was ten years older than me but seemed incredibly nervous. His hands trembled. He lay on me, his broad hairy chest warm and soft on my skin. At first it felt like we were two land masses barely touching, but then it became more frictive, stressed. In minutes he had completed himself. It had been an entirely external event and he rolled over, staring at one of the photographs on the wall. "That's my ex," he said. "He left me."

"That's terrible," I said.

"I have AIDS," he half confessed, half blurted.

I thought instantly of his semen across my abdomen and chest. It did not have teeth, was not burrowing into me. Indeed, the house was not collapsing around us nor the world ending. This was not the "big one."

"That's okay," I finally said.

"You don't care? He did. That's why he left. I think he gave it to me. I never cheated on him once." Travis kept his arms at his sides. He reached for the television remote. "Oh," he said, setting it back down. "I'm not allowed." When I asked him why, he explained that his counselor told him not to watch television or read any kind of newspaper or magazine that might have reports about AIDS. Essentially, he was told to disconnect from the world. I was still thinking about the sex. It was my currency. Though, it doesn't escape me now, that mined salt was once a precious mineral for exchange.

The Earth bucks and boils beneath us, vents gasses and steam, hot lava, disrupts, over time, the stability of its own surface. The manifestations of order we produce, our concrete and steel applications, our best-laid plans, are, as far as the Earth is concerned, only skin deep. In the El Centro earthquake, a cross-section of citrus trees in one grove shifted nineteen feet, row after row perfectly straight, then curved, a seismic doodle on the landscape.

In 1992, my boyfriend Roland and I attended an AIDS awareness conversation at a private home. The house sat above Silverlake reservoir, a picturesque body of water surrounded by expensive homes atop a ring of hills thrust up by one of LA's minor faults. The community of Silverlake itself was then a place of bath houses and leather bars, and where older gay men settled down after the faster-paced lifestyle of West Hollywood no longer suited them, the kind of sex they preferred or could procure.

Roland and I went to the meeting because, even then, we were unsure exactly what "safe sex" meant. Most of the others who attended were around our age, in their midtwenties, all of us part of that fortunate generation that began our sexual careers before or in the midst of watching the previous one besieged by what was then commonly called "the gay cancer." It was not unusual, in those days, to see men in their thirties splotched purple with Kaposi's Sarcoma or to know someone who'd gone in the hospital with pneumocystis pneumonia. Sick men became, in their last months, bluish, downy haired, increasingly still as if involved in some sort of process of lithification.

At one point late in the meeting, the oldest of the attendees spoke up. He was a handsome, mustached man in his late thirties, a lemming that had somehow missed the cliff leaping. "Maybe you guys are too young to remember, but we used to have fun," he said. "We've been sitting here the whole time talking about safe sex. But I miss the old days. I liked the anonymity and I want it back."

I'm eight, maybe, and a big orange book is thrust in my lap, a big orange book with a loopy illustration of an elephant. It is read to me and I read it. Over and over; ". . . even though you can't see or hear them at all, A person's a person no matter how small." Wow.

After the man, that lost soldier at the AIDS conversation, spoke, the room was quiet. Even the moderator remained silent. The very air seemed cleaved, all of us caught in a divergent boundary. On one side, our past, the era of empowerment from living one's sexuality, on the other side a future, it seemed, of caution and blandness, the price of self-preservation. We were adrift, solitary beings. Because, in crisis, in epidemics, it seemed to me then, heterosexuals could turn to God, the

Bible, and their love for a spouse, a girlfriend or boyfriend. But that was not part of our vocabulary. It could not be. All of us in that room, even the couples, were a community of single beings. Sex, not love, was our purpose, and without that, we'd lost our epicenter, the place from which all our energies emanated. We had no Bible. Perhaps someone might have pointed me to David and Jonathan or the work of Mark Doty.

During a college sophomore workshop a famous Southern California writer, feminist, and self-mytholgizer dismisses my work. In the next class, when I mock her style with my angry reading of what I think is a duplicate of her writing, the reflection she wants, I end by slamming the paper on the desk and asking "Is that it? Is that what you want?"

"Yes," she says, calmly, simply. "Yes."

The light goes on. She doesn't want me to be her. She wants me to care.

A year later, knowing I'm transformed, she nods at a piece of mine that will, a decade later, appear in my first book as "Firewalk: An Old Fashioned AIDS Story," and says, "Send it out."

By the day of the 6.7 Northridge quake hit, my boyfriend Tom and I had gotten serious. That is, we had moved in together after having met in a literature course. I was at the point where I wondered exactly where we were headed. I had in my mind, even then, no role models, no pathway. My English courses had tickled over Wilde, dangled "Sonny's Blues," blushed with Stein and Forrester sans *Maurice*, none of them, in fact, even remotely introduced as part of an LGBT cannon.

She pulls me out of a master's graduate seminar. "You have to write about this," she says, pointing to my story.

"Really?"

She is a notable Latina writer telling me my subject is about being half-Chinese.

The Northridge quake had been the result of a blind thrust fault, which is to say the actual breach in the continuity of the earth was well below the surface. In this case, eleven miles underground, at 4:30 in the morning, the fault gave way. Tom and I were asleep in our apartment near downtown Los Angeles, twenty miles from the epicenter but hardly out of harm's way. At that point we had been together a little over a year, a time when I started wondering what we meant as a pair. Neither of us were dying lovers. We did not have the intensity of tragedy to bond us.

I woke just before the full force of earthquake struck. We lived in a bottom floor apartment of a converted three-story house built in 1923. The windows rattled and the bed quivered as the main shock rolled toward us and then struck as if something huge, solid, had slammed into our building. Tom startled awake and rolled off the bed, pulling me with him, fearing the mirror hanging on the wall above our bed would crash down on me. Plaster fell from the ceiling, our television and computer smashed to the ground. From the kitchen I heard dishes crashing down. Outside, the windows of the upper floors broke out of their panes. The sound was intense, a mix of the deep, rumbling groan of the earth and the high-pitched whine of every man-made thing straining, if not outright breaking, under the pressure. I lay on top of Tom, the shaking so violent it put inches of air space between us with each bounce. I was sure at any moment the two stories above would come down on us. In seconds, it all stopped as quickly as it began, a few lingering pieces of glass falling to the ground just outside our front door, rim shots after a bad joke.

While Tom surveyed the damage to the apartment I stepped outside into the oddly dark morning. Our apartment was at the top of a hill overlooking much of Los Angeles and out to Hollywood. Few lights were on, and except for bleating car alarms, I'd never heard the city so still, never thought about the fact that traffic noise was not a sound indigenous to the natural landscape. But more than that, I thought about Tom and me. As we rode out the earthquake I had not been worried so much about my own safety, or his, or any concern of our physical well-being. I worried, in those brief seconds of shaking, about what would happen to the couple that we were. We had become good together, something worth preserving. And as the earth shook us to what might easily have been the brink, I understood that the real tragedy would have been that two people in love would have been extinguished. And there it was, as plain as that. I was in love with Tom and the feeling was mutual. It was a strange realization, like trying on a new piece of clothing that fits you suspiciously well—there must be something wrong. But no, the feeling would not shake loose. There, suddenly, was that feeling I had never conceived of and I could speak its name. I had lived the lesson, not read about it.

At the Lambda Literary Awards: "Your writing's not gay enough." At a Modern Language Association Conference: "You're not Chinese enough. You shouldn't be writing about it."

After the Northridge earthquake, I discovered, the landscape I thought I understood suddenly heaved up, chock-a-block, familiar passages caved in, reliable landmarks upturned. Fidelity, for example, seemed anthropological, like an excavated antique lamp. What exactly does monogamy have to do with being in love with someone? But with all that uncertainty, I'd had my Elizabeth Bishop moment, "you are an I, / . . . / you are one of them." It was a final piece of the puzzle, that being in love, being loved, and not for the reasons one might suspect. Because, what Tom was in love with, I understood, was not that I was gay, but all parts of me that made a Brian, all the parts that would become subjects of my writing, my neighborhood of selves.

She reads it to me over the phone, the last phrase of the review, "first timer Leung offers stories almost radical in their humane inclusiveness."
I am, by then, an English professor, know what I should say, but . . . "That's all Mr. Rogers," I tell her. And I mean it.

The earth shakes everywhere, trips us up, topples our houses and re-routes our streams. All of us, even in our stillest moments, are in constant motion whether we like it or not. The land carries us along, dips before our very eyes, or rises up. We are, in a way, parasites on its back that every so often get shaken off. From up here, on the surface, we convince ourselves of what is right for us and others, cling to the illusion of control, forgetting about the forces below, the inevitability of rupture and sudden shifts. But whether we pay attention or not, this is how things are. Just so, to each of us on an equal basis, if in different ways, through fissure and force, love and letters happen.

Botticelli Boy

Rick Barot

1

Here are two images of influence. In the first, picture someone walking in the galleries of a museum in a European city. He is feeling what the other tourists in the museum are feeling: just a bit bored, but also anticipating a moment of revelatory sight. Ornate religious scenes, classical scenes on canvases the size of the sides of houses, still lifes, kings and queens. And then he sees the painting: the painting of the boy. The boy is so particular, so himself, that he stops the tourist in his tracks. The tourist seems to be the only one experiencing this. Around him, the others pass by the painting, then move on to the next painting, then on to the next. But the tourist feels fastened to the painting, to the moment. This is the experience that the days of the trip have led up to: this one painting of a boy. A five-hundred-year-old boy.

And this is another image of influence. In the classroom, in the undergraduate seminar on American poetry, the student is listening to the discussion about Walt Whitman. He doesn't get it. He has done the reading, he has written the response paper. But the poems don't mean anything to him: they are saccharine, loud like certain happy uncles, insufficiently dark. What the student wants is dark things: dark poems, dark relationships, dark weather in his mind. Whitman goes past him, as unacknowledged as a sunny day. Years later, many years later, he is reading Whitman again. This time he is in another seminar, a graduate seminar. Reading the thick volume of Whitman's poems, he feels like that tourist in the museum: bored, but open to being moved. And then there is the poem he flips to: the poem about the dead things roiling underneath the green grass of spring. The poem is so unexpected, so black in its mood, that he returns to it for weeks and months afterward. The poem is like a worn photograph or an old ticket stub kept in a wallet: it goes with him everywhere.

2

Whitman was his voice. It is this voice we know when we know Whitman. Part aesthetic program and part social thesis, his barbaric yawp inflects his poems' intonations even when the poems are at their quietest. At the start, the voice was pitched as it was because it was the outsider's call into the silence around him. Young, doing odd new things in his poetry, with no audience he could see, Whitman was loud because the loud was a species of self-motivation; the zeal was born out of being at the margin. Later, with his place assured, Whitman's voice stopped being the outsider's bold salvo and became the great poet's counsel to the audience he loved. He had become Wordsworth's definition of the poet: "a man speaking to men."

Among the many things that it is, "Song of Myself" is a song. But if it is voice that is the recognizable given of Whitman's poetry, to me it is the quality of his seeing that gives charge to the most lingering of his poems. Glimpse, gaze, catalogue, juxtaposition, panorama, close-up—Whitman's seeing has a tensile variety that is coincident with the many textures of his thinking. Whitman's voice can be tiresome, which is to say that his personality, bluff as a salesman's, can be tiresome. But his looking, trained outward and identifying the multiplicities beyond the self, is never so. It was seeing that checked the ego, even as it validated the ego's claims.

Whitman's glimpse. I have specifically in mind this passage and its play of perspectives, the way the seeing enacts the longing:

> A glimpse through an interstice caught,
> Of a crowd of workmen and drivers in a bar-room around the stove
> late of a winter night, and I unremark'd seated in a corner,

Of a youth who loves me and whom I love, silently approaching
        and seating himself near, that he may hold me by the hand . . .

   The emotion here may be quite simple, even verging on the sentimental, but the dynamics of seeing in the first lines is remarkably
dramatic. The first line is fluidly abstract: we don't know what the
"glimpse" comprises, or what the "interstice" indicates; the word
"caught" emphasizes the fleeting quality of the act of the glimpse, and
of what has been glimpsed. In the first line, it's also unclear who is doing
the glimpsing, though we naturally assume that it is an unnamed "I," a
narrator who has seen something. After the opacity of the first line, in
the next lines we get a scene that is immediately concrete: a "crowd of
workmen and drivers" in a bar, with a stove serving as a kind of hub,
warming up the room on a late winter night. The scene is vivid: we
imagine that the room is smoky, perhaps dim, and gregarious.
   Then, out of the crowd, the narrator appears, "unremark'd seated in
a corner." Scanning the scene in the bar, it is startling to see the narrator
in the scene, because we had thought he was beside us, narrating the
event of the glimpse. But somewhere between the first line and the
appearance of the "I," the narrator has slipped away from us and has
joined the crowd, which is where we see him, quietly holding hands
with the "youth who loves me and whom I love." That slipping away of
the narrator, that shift in roles from observer to the one observed, is as
moving as it is strange. What the poem enacts is something like a wish
fulfillment. The image of the narrator and his companion is so sweet
that it is like a fantasy that is at first glimpsed and then fully inhabited.
Like an ache, the glimpse propels the narrator through the interstice—an
interstice that is as much an opening in the narrator's imagination as it
is a brief opening of the barroom's door—and into the life he sees for
himself.

                                    3

Who is he? The young man in the portrait by Botticelli has never been
identified. He is between seventeen and twenty-five, and it could be
said that he is as generic as the title that the National Gallery in London
has given the painting of him: *Portrait of a Young Man*. The museum

dates the painting to the early 1480s, and a historian of the material culture of the Quattrocento could probably read a good amount into the man's red hat, his brown jacket, and the disposition of his hair, telling us something about his class, his occupation, maybe even the family he belonged to in Florence. Otherwise we have simply his face, and our speculation.

A handful of Botticelli's paintings are now so iconic—*La Primavera*, *The Birth of Venus*—that it's stunning to learn that for almost four hundred years his work and name were virtually lost. He was born in 1444 or 1445, and died in 1510, in Florence. The early part of his career was steadily acclaimed: he had the favor and patronage of the Medicis and their circle; he painted sections of the Sistine Chapel. But his later years were troubled, even painfully so. He became a follower of Savonarola, the Dominican preacher who railed against the political and moral values of the day, and the association seems to have made Botticelli disavow his beautiful early style, for work that was by contrast severe and leaden. The figures of the High Renaissance, Leonardo and Michelangelo and Raphael, were also coming into focus; their new aesthetics made Botticelli's classicism seem tired. Walter Pater, the late nineteenth-century critic, almost single-handedly revived Botticelli's reputation. Reality, Pater writes, comes to Botticelli and awakes in him "a mood which it awakes in no one else, of which it is the double or repetition, and which it clothes, that all may share it, with visible circumstance" (Pater, "Sandro Botticelli," 39).

When I first saw Botticelli's portrait of the young man, what I felt was the surprise of familiarity. In the galleries that I had been walking through, it was clear enough that the set pieces—a Madonna and Child here, an Apollo and Daphne there—had didactic reasons for being. And the many portraits, too, had their legible reasons for portraying the men and women they portrayed—each portrait was something like proof of the sitter's place in some social order; it was wealth, ultimately, that each portrait spoke for. But Botticelli's young man didn't have the stylized impression that the other paintings gave. The painting is stark: the young man stands in front of a plain black background. He is facing fully forward, when the other portraits show subjects in profile, or at least in a sort of contrapposto angle toward the viewer. The young man's clothes seem reserved, unadorned. He wears a red cap, something that I would later learn was called a *beretta*. The rich redness of the cap is the one effusion in the otherwise dark palette of the painting.

And then there is the young man's face, which has a specificity that was disarming. A square jawline, a bluntly square nose, liquid brown eyes the same brown as his jacket and his full hair, and lips whose corners are expressively down-turned. The young man was familiar because he was alive. While the figures in the other paintings had been fulfillments of different prescribed types, the young man had his own actuality; he had a presence that was simple and intense. He could have been any one of the teenagers goofing around in Trafalgar Square, or looking around quietly in a Charing Cross record store. He seemed alive because, it was certain, at one point he had lived. Walking through those gallery rooms, I was so young myself. Twenty years ago now. Time was the interstice—and the painting's boy there.

4

That image in Whitman's poem, of the poet imagining himself into the life he yearns for. The permission Whitman gives us to dare ourselves into imagining who we want to be. Whitman's affirmative vision. That is one thing to be taken from Whitman. But what about that poem I opened to in the graduate seminar, the poem that contained one of the most terrifying utterances in all of Whitman's work. Here, the first section of "This Compost":

> Something startles me where I thought I was safest,
> I withdraw from the still woods I loved,
> I will not go now on the pastures to walk,
> I will not strip the clothes from my body to meet my lover the sea,
> I will not touch my flesh to the earth as to other flesh to renew me.
>
> O how can it be that the ground itself does not sicken?
> How can you be alive you growths of spring?
> How can you furnish health you blood of herbs, roots, orchards, grain?
> Are they not continually putting distemper'd corpses within you?
> Is not every continent work'd over and over with sour dead?
>
> Where have you disposed of their carcasses?
> Those drunkards and gluttons of so many generations?

Where have you drawn off all the foul liquid and meat?
I do not see any of it upon you to-day, or perhaps I am deceiv'd,
I will run a furrow with my plough, I will press my spade through
the sod and turn it up underneath,
I am sure I shall expose some of the foul meat.

Whitman is not often alarming. Our poet of connectivity and encouragement, he has a vision of manifest destiny for the American soul, a program that sweeps the various dappled qualities of the country's democracy into a cosmos held in place by enthusiasm. It is a messy cosmos, but within it, as Randall Jarrell points out, there are "little systems as beautifully and astonishingly organized as the rings and satellites of Saturn" (*Poetry and the Age*, 126). Notwithstanding those lucid little systems, however, in Whitman's work there are moments of chaos and vertigo that are incongruous and thrilling. These moments amount to a description of what happens when vision slips, when the visible is inundated by darker elements that sight cannot grasp. Looking at an ostensibly vital springtime scene, where "herbs, roots, orchards, grain" are carrying out the season's awakening, the speaker in "This Compost" is agitated into a freefalling set of thoughts regarding the dead things under the ground, the generations of decomposing flesh still festering there. As the section proceeds, the speaker goes into a kind of frenzy, repulsed and avidly curious at the same time. We're not told what has led the speaker to the moment—only that "Something" startled him into the nightmare reverie.

For a long time, reading "This Compost" over and over again, I thought of the first section as a kind of Freudian slip on Whitman's part. In my early engagements with Whitman's work, I mostly equated his long lines and his optimism with long-winded superficiality. The real interest I had in his work was in his homosexuality, and the occluded, brave, and heartbreaking ways the poems seemed to depict that homosexuality. Ideal images of masculine beauty—whether the athlete's refined movements, or a laborer's rough-hewn gracefulness—turn up with undeniable regularity in Whitman's work. Whitman is at pains to also show female beauty, and, in service to the larger pluralistic ideal, he also acknowledges the homely and damaged people around him. Nevertheless, the healthy male is always his ideal American figure. To my eyes, the homoerotic moments in his poems were proof enough of Whitman's homosexuality; these moments sometimes had a sweaty sensuality that was uninhibitedly frank, and thus conclusive.

It wasn't as simple as that, of course. If Dickinson, Whitman's contemporary, had *circumference* as the one-word code for her poetic project, *camaraderie* was the word meant to contextualize the moments I saw too eagerly as the evidence of a gay identity. Where I was wont to see the homoerotic, it could be argued that Whitman saw camaraderie. In that way, Whitman's times seemed increasingly different from ours, in that the close friendships between men and between women could be conducted with an intimacy that, to our postmodern eyes, reads as something less innocent than it was. And yet—there remain the heated scenes in his poems, which seem to speak so plainly about the affections being traded between speaker and beloved, beloved and speaker. Reading Whitman's work with all these angularities in mind, with the poems' tensions multiplying as I read them more deeply, I saw the body of his work as no longer just a system of inclusions but also as a system where the unacknowledged counted for as much as what was being shown. The first section of "This Compost" seemed like a release of hidden pressure, wherein the terror of a suppressed truth came out momentarily, bringing with it an abattoir's foulness.

5

Botticelli's boy is beautiful because he is young. But not so young that experience has not made its marks on him, imperceptible in the details but contributing nonetheless to an affect that is unmistakable in his expression. He is serene, he is melancholy—both. He is a little weary, but he knows that there is more. His brown eyes are lustrous in their sad intelligence, and absolutely confident in their gaze toward us. The trace of melancholy in his mouth is met by a trace of something like petulance. His hair, abundant behind him, is the color of walnut hulls.

Every work of art, as it exists through time, gains and wanes in meaning depending on the aesthetic, social, and historical forces that surround it. Context is very nearly all. Where the Medici-era viewer might have seen Botticelli's young man as the exemplar of an aristocratic lineage, the Paterian gallery-goer would have valued the artistic apotheosis that the painting represented. Today, an anthropologist is likely to have a wildly different perspective on the painting than, say, a literary scholar who specializes in postcolonial critical theories. A powerful work of art is a kind of mirror, reflecting back to the viewer the elements of whatever zeitgeist might be in currency during a given period. A work of art is also a vestige—that is, it is the fragment of a moment that has disappeared. That moment is, first of all, the civilization that produced the artwork, and which the artwork now exemplifies. The moment is also the particular artist's life, and the vectors of heart and mind that converge in that life. Nearly all of Botticelli's paintings have self-evident values attached to them: the paintings of religious scenes were meant to be installed in churches and chapels, the paintings of secular subjects were meant to be ornamental flourishes for his patrons' houses and villas. But for *Portrait of a Young Man*, we can't so easily designate a category of significance.

There are eight portraits attributed to Botticelli. Two of these are of Medici men: one portrait was destroyed in a Naples museum bombed during World War II; the other portrait, of Giuliano de Medici, is now in the National Gallery in Washington. If Botticelli did in fact paint *Portrait of a Young Man* in the early 1480s, he would have been in his early forties—in his prime. Why would Botticelli paint this painting? It's likely that the man was from a prominent Florentine family; the painting would have been intended for the house of the man's family. This would also have meant that the enigmatic aura now projected by the man was, during Botticelli's time, part of a perfectly legible identity. The man has a noble bearing, but the plainness of his clothes gives me pause. Notwithstanding the white, fur-like trim on his brown jacket, his clothes don't have the fineness I would expect in the attire of a nobleman. His clothes look like a workman's—sensible and comfortable. Was the man an assistant in Botticelli's studio? Was he a member of Botticelli's own family? If you look closely at the man's hairline, you will see messy tendrils there, as though he had quickly put on his red cap, as though he had only momentarily stopped what he was doing to present himself to the artist's gaze. The painting has an informality that makes it luminous and private.

The vestige of a culture's essence and an artist's sensibility, Botticelli's painting is also the vestige of a meticulous artisanal procedure. As an image, the painting has an immediate wholeness that is, as in a poem, felt before it is understood. This wholeness, however, belies the hundreds, if not the thousands, of small moves needed to take the painting to that place of totality. We may have only a speculative sense of what Botticelli intended with the painting, but we can at least get a nearly full sense of its profound materiality. The painting was executed on a poplar panel that is fifteen inches high and eleven inches wide. Botticelli used tempera paint, which was the dominant medium until oil paint superseded it late in the Renaissance. Tempera is created by mixing egg yolks with powdered pigments—azurite, for example, to make blues, and malachite and copper to make greens. Because it is fast-drying, tempera needs exquisite skill to handle. Before the actual paint was applied, however, the panel would have been heavily prepared. Several layers of gesso— powdered chalk mixed with glue—would have been applied on the panel to prime it, making a white ground. Botticelli would have then drawn the painting's design on the gesso, applying black paint or ink with a quill. And then the actual painting: the application of layers of various colors that built toward the particulars of the design. If we were at hand to see Botticelli painting the flesh on the young man's face, we would have seen him first apply an ochre wash on the gesso, followed by a layer of nearly transparent white, followed by adjusted layers of pink, leatherlike yellow-brown, and more white. Watching the man's face come into being, we would have gotten a keener sense of what Victor Hugo meant when he wrote, "Form is depth brought to the surface" (*Utilité du Beau*, 481).

6

By now I've carried that portrait in my mind for many years. It's like a talisman there. For a long time I didn't think much about the artist himself, Botticelli. What I know most of the time is that the artist is so metabolized into the work of art that only the work of art remains. The artist does not last; the work of art, if it is lasting, lasts. But I also know that transmitted into the artwork are the innumerable particles of experience, expertise, emotion, and fantasy that every person generates. And so I started looking into the life behind the art.

In Botticelli's biography, there is one particle of experience that is as tantalizing as it is elusive. Soon after Botticelli was resurrected by Pater, a cottage industry of scholarship went to work on the painter and his paintings. In 1938 one of these scholars, sifting through old Florentine records, came across a magistrate's ledger that tersely noted for November 16, 1502: "Sandro di Botticello si tiene un garzone" (Mesnil, *Botticelli*, 98). That is: "Botticelli keeps a boy." Beyond that one sentence and its damning legal brevity, there are no other records about the circumstances of the charge. Botticelli was apparently never tried, perhaps due to the intercession of his Medici patrons. He would have been around fifty-eight at the time, well past his fame as a painter. A few years later, if we believe Vasari, Botticelli was crippled and impoverished, hobbling Florence's streets on two canes. He died in May 1510.

And in Whitman's case, in a coincidence that shocked me, there is one particle of life, so absurd that it is almost unbelievable. David S. Reynolds tells the story in *Walt Whitman's America*, laying out a riveting case for the story's plausibility. It is the winter of 1841, Whitman is twenty-one and working as a teacher in Southold, a village on the easternmost end of Long Island. This is one of the string of teaching jobs that Whitman has had; he detests the work and the villages where he feels he has been exiled, away from New York and the work in writing and publishing he would rather be doing. It was not unusual for a male teacher like Whitman to board with one of the town's families, often sleeping in the boys' quarters. As Reynolds narrates the story, on one Sunday that January, Whitman was publicly denounced by the pastor of Southold's First Presbyterian Church. Whitman was accused of sodomy. The congregants formed a mob and gathered hot tar, which was easily available for mending the village's fishing nets. After first going to one house, the mob found Whitman in another, where a housekeeper had helped him hide in the attic, underneath straw mattresses. "They seized him," Reynolds writes, "plastered tar and feathers on his hair and clothes, and rode him out of town on a rail" (70). By the spring, Whitman was at another Long Island school, in his last stint as a teacher. In the summer of that year he moved to Manhattan, intent on being a full-time writer.

You can be haunted by the beauty of the art. It turns out you can also be haunted by the ghosts of experience that informed that art—ghosts that are as dark as the other side of a canvas, the other side of an expanse of green spring grass.

Fourteen or so years after Southold, the first edition of *Leaves of Grass* appeared. Another edition was published the following year, in 1856. This second edition carried the first version of "This Compost," with the title "Poem of Wonder at The Resurrection of The Wheat." Over the years, in subsequent editions, the poem was trimmed and revised, though the unsettling arc of the poem's seeing was already fully inscribed in the first version. Reading again the grotesque meditation in the poem's first section, I am always surprised to remember that the poem was first published before the Civil War, well before the eloquent witnessing that Whitman experienced during that war. Notwithstanding the evidence of spring before him, Whitman has what amounts to a hallucination. What triggers the vertigo in the poem's first section is an unnamed internal horror, his recoil given rhythmic breathlessness in the opening stanza's series of negations: "I withdraw," "I will not go," "I will not strip," "I will not touch." Given his preference for touch and contact as the modes by which Whitman approached the world, the explicit physical repulsion in "This Compost" is remarkable.

The very opposite of his love-filled glimpse into the crowded barroom scene, the glimpse into the seething soil of "This Compost" is nonetheless as fleeting as that other glimpse. In the second section of "This Compost," something like reasonableness asserts itself, reminding Whitman of the fertility that is underwritten by so much death:

> Behold this compost! behold it well!
> Perhaps every mite has once form'd part of a sick person—yet behold!
> The grass of spring covers the prairies,
> The bean bursts noiselessly through the mould in the garden,
> The delicate spear of the onion pierces upward,
> The apple-buds cluster together on the apple-branches,
> The resurrection of the wheat appears with pale visage out of its graves,
> The tinge awakes over the willow-tree and the mulberry-tree,
> The he-birds carol mornings and evenings while the she-birds sit on
>   their nests,
> The young of poultry break through the hatch'd eggs,

The new-born of animals appear, the calf is dropt from the cow,
    the colt from the mare,
Out of its little hill faithfully rise the potato's dark green leaves,
Out of its hill rises the yellow maize-stalk, the lilacs bloom in
    the dooryards,
The summer growth is innocent and disdainful above all those strata
    of sour dead.

Here is our reassuring, list-making, openly gazing Whitman, re-assuring himself of the vitality of things. Residues of the earlier horror appear in the above lines, but in these lines we can see Whitman's seeing arguing down the invisible malaise that had startled him. The specificity of the landscape affirms the cycle that gives pluralistic value to everything, because everything is connected. It is, of course, death itself that had startled Whitman—the fact of it, the undeniable occurrence that is undeniable precisely because it feeds the new life that keeps appearing. Whitman's inherent optimism is so foundational that to see it wobble in the early section of "This Compost" is moving. But I am almost disappointed in the return of Whitman's good sense in the poem's later section. Still, that good sense is ultimately what makes Whitman Whitman. His notion of camaraderie extends even to the dynamic between life and death. "What chemistry!" he intones:

That the winds are really not infectious,
That this is no cheat, this transparent green-wash of the sea which is
    so amorous after me,
That it is safe to allow it to lick my naked body all over with its tongues,
That it will not endanger me with the fevers that have deposited
    themselves in it,
That all is clean forever and forever,
That the cool drink from the well tastes so good,
That blackberries are so flavorous and juicy . . .

Here, signaling a return to the health of the body and the mind, the body is naked and everything it touches is clean. Purpose and equilibrium and enthusiasm have been restored. In the last section of "Song of Myself," in one of the most affecting moments in our poetry, Whitman sees himself as part of the compost that finally takes everything into itself: "I bequeath myself to the dirt to grow from the grass I love, / If you want me again look for me under your boot-soles." Similarly, by the time we arrive at the last stanza of "This Compost," Whitman is far from the private darkness that initiated the poem, and he is in full awe of the earth, that "It renews with such unwitting looks its prodigal, annual, sumptuous crops," that "It gives such divine materials to men, and accepts such leavings from them at last." What started as nightmare has turned into a clear-eyed glimpse into change, dissolution, and renewal—a theory of immortality.

References

Hugo, Victor. *Utilité du Beau*. Reprinted in *Oeuvres completes: Philosophie*, vol. 2, 478–87. Paris: Librairie Ollendorff, 1904.

Jerrell, Randall. *Poetry and the Age*. New York: Knopf, 1953.

Mesnil, Jacques. *Botticelli*. Paris: A. Michel, 1938.

Pater, Walter. "Sandro Botticelli." In *The Renaissance: Studies in Art and Poetry*, 37–44. 4th ed. Mineola, N.Y.: Dover, 2005.

Reynolds, David S. *Walt Whitman's America: A Cultural Biography*. New York: Knopf, 1995.

Whitman, Walt. *Leaves of Grass*. 2nd ed. New York: Fowler & Wells, 1856.

Miss Thing

Paul Bonin-Rodriguez

M iss Thing and I were introduced properly at drama school in the
early 1980s. I cannot remember when exactly, or under what
circumstances, only that it was done and I knew her, and I found her
daunting. She was played in real life by Robert, who was older than
most of us and from El Paso. Robert was studying acting and dance and
planning on a career as a Broadway gypsy, if not as a major star of television and film. Naïve and newly out, I didn't know at first—and would
not know for some time—that Robert's alter ego, who accompanied
him everywhere, shared her name with many Miss Things across the
English-speaking world. At the time, I couldn't imagine her sharing
anything, especially a spotlight. To me, she was and will always be of an
era and of a type: an original and complex gay story embodied, an endless source of contradictions and intrigue. That is to say, she was of my
era and she carried my story with her, long before I was ready or able to
tell it.

Miss Thing inhabited the grueling, morally ambivalent world of
glamour, which kept her ever vigilant to her appearance. Her nails were
perfectly manicured and painted with a clear gloss. Her eyes were
almond-shaped and always clear, bordered by a deftly applied black
liner and mascara. Her dark beige foundation—her "matte finish," as

she called it—disappeared into her skin and returned with an even tone worthy of the most skilled mortician. Her naturally full lips were evenly pink and moist, not garishly coral or stupidly wet with gloss, as was popular then. Her black hair was blown and sprayed back in a helmet a la George Hamilton, Liberace, and Eddie Munster. Her moustache occupied the medium gauge between Robert Goulet and John Waters.

In the dance studio, as on campus, her style was both *Fame* and *Flashdance*. She wore black tights cut mid-thigh, and a gold T-shirt relieved of its collar. She wore the T-shirt belted at the waist, or tied at the bottom and tucked behind to hide her slight sway back. Frequently, she adjusted her junk to its best effect. She never hid her *candy*. She planned to live forever. We would remember her name. (Remember! Remember!)

Miss Thing spoke in third person, often beginning with an announcement about her appearance. *Miss Thing had to apply extra concealer this morning to hide her bags. Miss Thing is a wreck today; she didn't get her beauty sleep.* As Miss Thing was wrecked by many things—a pretty boy smiling at her, a rip in her tights, a difficult dance combination in a callback audition—the profane forever teetered on the brink of cataclysmic and needing of rescue. As with many things, Miss Thing's helplessness was just another layer of artifice. She was perfectly capable of many things, but very interested in finding out who might care to help her.

For professional reasons, Miss Thing cultivated and guarded her whiteness and her maleness, speaking of both as if they, unlike her beauty issues, were mechanisms under her complete control. Miss Thing Anglicized her Christian names: Roberto Antonio became Robert Anthony, who dropped his Latino surname. She spoke in carefully articulated English, paying close attention to the pronunciation of vowels. Although she answered to "Miss Thang," as she was hailed by the students who flaunted their Texas accents, she always introduced herself as Miss Thing. Only when impersonating her *abuela* did her El Paso came out: "Roberto, cántame como *Barbrra*."

Miss Thing could slide into the note just like Ms. Streisand. She knew every inflection and gesture in Barbra's delivery of "People" from *Funny Girl*, the movie, circa 1965. She rarely seemed to get past the point when Barbra turns and leans against a post, and delivers with a slight giggle, ". . . but I don't know" before those who watched her tried on their own impersonations, drowning out Miss Thing's well-rehearsed and clearly pleasurable chansonnier with brassy, even cacophonous versions of "Don't Rain on My Parade" and "My Man." In those moments, Miss Thing did not lower herself to compete with us, or even to look at us. The spotlight belonged to her, and in the public arena it could never stay off her for very long.

Being recognized by Miss Thing with a "hello!"—alternately performed as a giggly schoolgirl or a sultry chanteuse—coincided with being seen by a gaggle of drama majors who soaked up her affect and wit. "I'm so sure," she would often say to put someone in his/her place. She demonstrated her scrutiny and incredulity by pulling down on her lower eyelid with an index finger. *They're casting you in a butch role? I'm so sure.*

Over time, other west Texans, who came from areas closer to Midland and Big Spring/La Mesa (or "Big Sprang/La Meesa") than to El Paso appropriated the term and modified it: "So *damn* sure," they returned. As if answering a challenge, Miss Thing shortened the phrase to "SDS," and the lexicon was concretized. Same gesture, longer emphasis on the consonants, with the s hissed out as eye contact was broken, the eyelid released, and Miss Thing (and Miss Thing wannabes) walked away.

Sitting in the school lobby—one side dedicated to smoking, the other to ambient smoke—and engaging in cross-shouts and catcalls, the drama majors marked every passerby of note under their assiduous gaze. Although Miss Thing had set the tone and the parameters of practice, she rarely deigned to participate in this group activity. She calibrated her presence to maintain her mystique; she guarded her eye contact.

She wrote our scripts, and then disappeared.

This is all to say that Miss Thing was, effectively, the first bitchy, self-possessed queen in my life. Having been reared in rural Texas and the Deep South, I had little exposure to queer language and artifice, to the promiscuous exchanges or bloated performances of gender, to affected self-deprecation and vicious, biting humor—at least outside of liquor-fueled cotillions and powder puff football games. I had read a lot of Eudora Welty and Flannery O'Connor. I knew very little about Tallulah Bankhead, except for a girl at school named after her, and we called her "Tulie." But I was perceptive enough to get that Miss Thing had given herself her own name and that her ingenue status, her "Miss," like many things about her, was both ironic and serious.

In Mobile, Alabama, where I began college and my journey out of the closet at a little bar named David's, one button-shirted boy called me "Mary" over the din of dance music and happy chatter. "Who?" I asked, looking around, expecting, as always, a humble virgin figure, backlit, sloe-eyed, perhaps slightly uncomfortable. My companion hit me, making me turn around: "It's gay talk, what we do when we're having fun. We call each other Mary." Clearly I had much to learn. And learn I did a year later when I transferred to Austin and met Miss Thing.

Within a short time of meeting Miss Thing, Robert and I became friends and later, briefly, roommates. From the outset we had enough in common to share. We were both the youngest of all boy families. He had two older brothers; I had three. We were both Latino, both brought up Catholic, both close to our grandmothers. We both had our eyes on entertainment, particularly singing and dancing. But Miss Thing had something I did not—a willingness to be seen as the set of contradictions and surprises that she was. Her wit, her gestures, and her lexicon made her the punch line before others could deliver it at her expense.

In my view, Robert had tremendous power. He seemed to know when he was Miss Thing, and he could say definitively—as he often did—"That's Mister Thing to you." He was a chameleon-like but resilient figure, someone who announced a unique presence and who determined the course of the conversation. He was my first image of queer liberation. He challenged me to think beyond the codes under which I had grown up and to imagine a world, even write about one, where Miss Thing had friends, lovers, and family. He allowed me to see a person who was not defined by narrow gender, religious, and racial codes, at least for a time.

In the fishbowl of our environs, I also saw the Janus face of early 1980s Austin queer identity enabled by homophobia and, in this case, chicanophobia. We still kept our true identities from our families. In the still-conservative environment of the drama department, which we understood as the gateway to legitimate theater, we both had to negotiate, or rather hide, our easily effeminate behavior in classes and auditions.

Still, in hope we worked our assets off. I spent extra time in the studio and began to excel at dancing, which is where I took refuge until I could start telling stories. He had musical training; he could play the piano score to most musicals. But neither of us could pull off an all-American male. Save for a few, small roles, we were not often cast. I understood our Miss Things to be wallflowers, not stars, in the theater's limited imagination of the day. I left the department and pursued an English degree with a focus in writing, where I began to write about Miss Things. Robert graduated, to the pride of his family, returned to El Paso, and hosted a segment on a morning talk show, where, I am told, his bitchy chatter became the toast of El Paso.

Miss Thing planned on something like Lea Michele's career, but my friend was born too early for *Glee* and combination therapies against HIV. She would have made an excellent reality show contestant, a survivor of note who influenced the lexicon of the blogosphere. She would have made an excellent pundit. How might Bill O'Reilly, Ann Coulter, and even Andrew Sullivan wither under her searing "SDS"? But her star flashed and burned its image into the memories of those of us who knew her, those of us who in moments of collusion or private humor still reach up and still pull down an eyelid.

More importantly, perhaps, her spirit continues to show up, not only in my stories but also in my work as a teacher in the same department where Miss Thing and I first met. The lobbies are smoke-free now; the students are just as self-conscious, and often succumb to conservative notions of gender; but there are moments in production, in class, and in dialogue when the spirit of Miss Thing emerges and holds court.

And I welcome her every time.

Thirteen Ways
of Looking at My Father

K. M. Soehnlein

1

Six feet tall, 190 pounds, brown hair that had been blond when he was a boy, glasses with a strong prescription, a mustache for as long as I can remember, a strong physique from years spent running, inevitably thicker now around the middle—I look at him and see how I'm going to age.

2

I'm named after my father: a first name often misspelled; a middle name with a comical ring (Manfred); a family name everyone mispronounces. My birth certificate includes the Roman numeral II. Being "the second" implies a repetition of the first, the new version, the next in line: a bond, and a challenge.

3

After a semester away at college, I came home and declared myself an atheist. In our house, the Catholic Church was central, not dogmatically but as a means to a circle of friends: encounter groups and prayer meetings, church decorating committees and coffee socials. We attended mass every Saturday evening—"folk mass" with acoustic guitars and harmonizing, fresh-faced singers. For most of my teenage years I went to a once-a-week Prayer Meeting, where inspirational "talks" were followed by all of us holding hands in a circle, the room lit by a single candle, our personal, confessional prayers spoken aloud, often through tears. I gave several of these talks myself, including one titled "Is Life Fair?" during which I played ABBA's "The Winner Takes It All."

When I announced to my father I would no longer go to mass, it was dogma and hypocrisy I blamed. He'd urged me my whole life to think for myself, I said, but we let the Church do our thinking for us. My father in this conversation went through stages, like a dying patient. Anger gave over to an attempt to bargain, and then something like depression set in. "We thought you were going to be a priest," he said. Acceptance took longer, though eventually, he took the path of least resistance and gave in. This conversation was a preamble to the one about sexuality that would follow a year later—my coming out—with its own stages of grief.

4

The first person I ever told of my attraction to men was a priest. At a teen retreat, during a candlelit mass in a gymnasium, we went to confession, face to face in folding chairs set up around the room. "Bless me, Father, for I have sinned, I have violated my sexuality," I told Father Greg, a young priest from a neighboring parish. "Acts or thoughts?" he asked, and when I said, "Mostly thoughts," he gently pushed on. "Thoughts about sex? About girls?" There was a tiny pause and then he added in a very neutral voice, "About guys?"

The relief I felt—that he'd said this before I had to—opened the floodgates. "It's more than thoughts," I said, explaining how I'd "done stuff" with girls though my real sin was masturbating while thinking about guys. "A lot," I added, feeling braver now. He assured me that thoughts were okay, natural. "Most men do it," he said. "Teenagers, adults. Even priests."

In that moment I sensed his conflict between having to toe an official line and not fully believing it, because he, like me, existed in the real world of desire. "Think of it this way," he said. "It makes you feel guilty, and that's not worth it. Plus, all you wind up with is a mess on your hands." I chuckled in surprise, and also with an adult sense of collusion. The image he'd put forth was vivid enough to be its own kind of confession. I'd told him a story, and he, my audience, had identified with my protagonist.

5

"Who are your influences?" is the impossible question that writers get asked when they read or lecture in public. It offers no illumination to anyone if I cite a favorite writer, like Joan Didion, whose books line my shelves but whose prose sounds nothing like mine. (I admire Didion's power of rational assessment like a favorite cuisine that I'd never attempt to cook at home.) If I tell you Kerouac has been an influence, that his emotional openness and visionary reach have pushed me to loosen up my phrasing, do you automatically think that I write in run-on, improvisatory sentences full of self-pity?

If I cite a gay writer, an established elder, the answer will strike some as a better fit: gay writers are supposed to learn from other gay writers, bonded by subject matter, not style. But if I cite James Baldwin you wouldn't be wrong in asking, "Where is the preacher's cadence in *your* sentences? Where is the controlled, seething rage?" If I cite Edmund White, you might note how I fail at the observational specificity that arises from his unblinking candor. Every claimed influence reveals a lack. The son always fears falling short.

6

Around the time I took my first fiction workshop, I read Alan Hollinghurst's *The Swimming Pool Library*, mesmerized by its combination of contemporary sex and cultural history, its smart, dirty mind. I lingered too over Edmund White's cover blurb, comparing Hollinghurst to Nabokov and Genet. If only, I thought, the author of one of my favorite novels (*The Beautiful Room Is Empty*) would one day attest to my literary merit. Ten years later, it happened. My first novel was published with praise from White—secured through my agent, who had once been his student—and immediately I fretted that it was not enough. There were no comparisons to the greats of the past, no adding of my name to a hallowed lineage. Later, I attended a lecture at which White referred to himself as a "blurb slut," citing the countless novels that he'd endorsed as much out of duty—avuncular elder doing his part for the tribe—as enthusiasm. The praise I had craved was revealed at last for what it was: a transaction, when what I'd wanted was validation. Such craving is perhaps unavoidable in a culture that only understands quantifiable success, when our vocation is one that can't be measured. Indeed, I don't know a single writer—from those who've been praised in the *Times* to those who can't get published—who doesn't think that he or she is underappreciated.

7

My father built a tall, narrow bookshelf just inside the front door of our house. The first thing you saw when you entered were those shelves that held the Funk and Wagnalls encyclopedia, A–Z, gold spines suggesting treasure within; the Time-Life history of the presidents; the National Geographic atlas; the Merriam-Webster dictionary. If at any point a factual question arose, my father walked to the bookshelf and came back with an open volume. My sisters and I teased him for needing all the answers, calling him "Mr. Encyclopedia." We were of a generation that didn't see information as currency required for cultural participation. Back then, knowing it all was uncool.

But education was the other persistent current of our household, clashing at times with faith. My parents, married in their early twenties, each went back to college in their thirties. I typed their papers for them at twenty-five cents a page, on a new electric typewriter, which is how I first encountered *The Great Gatsby* and *To Kill a Mockingbird*, Foucault's *Madness and Civilization*, Kübler-Ross's *On Death and Dying*. I learned about psychology, philosophy, and literature by osmosis, the child-typist gaining an accidental subversive education.

8

In childhood, the nemesis of imagination was my paternal grandfather, whom we called Opa. He was an unschooled immigrant from the most conservative part of Germany, who worked most of his life as a baker in a supermarket chain, frugal with both money and emotion. He spoke in truisms, often reproachful: "If you're going to be a man at night, you have to be a man in the morning"; often banal: "It's nice to be nice." I considered it one of my teenage triumphs when he cornered me with one of his favorites, "Everything in moderation," and I had the wits to reply, "Yes, Opa. Even moderation."

Opa was not interested in reading unless produced by a company he owned stock in. He would corner me with an annual report, telling me to read the financial summaries and reminding me, "When I came to this country I had nothing." The through-line from impoverished youth to middle-class adulthood was hard work, a lesson largely lost on me, a suburban kid with his own bedroom, bicycle, and portable stereo spinning disco records. Opa's annual reports and the news stories of the same companies in the *Wall Street Journal* (skinny columns crammed with jargon) seemed impossibly complicated, but what he was trying to teach me was simple: work hard, save your money. That is success. The story he was most interested in was the American Dream, the cliché that explained his life.

The privilege of youth is to reject hard evidence in favor of emotional truth. Numbers, money, investment: none of this held sway. I was a daydreamer, trying to balm the confusion inside of me by making up worlds on paper. Unlike so many boys, my fantasies were not set in Middle Earth or faraway planets but in suburban towns not so different from the one I lived in, though more to my liking. The first short story I ever completed, called "King of the Roller Rink," was about a boy in a town like mine, hoping to win a roller-skating contest to get the attention of a pretty girl from school. Under the mentorship of an old-timer who works at the rink, he becomes a fast skater; but the girl turns out to be a phony, and our hero Learns a Lesson: working hard might give you a victory, but it won't guarantee happiness.

9

I'd been a reader since kindergarten: picture books with cartoon characters, biographies written for children (Paul Revere, Abraham Lincoln, Crazy Horse), mysteries (Encyclopedia Brown, the Hardy Boys, Nancy Drew). I owned a Bible called *The Way*, filed with photos of kids in contemporary clothes and passages likening today's problems to those of the Bible's heroes.

In fifth grade I read *Then Again, Maybe I Won't*, the book that changed forever what I wanted out of books. It was Judy Blume's first novel to feature a male protagonist. Tony's narration revealed secret opinions about his family, voyeuristic glances at the sexy girl next door, and unwanted middle-of-the-day hard-ons. Tony suffered eruptions of stomach pain when he felt anxious, and wet dreams that left his bed sheets sticky with the evidence of uncontrolled desire. He was the first character in literature who seemed like me.

My parents gave me a diary that same year, and it seems to me now that the keeping of the diary and the reading of *Then Again, Maybe I Won't* were two parts of the same breakthrough. I was being given permission to write in a daily journal, and I was being "given permission" by Judy Blume to do so in a voice that told the truth—or at least *a* truth—about being a boy in a boy's body.

10

The father in *Then Again, Maybe I Won't* is a financial provider, as fathers have always been expected to be. He invents an "electric cartridge," strikes it rich, and then moves his family from working-class Jersey City to the suburbs. The problems that ensue are all domestic—Mom becomes a status-conscious ninny, the new housekeeper is a tyrant, and young Tony is tormented by his friendship with a domineering rich kid. At no point does the story give a clue as to the pressures upon Tony's father, who has gone from self-employed electrician to company owner. Fathers in coming-of-age fiction frequently hover offstage. In my first novel, the teenage protagonist, Robin, isn't even sure what his father does for a living—a failure perhaps of my authorial imagination to fully engage with the particulars of the characters I'd created, not to mention a symptom of my own general disinterest in the realm of economics.

It's easier, perhaps, to move the parents offstage than to portray them in all their complexity. My father was not emotionally withholding—he was unafraid to say "I love you"—and could command great moral authority, as when he kicked his cousin out of our house for spewing anti-Semitic rhetoric. But his life as a provider—working for a single company for thirty years, moving slowly from entry level to middle management—was one of stress. During one dark period, he became the target of the workers he supervised, a crew that had always had the run of the place, who launched a campaign against him that culminated when they poured glue all over his desk after hours. It frightened me to hear about this organized bullying, which was so much like moments I'd faced at school. I'd counted on my father to take care of problems. But now he was being terrorized, and for a while the workers, like a gang with a code of silence, seemed invincible.

During this time, the stories I wanted to write emerged only as sketches. I created a hero named Brian, who made friends with boys and had crushes on girls—the inverse of my own existence. I'd outline the goings-on every day over a single summer between junior and senior year of high school, filling his schedule with parties thrown while parents were away. Some of these teenagers had bigger, fancier houses than the others, or drove new cars instead of hand-me-downs (as I did, inheriting Opa's old Chevy), but at no point did I stop to figure out what anyone's father or mother did for a living. There was something tribal about this world: teenagers operating free from authority, forging and breaking alliances according to whim. I created plenty of conflict: Brian would cheat on one girl with another, who might start dating his best friend. Eventually he made friends with a boy named Kyle, who slowly emerged as my first gay character. In this way, I kept advancing the plot.

11

My earliest mentors were women: Mrs. Bishack, the children's librarian who ran the summer reading program; Miss Piltz, a white-blonde,

K. M. Soehnlein

bone-thin, and fashionable middle-school English teacher (it was under her watch that "King of the Roller Rink" was written); the mothers of my friends, who sat around kitchen tables, smoking cigarettes, gossiping with relish. The first gay novel I read was Patricia Nell Warren's *The Front Runner*, assigned to me in a college sociology course called "Sexual Oppression," taught by an out bisexual (female) professor.

But when it came time to write—to push beyond the realm of my straight alter ego—I found the literary inspiration I needed in the world of men, gay writers illustrating the path of a particular subculture. I needed models for one main reason: I had never written honestly about desire. I had imposed a silence upon myself that went all the way to my diary, which remained muffled and coded. Wordless fantasy—pictures in my mind—had been the only place I allowed myself to author queer stories. I had told no one of this but Father Greg.

"As one reads more and more you get more fathers in your hierarchy of fathers. And then, after summoning twenty or thirty fathers, perhaps *you* are born . . ." So said the writer Donald Barthelme (*Not-Knowing*, 211). For the aesthetically driven (and heterosexual) Barthelme, whose short stories were marked by an ironic, obfuscating style, a father was a literary forebear who taught that language should allude to, but not express, story. For me the issue was not stylistic experimentation but communication of content. The emergence of gay fiction in the '80s and '90s revealed a necessary point of view and mapped out a new terrain, a new tribe. I could list the writers who became important to me, though the point is not any single author's influence but the collective under-standing that we had our own literature, that we were accountable to each other, not to authority.

12

The first story I completed as an adult grew out of the experience of watching my mother die of cancer. I gave the story to my family as a gift. My father, devastated by the loss, treated the story as a holy relic: a tribute to her and a testament to her survivors muddling through our stages of grief. But when he read my second story, more purely a work of fiction, he was uncertain what to make of it. The story was about a boy who is called a faggot and beaten up in the woods behind his school.

He comes home, locks himself in his bedroom, and refuses to come out. His mother is a dizzy character, short-tempered and unable to cope with the crisis. After reading this, my father remarked, "That's not your mother."

"Of course not," I protested. "She's a fictional character." I was frustrated in the moment, but in time, and after more stories, I came to understand that fiction arising from elements of personal experience (sexuality, event, setting) will always be judged according to how true it seems, no matter how fabricated the plot.

For my second novel—the story of an unreconciled relationship between a homophobic father and gay son—I put this dedication at the front: *To my father, for not being the father in this book.* Indeed, the father in the book is already dead on page 1. He's been deteriorating for years from something like Alzheimer's that has led him to forget many things, including the trouble with his son. I knew a little about this disease from what happened to Opa, who died this way, his mind erased but his bank account full enough to pay for the health care he needed at the end of his life.

13

Influence is impossible to quantify. How much of my literary voice belongs to Judy Blume, to Edmund White, to Miss Piltz, to the New Testament gospel writers and their contemporary translators? How much belongs to my father, who was in his own way a storyteller—those terrible tales from work—but who more significantly allowed me to close my bedroom door and write in my notebooks uninterrupted, who let me persuade him of my need for independence (from religion, from heterosexuality), who opened himself up to the notion that as a writer I might cast him in a new role, that of muse, as in one novel after another I have struggled to unlock the mystery of what happens between gay sons and their straight fathers—men who are sometimes like him and sometimes the opposite of who he is, the father he might have turned out to be had he been less tolerant, less inquisitive, less loving. Encouragement—it must be said—is its own form of influence. So is getting out of the way. So is letting go, so that other influences can emerge to complicate the stories that must be told.

Contributors

Noël Alumit is the author of the novels *Letters to Montgomery Clift* (2002) and *Talking to the Moon* (2007). His website is www.noelalumit.com.

Rick Barot has published two books of poetry: *The Darker Fall* (2002) and *Want* (2008), a finalist for the Lambda Literary Award and winner of the 2009 Grub Street Book Prize. He has received fellowships from the NEA, the Artist Trust of Washington, the Civitella Ranieri, and Stanford University. His poems and essays have appeared in numerous publications, including *Poetry, Paris Review, New Republic, Ploughshares, Tin House, Kenyon Review, Virginia Quarterly Review*, and *Threepenny Review*. He lives in Tacoma, Washington, and teaches at Pacific Lutheran University and in the Program for Writers at Warren Wilson College.

Mark Bibbins is the author of two books of poems: *The Dance of No Hard Feelings* (2009) and the Lambda Award–winning *Sky Lounge* (2003). His third collection, *They Don't Kill You Because They're Hungry, They Kill You Because They're Full*, is forthcoming. He teaches at The New School, where he cofounded *LIT* magazine, and at Columbia University. He edits the poetry section of *The Awl*.

Richard Blanco's acclaimed first book, *City of a Hundred Fires* (1998), received the prestigious Agnes Starrett Poetry Prize. His second book, *Directions to the Beach of the Dead* (2005), won the 2006 PEN / American Center Beyond Margins Award. His third, *Looking for The Gulf Motel* (2012), was published through the Pitt Poetry Series. His poems have appeared in *The Best American Poetry 2000*, *Great American Prose Poems*, and have been featured on National Public Radio's *All Things Considered*. He is currently at work on a memoir about growing up bilingual, bicultural, and bisexual in Miami.

Paul Bonin-Rodriguez is a writer-performer who teaches in the Performance as Public Practice Program at the University of Texas at Austin.

Justin Chin is the author of three books of poetry, three books of essays, and a short story collection. He lives in San Francisco, California.

Peter Covino, poet, translator, and editor, is the author of *The Right Place to Jump* (2012) and *Cut Off the Ears of Winter* (2005), winner of the 2007 PEN America/Osterweil Award and finalist for the Paterson Poetry Prize and the Thom Gunn Award. Recent poems have appeared in *American Poetry Review*, *Colorado Review*, *LIT*, the *Paris Review*, the *Yale Review*, and other publications. He is coeditor of *Essays on Italian American Literature and Culture* (2012). He is associate professor of English and creative writing at the University of Rhode Island.

Mark Doty's *Fire to Fire: New and Selected Poems* won the National Book Award for Poetry in 2008. He teaches at Rutgers University and lives in New York City. His essay in this volume is drawn from the forthcoming *What Is the Grass*, a meditation on Whitman, desire, death, and the ecstatic.

Jim Elledge's *H*, a collection of prose poems about outsider artist Henry Darger, was published in 2012, and his biography of Darger, *Throw-Away Boy*, will be issued the following year. His *A History of My Tattoo: A Poem* (2006) won the Lambda Literary Award for gay male poetry. He directs the MA in Professional Writing Program at Kennesaw State University and lives in Atlanta.

Kenny Fries is the author of *The History of My Shoes and the Evolution of Darwin's Theory* (2007) and *Body, Remember: A Memoir* (1997). He is the editor of *Staring Back: The Disability Experience from the Inside Out* (1997). His books of poems include *Desert Walking* (2000) and *Anesthesia* (1996). He was a Creative Arts Fellow of the Japan/U.S. Friendship Commission and the National Endowment for the Arts and a Fulbright Scholar to Japan, and he received the Creative Capital Foundation grant in innovative literature for his forthcoming book, *In the Province of the Gods*. He teaches in the MFA in Creative Writing Program at Goddard College. His website is www.kennyfries.com.

Thomas Glave is the author of *Whose Song? And Other Stories* (2000), *Words to Our Now: Imagination and Dissent* (Lambda Literary Award, 2005), *The Torturer's Wife* (2008), and *Among the Bloodpeople: Politics and Flesh* (2013). He is editor of the anthology *Our Caribbean: A Gathering of Lesbian and Gay Writing from the Antilles* (Lambda Literary Award, 2008). His most recent work appears in the *New York Times, Kenyon Review, Callaloo*, and in the anthologies *Kingston Noir; Love, Christopher Street;* and *Why Are Faggots So Afraid of Faggots? Flaming Challenges to Masculinity, Objectification, and the Desire to Conform*, all published in 2012. Glave has been Martin Luther King Jr. Visiting Professor at MIT, and is a 2012 Visiting Fellow at Clare Hall, Cambridge University.

Rigoberto González is the author of ten books, including the memoir *Butterfly Boy: Memories of a Chicano Mariposa* (2006). The recipient of fellowships from the Guggenheim and NEA, the American Book Award, a New York Foundation for the Arts fellowship, and the Shelley Memorial Award from the Poetry Society of America, he writes a Latino book column for the *El Paso Times* of Texas. He is also contributing editor for *Poets & Writers*, on the Board of Directors of the National Book Critics Circle, and on the Advisory Circle of Con Tinta, a collective of Chicano/Latino activist writers. He lives in New York City and is associate professor of English at Rutgers–Newark.

David Groff's book *Theory of Devolution* (2002) was selected by Mark Doty for the National Poetry Series. He is also the author, with the late Robin Hardy, of *The Crisis of Desire: AIDS and the Fate of Gay Brotherhood* (1999), and, with Philip Clark, edited *Persistent Voices: Poetry by Writers Lost to AIDS* (2009). His forthcoming book of poems, *Clay*, was chosen by Michael Waters for the Louise Bogan Award. An independent book editor, he teaches in the MFA Graduate Writing Program of the City College of New York.

Benjamin S. Grossberg is an associate professor of English at the University of Hartford. His books are *Sweet Core Orchard* (2009), winner of the 2008 Tampa Review Prize and a Lambda Literary Award, and *Underwater Lengths in a Single Breath* (2007). His poems have appeared in many venues, including *New England Review, Paris Review, Southwest Review*, and the *Pushcart Prize* and *Best American Poetry* anthologies. *Space Traveler*, his third collection, will be published in 2013.

James Allen Hall's first collection of poems, *Now You're the Enemy* (2008), received awards from the Lambda Literary Foundation, the Texas Institute of Letters, and the Fellowship of Southern Writers. A recipient of fellowships in poetry from the National Endowment for the Arts and the New York Foundation for the Arts, he teaches creative writing and literature in upstate New York.

Aaron Hamburger won the Rome Prize of the American Academy of Arts and Letters for his story collection *The View from Stalin's Head* (2004), also nominated for a Violet Quill Award. His novel, *Faith for Beginners* (2005), was nominated for a Lambda Literary Award. His writing has appeared in *Poets and Writers*, *Tin House*, *Details*, *The Village Voice*, *The Forward*, and *Out*. He has received fellowships from the Edward F. Albee Foundation and the Civitella Ranieri Foundation in Umbria, Italy, and residencies from Yaddo and Djerassi Resident Artists Program. He teaches writing at Columbia University and Stonecoast's MFA Program.

Greg Hewett is the author of four books of poetry, most recently *darkacre* (2010), which was a finalist for a Lambda Book Award. *Red Suburb* (2002) won the Publishing Triangle Award for poetry. He has been a Fulbright Fellow to Denmark and Norway, and a fellow at the Camargo Foundation in Provence. He teaches at Carleton College in Northfield, Minnesota.

Martin Hyatt was born just outside of New Orleans. His debut novel, *A Scarecrow's Bible* (2006), was named a Stonewall Honor Book by the American Library Association and won the Edmund White Award for Debut Fiction; it was also a finalist for the Ferro-Grumley Award, a Lambda Literary Award, and the Violet Quill Award. *New York Magazine* named him a literary "star of tomorrow." He has just completed a new novel, *Beautiful Gravity*, and is currently working on a memoir, *Greyhound Boy, 1976*. He has taught writing at such places at Hofstra, Parsons, and St. Francis College, and is an associate professor and the director of the Writing Center at ASA College in Brooklyn, New York.

Charles Jensen is the author of the poetry collection *The First Risk* (2009). His poems have appeared in *Bloom*, *Columbia Poetry Review*, *Field*, *The Journal*, *New England Review*, *Prairie Schooner*, and *Willow Springs*. He serves on the Emerging Leader Council of Americans for the Arts and is the Development & Communications Manager for Arts for LA. He lives in Los Angeles.

Saeed Jones received his MFA in Creative Writing at Rutgers University–Newark. His poetry has appeared or is forthcoming in such publications as *Hayden's Ferry Review*, *Jubilat*, *West Branch*, *The Collagist*, and *Line Break*.

He is a regular contributor to Lambda Literary and *Union Station Magazine.* *When the Only Light Is Fire* (2011) is his chapbook of poems.

Dave King's bestselling debut novel *The Ha-Ha* (2005) won the 2006 Rome Prize Fellowship from the American Academy of Arts and Letters and was named one of the best books of 2005 by the *Washington Post*, the *Christian Science Monitor*, the *Pittsburgh Tribune-Review*, and Amazon.com. King's work has appeared in the *Paris Review*, the *Village Voice*, and the Italian literary journal *Nuovi Argomenti*. He teaches at New York University's Gallatin School of Interdisciplinary Studies and divides his time between Brooklyn and the Hudson Valley. A new novel, tentatively titled *The Beast and Beauty*, is forthcoming.

Michael Klein's second book of poems, *then, we were still living* (2010), was a Lambda Literary Award finalist and two of his other books, *1990* (1993) and the edited collection *Poets for Life: Seventy-Six Poets Respond to AIDS* (1989), won the award. He has also written Lambda finalist *Track Conditions* (1997) and *The End of Being Known* (2003), a book of linked essays. His collection of short essays, *States of Independence*, won the inaugural BLOOM Chapbook Prize in nonfiction judged by Rigoberto González and will be out at the end of 2012, and his third book of poems, *The Talking Day*, will be published in early 2013. His recent work has appeared in *Poets & Writers*, *Bloom*, *Fence*, *The Awl*, *Ploughshares*, and *Tin House*. He teaches in the MFA Program at Goddard College and lives in New York with his boyfriend, Andrew Hood, Cyrus the yellowish cat, and Ruby the fearless and smiling French bulldog.

Brian Leung is a recipient of a Lambda Literary Award for Outstanding Mid-Career Novelist. He is the author of the historical novel *Take Me Home* (2010), which centers on the historical event of a massacre of Chinese Miners in 1885 Wyoming Territory. The novel earned a Willa Award for Historical Fiction. Leung is also the author of the novel *Lost Men* (2007) as well as the story collection *World Famous Love Acts* (2004), a winner of the Asian American Literary Award and the Mary McCarthy Prize in Short Fiction. His poetry, creative nonfiction, and short fiction have appeared in numerous journals and anthologies. He is Director of Creative Writing at the University of Louisville.

Shaun Levin is the author, most recently, of *Trees at a Sanatorium* (2011) and *Snapshots of The Boy* (2009). His other books include *Seven Sweet Things*

(2003), *A Year of Two Summers* (2005) and *Isaac Rosenberg's Journey to Arras: A Meditation* (2008). He is the founding editor of the queer literary and arts journal *Chroma* and teaches creative writing in London. His website is www.shaunlevin.com.

Paul Lisicky is the author of *Lawnboy* (1999), *Famous Builder* (2002), *The Burning House* (2011), and *Unbuilt Projects* (2012). His recent work appears in *Fence, Tin House, The Iowa Review, The Rumpus, Story Quarterly*, and elsewhere. He has taught in the writing programs at Cornell University, New York University, Sarah Lawrence College, and the University of North Carolina at Wilmington. He is currently the New Voices Professor at Rutgers University. A memoir, *The Narrow Door*, is forthcoming in 2014.

Timothy Liu is the author of eight books of poems, most recently *Bending the Mind Around the Dream's Blown Fuse* (2009). He lives with his husband in Manhattan.

Chip Livingston is the author of the poetry collections *Crow-Blue, Crow-Black* (2012) and *Museum of False Starts* (2010) and the chapbook *ALARUM* (2007). Recent poems, essays, and stories appear in *Court Green, Potomac Review, Cimarron Review, The Florida Review, Ploughshares*, and *Hinchas de Poesia*. After nine years in New York City, Chip now lives in Montevideo, Uruguay. His website is www.chiplivingston.com.

Raymond Luczak is the author and editor of fifteen books, including *How to Kill Poetry* (2013), *Among the Leaves: Queer Male Poets on the Midwestern Experience* (2012), and *Assembly Required: Notes from a Deaf Gay Life* (2009). A playwright and filmmaker, he lives in Minneapolis, Minnesota. His website is www.raymondluczak.com.

Jeff Mann's books include three collections of poetry, *Bones Washed with Wine* (2003), *On the Tongue* (2006), and *Ash: Poems from Norse Mythology* (2011); two books of personal essays, *Edge: Travels of an Appalachian Leather Bear* (2008) and *Binding the God: Ursine Essays from the Mountain South* (2010); two novellas, *Devoured*, included in *Masters of Midnight: Erotic Tales of the Vampire* (2003), and *Camp Allegheny*, included in *History's Passion: Stories of Sex Before Stonewall* (2011); two novels, *Fog: A Novel of Desire and Reprisal* (2011) and *Purgatory: A Novel of the Civil War* (2012); a collection of poetry and memoir, *Loving Mountains, Loving Men* (2005); and a volume of short fiction, *A History of Barbed Wire* (2006), winner of a Lambda Literary Award. He teaches creative writing at Virginia Tech in Blacksburg.

Randall Mann is the author of three collections of poetry, *Complaint in the Garden* (2004), *Breakfast with Thom Gunn* (2009), and the forthcoming *Straight Razor*. His writing has appeared in the *Washington Post*, the *Paris Review*, *Poetry*, the *New Republic*, and the *Kenyon Review*. He lives in San Francisco.

Richard McCann is the author of *Mother of Sorrows* (2005), an award-winning collection of linked stories, and *Ghost Letters* (1994), a collection of poems. His work has appeared in such magazines as *The Atlantic*, *Esquire*, and *Tin House* and in such anthologies as *The O. Henry Stories 2007* and *Best American Essays*. A professor at American University, he lives in Washington, D.C. He serves on the Board of Trustees of the PEN/Faulkner Foundation and the Corporation of Yaddo.

Alistair McCartney is the author of *The End of the World Book: A Novel* (2008), a finalist for the 2009 PEN USA Fiction Award and the Publishing Triangle Edmund White Debut Fiction Award as well as the *Seattle Times*'s Best Ten Books of 2008. McCartney's writing has appeared in *Fence*, *Bloom*, *Lies/Isles*, *Crush Fanzine*, *1913*, *James White Review*, and other journals and anthologies. Currently at work on the second novel in a projected six-book cycle, he lives with his partner Tim Miller in Los Angeles, teaching creative writing and literature in the BA and MFA Programs at Antioch University.

David McConnell is the author of the novel *The Silver Hearted* (2010). His short fiction and journalism have appeared widely in journals and anthologies. A nonfiction book, *American Honor Killings*, will appear in early 2013. He is the co-chair of the Lambda Literary Foundation and lives in New York City.

Tim Miller's solo performance work, hailed for its humor and passion, has delighted and emboldened audiences all over the world. He is the author of the books *Shirts & Skins* (1997), *Body Blows* (2002), and *1001 Beds* (2006), an anthology of his performances and essays that won the 2007 Lambda Literary Award for best book in Drama-Theatre. Miller has taught performance at UCLA, New York University, and Claremont School of Theology. He is the cofounder of Performance Space 122 in New York City and Highways Performance Space in Santa Monica, California. His website is www.TimMillerPerformer.com.

Dale Peck is the author of *Martin and John* (1993), *The Law of Enclosures* (1996), *Now It's Time to Say Goodbye* (1998), *What We Lost* (2003), and *Sprout* (2009), which won the 2010 Lambda Literary Award for young adult fiction. His most recent novel is *The Garden of Lost and Found* (2012).

Charles Rice-González, born in Puerto Rico and reared in the Bronx, is a writer, community and LGBT activist, and Executive Director of BAAD! The Bronx Academy of Arts & Dance. He is the author of the debut novel *Chulito* (2011) and coeditor of *From Macho to Mariposa: New Gay Latino Fiction* (2011). His work appears in *Pitkin Review* (2008), *Los Otros Cuerpos* (2007), *Best Gay Stories 2008, Best of PANIC!: En Vivo from the East Village* (2010), *Ambientes: New Queer Latino Writing* (2011), and *Love, Christopher Street* (2012). He's written several plays, including *Pink Jesus* (1997), *Los Nutcrackers: A Christmas Carajo* (2004), and the award-winning *I Just Love Andy Gibb* (2007).

K. M. Soehnlein is the author of the novels *Robin and Ruby* (2010), *You Can Say You Knew Me When* (2005), and *The World of Normal Boys* (2000), which received the Lambda Literary Award for Gay Men's Fiction. His recent publications include "Proof," a short story in *Routes: An Achiote Press Fiction Anthology* (2011), and essays in the anthologies *Bookmark Now: Writing in Unreaderly Times; Girls Who Like Boys Who Like Boys;* and *Love, Castro Street.* He lives in San Francisco with his husband, Kevin Clarke.

Brian Teare, a former National Endowment for the Arts Fellow, is the recipient of poetry fellowships from the MacDowell Colony, Headlands Center for the Arts, and the American Antiquarian Society. He is the author of *The Room Where I Was Born* (2003), *Sight Map* (2009), the Lambda Award–winning *Pleasure* (2010), and the forthcoming *Companion Grasses* (2013). An assistant professor at Temple University, he lives in Philadelphia, where he makes books by hand for his micropress, Albion Books.

Ellery Washington teaches creative writing at the Pratt Institute, in Brooklyn, New York. His fiction and essays have appeared in numerous collections, journals, and magazines, including the *New York Times, Ploughshares, OUT Magazine, International Review, Frankfurter Allgemeine, Nouvelles Frontières,* and the national best seller *State by State—A Panoramic Portrait of America.* He currently divides his time between San Francisco and New York.